D1243838

THE NEWMAN MOVEMENT

THE NEWMAN MOVEMENT

*Roman Catholics in
American Higher Education, 1883–1971*

JOHN WHITNEY EVANS

UNIVERSITY OF NOTRE DAME PRESS

NOTRE DAME   LONDON

Library of Congress Cataloging in Publication Data

Evans, John Whitney, 1931–
  The Newman movement.

  Bibliography: p.
  1. Newman clubs–History. 2. Church work with
students–Catholic Church. 3. Church work with students
–United States. 4. Church and college in the United
States. 5. United States–Church history. I. Title.
BX810.E9   267'.62'2   79–18214
ISBN 0–268–01453–1

FOR
MARTHA AND HENRY

Contents

Foreword

"To be . . . worthy the historian must have not only erudition but zeal for what he is doing."[1] Thus did Sebastien LeNain de Tillemont (1637–1698), the learned French priest-historian, upon whose scholarship Edward Gibbon leaned so heavily for *The Decline and Fall of the Roman Empire,* describe in part the qualities that should characterize the ecclesiastical historian. Among recent works in the history of American Catholicism, I know of none that better exemplifies what Tillemont here had in mind than Father Evans' thorough and scholarly account of the Catholic apostolate for students in non-Catholic colleges and universities, an apostolate that has generally been known as the Newman Movement.

The great Jesuit scientist Pierre Teilhard de Chardin once remarked that "everything is the sum of the past and . . . nothing is comprehensible except through its history."[2] The movement of Catholic students toward the non-Catholic campuses of the United States is no exception, and when one considers the distance travelled since the feeble beginnings of this movement adumbrated in the founding of the Melvin Club at the University of Wisconsin in 1883, and contrasts its present nationwide character, which embraces approximately 2,000 chaplains and members of religious sisterhoods working on 1,500 non-Catholic campuses with an estimated 2,700,000 Catholic students as their potential clientele, one begins to comprehend the extent and significance that this movement has assumed. For it is a matter of common knowledge that the estimated 458,000 students on the 238 Catholic college and university campuses at the start of the 1980s are with each passing year being more and more outdistanced proportionally by their coreligionists in the non-Catholic institutions of the country.

A further factor that lends a note of genuine timeliness to Father Evans' work is the rising interest in religious studies in general on American campuses. It would be absurd to suggest that the college population's search for values and ideals outside themselves has found its resting place in courses dealing in one way or another with religion in the curricula of the colleges and universities. But it is certainly true that courses and programs of this kind are today finding an increasingly hospitable reception among young Americans, a fact that adds one more paradox among the countless number that have made our age so complicated and difficult to understand. When 20 percent of the public universities of the United States have departments of religious studies and over 90 percent of these same universities offer courses dealing in one aspect or other with religion, one is warranted in believing that a considerable number of collegians are showing a deepening theological concern.

If such trends are to be properly analyzed it is necessary to know how Catholics, the largest religious body in the nation, came to participate in them, especially since the American members of the Church of Rome have advanced beyond their immigrant and ghetto past and have entered the mainstream of American life. As one reads this richly documented story of the Newman Movement it becomes evident — at times painfully evident — how gradual and cautious was the recognition given to this movement by most of the ranking officials of the American Church. The relevance of Father Evans' book for one who wishes to be not only *au courant* with the religious and educational aspects of the revolution through which both Church and State are now passing, but also equipped with helpful data for offering fully informed remedies toward their solution, must be obvious.

Since the end of the 1960s Catholic youth have averaged 33 percent of the overall enrollments of all institutions of higher learning in the United States. It will not be thought rash to predict that the remaining decades of the twentieth century will see this condition reflected in most literate, social, professional, and political circles.[3] What part, if any, their Church played in their lives as collegians will not be without importance in assessing the public careers of these men and women. The reader of this volume will find here the evidence of how this aspect of the Catholic apostolate evolved, the obstacles it had to overcome to reach its present impressive status, and the suggestion as well of the distance that the Newman Movement has yet to traverse before it can afford to rest on the laurels of its achievement. And all of this has been, is, and will continue to be part of one of the most obsessive problems that confront Americans generally in this extraordinarily disturbed and uncertain time in their country's history.

Solid research can and often does make insufferably dull reading. Father Evans' mastery of the elements of literary style and his keen sense of the beauty of the English language have elevated his prose far beyond the dangers that all too frequently overtake works of careful scholarship. Here, in a word, the reader will find meticulously accurate history, highly informative content, and a graceful literary style combined to furnish one of the most attractive books that it has fallen to this writer's lot to read in his more than forty years as a member of the American academic community.

John Tracy Ellis
Professorial Lecturer in Church History
The Catholic University of America

Preface

*...A Church made up of those who have struggled
against their environment in order to reach a personally clearly and explicitly responsible decision of faith
... will be the Church of the future or there will be no
Church at all.*

Karl Rahner, S.J.,
The Shape of the Church to Come, 1972

The Newman Movement is a success story. The Church does not adopt
new policies, disciplines, and ministries automatically. Its members
must take responsibility to believe and hope, to work and wait for
renewal to become reality. That is what the young men and women
who lived this story, and the few clergy who served them, did.

Their hopes were very personal. Sons and daughters of immigrants in many cases, these protagonists sought to enter the mainstream of American life through higher education. Because the institutions available to them were secular, these young Catholics had to
make extraordinary efforts to permeate their training with the faith
they brought from home and parish. Because they could not accomplish this alone, they looked for spiritual guidance and religious
instruction from their priests. And because such a program ran
counter to Church law, and yet was legislated by the circumstances of
modern life, they awaited recognition from their bishops: not merely
for assurance that they were approved as loyal Catholics but, more
significantly, for authorization as agents helping to evangelize the
contemporary world represented on campus.

Thus, their hopes were also inevitably public, expressed in what
has come to be known as the "Newman Movement." In researching
this movement, I have found that it is much broader in conception and
form than can be represented by the idea of the Newman Club or the
Newman Federation or even the Newman Apostolate itself, although
each of these approximates the fuller reality. In the present study,
"Newman Movement" identifies attempts, often drawing inspiration

from the life and writings of John Henry Newman, by Catholic
students, campus officials, and clergymen to supply pastoral care and
religious education in non-Catholic colleges and universities. These
efforts have passed through three stages that correspond roughly to
changes within both the secular campus and the American Church.

The first phase opened in 1883 with the founding of the Melvin
Club at the University of Wisconsin and came to a climax shortly after
the turn of the century when Catholic bishops began to augment the
growing number of such societies, some already known as Newman
clubs, with their own chaplains and halls. During these pre–World
War I years, non-Catholic colleges and universities remained generally receptive to Christian influences, although they were not always
friendly to Catholicism. This same period witnessed the first effects of
the Americanism controversy on the Church in the United States. The
emergent conservatism took a dual form: nervousness about the role
of lay people in Church affairs, and withdrawal from engagement with
American institutions. It found one expression in 1907 when leaders
of the Catholic college movement successfully challenged the idea
that chaplaincies and "Catholic halls" at state universities could
provide adequate spiritual and intellectual nurture, despite the fact
that a papal decree had authorized such initiatives.

The second stage of the Newman Movement began in 1908 with
the founding of the first national student federation. What would
become the National Newman Club Federation replaced this first
effort about the time of World War I. For half a century such student
groups represented the principal expression of Catholic concern for
religion on the non-denominational campus. From this period came
identification of the movement with the Newman Club, largely due to
the heroic efforts of Father John W. Keogh, for eighteen years chaplain
of the Federation. In contrast to the first phase, which was characterized
by a strong educational and missionary as well as apologetical fervor,
this phase presented a sorry picture of students and priests combatting
secularism in what had become in most instances a hostile campus
atmosphere, while also defending their efforts before Catholic leaders
who were increasingly suspicious and withdrawn. In 1941 the movement received semi-official recognition from the bishops, and in 1962
it was mandated as the National Newman Apostolate "to perform the
work of the Catholic Church in the secular campus community."
During these years bishops once again began to assume leadership as
they appointed priests and sisters to serve the movement and contributed to the erection of chapels and student centers. Because these
efforts strengthened local bases of the movement in the spirit of

Vatican II, which called for decentralization and an increased sharing of responsibility at diocesan and parochial levels, the Newman Apostolate as a national superstructure waned in effectiveness.

In 1969 the movement entered its third and present stage. It has once again become a diocesan-centered enterprise reflecting many of the features it incipiently manifested prior to 1907. It is most conspicuously different from its previous phases, perhaps, in the way Newman centers and other campus communities have replaced the Newman Club; in the degree of acceptance by the clerical establishment revealed by the presence of over 200 diocesan directors of the work; by the strong and vigorous professional corps of chaplains, the Catholic Campus Ministry Association, which carries out most of the functions earlier performed by youth and educational offices in the Washington secretariat of the Church; by the receptiveness to religious learning and influence on most secular campuses; by the ecumenical spirit among chaplains and students; and by the readiness of Catholic college leaders to cooperate with the Newman Movement.

It would be a mistake to see in this development from local to national and back to local leadership a complete fulfillment of the hopes of Newman leaders. They have achieved *in principle* recognition of their ministry; but this does not mean that *in fact* the movement flourishes everywhere. Indeed, having arrived at the point it had attained organizationally seven decades earlier, the pastoral and educational mission of the Church in American post-secondary education, in a sense, is just beginning. This certainly becomes evident upon reviewing events since 1971, the end point of this study, when the outlook appeared very optimistic. For example, the research department and training institute mentioned in the final chapter no longer exist; budgets have been cut, at times disastrously; older chaplains have moved on and younger ones are recruited with increasing difficulty; some observers insist that the Church is continuing to lose its most educated young members; and it is experiencing a wrenching crisis of credibility in its leadership while at the same time undergoing a remarkable renewal among various sectors of its membership. Only the passage of time and further investigation will tell with relative assurance whether or not Newman's apostles of hope labored in vain or, as I tend to think, achieved more of their aims than anyone would have thought possible.

Many persons have contributed to the preparation of this study. I owe thanks to George Garrelts, former Newman Chaplain at the University of Minnesota, and Richard Butler, O.P., former National Chaplain, for suggesting the project in 1963 and securing initial financial aid; to many archivists who made collections in universities, dioceses, and historical societies available; to the National Newman Foundation and the University of Minnesota for travel grants that carried me some 15,000 miles to these sources; to my friend, Monsignor John Tracy Ellis, Professorial Lecturer in Church History at The Catholic University of America, for warning me at the outset that "not much material on this subject is available" and then for carefully criticizing the 800 pages that comprised the original draft; to another good friend, Professor Timothy L. Smith, Director of the Program in American Religious History of The Johns Hopkins University, who also offered meaningful criticism as my mentor during his years at Minnesota; to Mildred Cavanaugh who typed the final draft; and to my colleague, Sister Mary Richard Boo, O.S.B., who edited the final version of the manuscript. There remain others who, like those mentioned, tried to assure the accuracy and coherence of my efforts. All have my gratitude along with the acknowledgement that I remain accountable for lapses.

PART ONE

ASPECTS OF AN IDEA

The idea which represents an object or supposed object is commensurate with the sum total of its possible aspects ... all the aspects of an idea are capable of coalition.

John Henry Newman,
*An Essay on the Development
of Christian Doctrine*

ONE

Religion Stayed in College

... A university ... is not a convent, it is not a seminary; it is a place to fit men of the world for the world.

John Henry Newman
The Idea of a University

Shortly after the turn of the century observers of American higher education clearly discerned what they termed a "shifting of the field." By this they meant that denominational schools, which for so long had prepared the majority of American youths for leadership in the affairs of the nation, would no longer do so. This trend was especially prominent in the Midwest, where church-sponsored schools were growing at only about half the rate of their public counterparts.[1] Everywhere the latter were expanding at dizzying speed. Opening with 238,000 students in 1900, state institutions more than doubled in size by 1920, and during the next two decades swelled to 1.5 million, increases on campus far greater than for the nation as a whole. Furthermore, the number of women going to college was rising. About one-third of the campus totals in 1920, they constituted over 40 percent of student bodies on the eve of World War II.[2]

For many onlookers the concentration of young American men and women in schools devoid of denominational control spelled disaster. Said a widely read Protestant fundamentalist in 1909, the state universities were "blasting at the rock of ages" by promulgating doctrines that, "if universally applied, might overturn religion, society, and civil law."[3] Said an American Jesuit fresh from a public campus in the Midwest, if true Christians expected to go "through a secular university with faith unshaken and morals unimpaired," they had better "possess the courage of a saint and the mental training of a Catholic doctor of philosophy."[4]

Evidence of a worldly spirit in U.S. post-secondary institutions leapt from behind nearly every tree of academe. The University of Missouri offers one example. In 1904 its bulletin cited the Northwest

3

Ordinance as authority for holding voluntary religious exercises, which included hymn singing, readings from the Old and New Testaments, and prayer, in connection with its voluntary daily assemblies. In less than a decade the "Home of the Tigers" deleted from its catalogue all reference to the Ordinance, substituted "religious influences" for "religious exercises," and no longer announced fixed dates for the assemblies.[5] Between 1910 and 1920 the number of college catalogues assigning religious aims to higher education dwindled by more than half.[6]

And why not? College administrative boards now seated businessmen, not clerics. Their presidents were no longer preachers, but lawyers, or natural scientists, or public relations experts. Professors set up specialized departments that explored phenomena, not as the writing of God in nature or on the hearts of men, but as manipulable data. Personnel workers separated guidance from moralizing and questioned the value of prayer for well-rounded human beings. By 1923 President William O. Thompson of Ohio State University could declare that he was "in no way untrue to state institutions" when he asserted that a student might take a degree "in almost any one of the best of them" and be as ignorant of the Bible and religion "as if he had been educated in a non-Christian country."[7] But something more dramatic than the mere elimination of traditional religion seemed to be taking place. Early in the century, Nicholas Murray Butler of Columbia University noted that "the university has succeeded to the place once held by the cathedral as the best embodiment of the uplifting forces of the modern time."[8] Lacking a church, the university had to create one—itself.

As we might expect, students appeared to be the chief victims of this usurpation. One state university, which had accredited Bible study around the time of World War I, warned its freshmen classes forty years later of "the difference between acquiring facts about life and grasping some clues to the meaning of life. . . . Your academic pursuits . . . will take you a long way toward the former, but progress toward the latter will be up to you."[9] Such a campus deserves some credit, at least, for practicing truth in advertising; and more credit for untypically recognizing the problem. But what did this widespread condition of indifference to the religious dimension of human existence suggest for the rigorous exploration of religious history and thought—key elements in western civilization, American culture, and international understanding—as a traditional pursuit among persons seeking advanced learning?

What we are talking about has been named "secularization."

This is a fuzzy term and deserves some clarification; especially so because, though asked to leave, traditional religion simply would not drop out of American higher education.

PROBLEMS OF "SECULARIZATION"

The term "secular" and its related forms fit nonsectarian campuses in different ways. One of these is quite harmless. It simply identifies an institution under lay control as compared with one sponsored by some religious group. In this case "secular" is a quite innocent descriptive term, much the way "secular priest"points out one working in the world and not removed to a monastery or committed to all the vows of a "religious priest."

A second usage includes a distinctly ideological note. It describes a campus not only no longer under religious control, but also more or less antagonistic to religious influences and pursuits. In contrast with the "secular" campus, we here discover the "secularistic" one. That is, one dominated by the world view of "secularism"—that revolt against theological absolutes culminating in "the attempt to establish an autonomous sphere of knowledge expunged of supernatural, fideistic presuppositions."[10]

Another derivative, "secularization," has a double meaning. Traditionally this term signified a negative process by which cultural and social change rendered religion and its forms in one way or another obsolete.[11] Since the 1960s in the United States "secularization" identifies a theory explaining how the *process* results in a desirable *outcome;* religious and secular persons, ideas, institutions, etc., coexist in a creative tension and participate in the kind of courteous dialogue any neutral situation makes possible.[12]

I believe this last notion to be only minimally helpful in trying to understand what has happened in American higher education since the Civil War, and especially since about the turn of the century. Secularization theory can be invoked to illuminate contradictory world views; it errs in denying the persistence of religious experience and concern for ultimate values among people, including intellectuals; and it fails to take into account continuing pressures of a dominant this-worldliness that negāte the supposed "neutrality" of secularization.[13] In the present discussion I shall use "secular" and its forms not as applications of this theory, but simply in the first two descriptive senses mentioned above.

Although American colleges and universities have become more and more secular during the twentieth century, religion has, in the main, been more present than absent to them. One way to see this is to follow its fortunes over the years. Prior to World War I Christianity strongly influenced the mood on all campuses. Naturally, this most characterized church-related colleges. Among independent schools, Harvard was said to be the most indifferent to religion, but more as a gentleman snubbing an inferior than as a janitor removing trash. Depending upon region, state universities tended to establish a kind of liberal Protestantism. These years gave us a campus institutionally secularized but still enfolded, with varying intensity, in American Protestantism.

Between the wars a secularistic mood grew quite dominant. For example, in 1927 researchers at Northwestern University hesitated to publish results of a survey tabulating the number of denominational and independent schools offering courses in religion because enrollments were so small it was feared "such information might play into the hands of administrators" seeking "justification for cutting out the [religion] department entirely."[14] About the same time, efforts to set up "schools of religion" in state universities came to an end. Institutionally secularized, the campuses seemed now under the power of secularism as a guiding philosophy. During the 1930s student indifference as well as administrative and faculty hostility put campus religiosity and religious study into its deepest decline.

Religion began to become more prominent in campus life after 1940 and was definitely in the ascendant following World War II. The revival of the 1950s phased into the reinstatement of religious studies in state universities during the 1960s. We shall examine this phase of the story in a later chapter.[15] The remainder of this chapter will begin to flesh out our summary of the first two periods.

THE RELIGIOUS SPIRIT OF STUDENTS

Throughout the years 1900 to 1940 statistical evidence of church attendance, scientific surveys of student religious opinion, and modest activism among students themselves support the conclusion that American undergraduate life showed "a deep current of seriousness and religious feeling" and that, although the average student cared little for religious systems, he remained "enormously" concerned about "the fundamental truths of religion."[16]

Church membership and attendance figures suggest no massive falling away from religion among students. In 1900 a twenty-state canvass found that 50 to 80 percent of enrollees on nonsectarian campuses actively embraced Christianity. In 1924 officials at twenty-one state universities claimed that 85 percent of their student bodies belonged to some church. At the end of the 1930s, admittedly a bad decade for campus piety, a survey of 800,000 students disclosed that only 6 percent had no definite religious preference, while 88 percent did.[17]

One might argue that congregational membership was simply social conformity, not religious profession. The facts do not support this contention. The proportion of Americans over thirteen years of age who belonged to churches dropped from 55 percent in 1906 to 50 percent in 1940, significantly below the participation of college students. Furthermore, except for a handful of campuses, students tended to be more church-going than citizens of the local community, and they were at least "on a par with the social group from which they came."[18] Because of religious pluralism and occasional attacks on religion within the campuses, students had to think out their faith and behavior more deliberately than townspeople. It would seem fairer to say that, as a result, students constituted a group of comparatively stronger believers.

Or would they be better characterized as searchers? A number of studies appearing during these years explored the faith of college students and indicated their serious-minded concern. Those in the 1920s visualized God in ways sharply different from notions characteristic among previous generations. In 1908, 70 percent of students surveyed affirmed their belief in God as a Person and 61 percent felt they needed Him for successful daily living. Two decades later this outlook had undergone a complete reversal. Nearly 70 percent saw God as an "Impersonal Force" and less than 40 percent believed prayer could alter the course of human affairs. Acceptance of the Bible had also changed dramatically. What around the turn of the century had been a divinely inspired message to mankind by 1930 was an important but obscure collection of literary, historical, and allegorical materials subject to the same kind of analysis as Shakespeare or Confucius. Similarly, Jesus had declined from a Divine Authority to be obeyed to a good example to be imitated.[19]

The scientifically trained student, wrote one observer, tended to doubt the power of the mind to know God and religious truth and preferred to find "the higher values of religion . . . in the realm of appreciation and affection."[20] A student at the University of Michigan concluded that his peers had to move from a literal to a "literary faith," and build a new moral code based on "convention or convenience rather than . . . conviction."[21] Yet the search went on. In 1924 less than

30 percent of college students concluded that science posed decisive obstacles to their faith. During the years that followed, a rising number claimed that religion held meaning for "intelligent, scientific people."[22] Unfortunately, clarity and consistency did not characterize these views. As early as 1916 one researcher complained that so far as faith in God and immortality were concerned, "students are grovelling in darkness."[23] Fifteen years later another study concluded that the religious thinking of the graduates of American nonsectarian colleges had the quality of "uninformed public opinion."[24]

Realizing that such outcomes were not only harmful but also belied claims about receiving liberal and truly "scientific" education, a few students reacted sharply. One graduate of the 1920s recalled that college instruction had never demonstrated how American democracy depended upon "the religious concept of the sacredness of the individual soul, and the existence of certain inalienable rights conferred upon man by Almighty God."[25] In 1927 Purdue's undergraduate Committee of Sixteen called for more stress on the teaching of ethical and moral values and asked every professor to evaluate his courses against the standard of how well they helped the young person to "orient himself in the world."[26] About the same time the Harvard Undergraduate Report addressed itself to "the confusion of thought" attending upon "the modern conflict between science and religion." The students asked the university not to leave them "in a state of negation and skepticism deprived of whatever Religion did offer." They also requested two new courses, one "to offer the student a sound basis upon which to build his own philosophy," the other an investigation of Christianity, in order to remedy "the prevailing ignorance concerning so important a subject."[27]

As did their less articulate peers, these American college students, said Chancellor Elmer E. Brown of New York University, lived "at a time of tension and of readjustment of the religious habits of men everywhere." Brown realized that "the religious spirit is quickened when it finds direction and companionship."[28] Supposedly, faculties provided the former and administrative personnel the latter. How much help did they offer?

UNIVERSITY PRESIDENTS AS PASTORS

No university president summarized the mission of the state university around the turn of the century more concisely than did Richard Henry Jesse of the University of Missouri: "Our aim must be to make good and intelligent citizens for Missouri, whatever the party, and good Christians, whatever the Church . . . patriots but not partisan, Christian but not sectarian."[29] During these years administrators labored to keep old-time college intimacy and influences alive amid the spreading bigness of their campuses. They promoted athletics and ascetical codes of conduct, fraternities, honor societies, and student government—all in the interest of morality and scholarship. A few also advocated student unions and dormitories to curb loneliness and to end undemocratic divisions within student bodies.[30]

Expectedly, these presidents also reached for traditional forms of religiosity. President Prince L. Campbell of the University of Oregon typified his nineteenth-century counterpart. From 1902 to 1917 he taught freshman classes in ethics, made himself readily available to students for counseling, and sent nearly every senior into the world with a personal pep talk on reverence for American and religious values. Many presidents also deplored the drop in chapel services after 1900. Only seven of 144 state institutions retained compulsory religious exercises. To encourage attendance at chapel Indiana University offered a half credit for going to morning prayers, while Frank H. Strong of the University of Kansas offered powerful preaching. For almost two decades after 1902 Strong's "The Bible, the Text Book of Democracy" and similar sermons filled Fraser Hall once each week with undergraduates and professors alike. At the University of Pennsylvania, Edgar Fahs Smith not only reimposed compulsory chapel on Protestants but offered to have university personnel check on how well Catholics attended Mass in nearby parishes. As Thompson of Ohio put it in 1905, the church was no longer "the only agency interested in religion."[31]

Yet, as Jesse observed, few university men could be "profoundly intellectual and profoundly spiritual at the same time."[32] Accordingly, administrators began to rely more and more upon what George MacLean of Iowa called "the voluntary cultivation of the religious and moral life of the college community."[33]

Between 1890 and World War I the campus chapters of the Young Men's Christian Association and Young Women's Christian Association filled this function. By 1900 over 600 YMCA and YWCA chapters enrolled over 32,000 students and had sixty-four secretaries organizing programs of moral welfare.[34] When Charles Van Hise praised the "Ys" for their "deep and broad influence on the intellectual and spiritual development" of students at the University of Wisconsin,[35] he reflected the attitude of many presidents. As late as 1921 two dozen tax-supported institutions still subsidized the Association with amounts ranging from $250 a year at Nebraska to $5,300 at Pennsylvania State. At some of these schools the transition from YMCA to services provided by a student affairs office meant little more than changing the nameplate on a door.[36]

But the presidents gradually lost this valuable adjunct. Roman Catholics, Unitarians, Jews, and Universalists complained about official university sponsorship of an organization so fully in the tradition of evan-gelical Protestantism. Even the nondenominational Disciples of Christ felt miffed when Missouri afforded the Association exclusive use of university classrooms for Bible courses. As more and more students from mainline Protestant denominations entered the campuses after 1900, local pastors joined in these complaints. Presidents were soon faced with the development of the "campus pastor movement" which swept all denominations outside the Roman Catholic after 1905.[37]

During these years some presidents could also rely upon faculty members to keep religion and morality viable on campus. Professors served on discipline committees, monitored the growing number of denominational clubs, and drafted codes to create "morally and spiritually as well as intellectually stimulating" campus climates.[38] More in line with their academic commitments, some rallied to the new hybrid "science of religion." Around 1910 teachers of comparative religion exploited history, linguistics, anthropology, and art to illuminate Christian civilization and, at times, to assert its superiority over that of paganism. Sociologists and psychologists taught short courses to religious professionals in the hope of generating new strategies of catechetics and conversion. Professors also served in the Y-sponsored Bible courses. In 1908, for example, over 1,400 professors in 400 schools were instructing nearly 50,000 men and 20,000 coeds. But by 1915 this zeal had passed. That year reports of campus secretaries registered a sharp decline in professorial help and noted that recruiting efforts were turning up "immature and incompetent" replacements.[39]

Besides giving evidence of the spread of the worldly spirit, changes in the composition and role of the university presidency contributed to it. The practice of drawing administrators less and less from the clergy or the humanities and more from the scientific disciplines or the professions resulted in the installation of university presidents who wanted to test the stars before following them. As paternalistic overseers of student life and morals gave way to bureaucratic balancers and institutional apologists, presidents also had to learn how to test the wind. But of themselves, these new expectations, distractions, and pressures on administrators could not subvert religious influences on campus. As student life showed, religion was vital enough to survive expansion, complexity, coeducation, fraternities, football, and the scientific movement. Only one thing carried enough clout to eliminate officially fostered religion from the state university: sectarianism. As one churchman noted in 1907, only the sensibilities of parents and church groups erected the "insuperable barrier against those forms of aggressive religious culture which none could be more anxious to inaugurate than the authorities of state universities."[40] Be they compulsory chapel services or accredited courses treating religion in a "frank and honest and intelligent way," concluded President D. L. Crawford of the University of Hawaii, sooner or later the churches would successfully remove them from the campus through the legislatures.[41]

Problems of religious pluralism, sectarianism, and legal interpretations complicated the lives of presidents seeking to maintain or reintroduce religious elements in nondenominational higher education prior to World War I. Such considerations also threw up obstacles for professors favorable to religious influences and studies. This latter group faced their own unique and destructive problems and we shall examine them when we catch up with the period between World War I and World War II. For now, we shall look at the Catholic setting in which the Newman Movement appeared.

CATHOLIC STIRRINGS

Around 1900 American Catholics were experiencing their own "shifting of the field." During the years leading up to the Third Plenary Council of Baltimore, whose decrees received Vatican approval in 1885, Catholic bishops addressed themselves primarily to perfecting their own hierarchical structures and developing parochial life. Such concerns, especially the latter, would remain paramount for decades to come.

Between about 1885 and the end of the century, however, lay Catholics and a new generation of prelates devoted much time and energy to an attempt to clarify the larger role their Church should play in the life of their adopted nation. For the lay Catholic this program appeared most prominently in connection with two great lay congresses. In 1889 a congress in Baltimore attracted 1,500 delegates who placed themselves on record in favor of the American separation of church and state, expressed the need for Catholics to become

involved in alleviating social problems related to immigrants, workers, and minorities, and encouraged the development of Catholic
writers who could present the true position of the Church. Four years
later 2,500 delegates gathered in Chicago for the Columbian Catholic
Congress that gave even greater stress to the pursuit of social justice.
Such monster manifestations reared themselves upon local islands of
new Catholic affluence, awareness, and commitment in such cities as
St. Paul, Detroit, St. Louis, and Chicago, and took nourishment from
publications like Milwaukee's *Catholic Citizen* and Brooklyn's *Examin-
er,* from *The Catholic World,* and from the *American Catholic Quarterly
Review.*[42]

Meanwhile, some bishops turned their attention to examining
American institutions and values with a two-fold purpose in mind: to
discover where these accorded with Catholic principles and to accommodate their immigrant-dominated Church to its new situation.
One observer framed the question sharply: "If Democracy, which has
learned in its own order the secret of self-government, is to be
reconciled with Rome, can the temper, the methods of the sixteenth
century avail under circumstances so novel and unprecedented?"[43]
Clerical leaders like Archbishop John Ireland of St. Paul; Cardinal
James Gibbons of Baltimore; Bishop John Lancaster Spalding of
Peoria; Bishop John J. Keane, Rector of The Catholic University of
America; Monsignor Denis J. O'Connell, Rector of the American
College in Rome; and the Paulist Fathers believed that their Church
had to discern what religious pluralism, democratic forms of political,
economic, and social life, interfaith cooperation, higher education,
and religious liberty meant for Catholic structures and piety. They
also believed that unless they updated their Church, it would fail not
only to convert America but even to survive as a source of life and
hope for the modern world.[44]

In other words, the years prior to 1900 saw a promising reappear-
ance of earlier lay leadership within Catholic ranks and a simulta-
neous, equally serious engagement with modernity stirring among
prominent members of the hierarchy. Historians have termed this
two-fold development "a nascent cultural renaissance"[45] or "the emergence of liberal Catholicism."[46] Its two phases were interdependent.
As Archbishop Ireland told the Columbian Congress: "Lay action
today particularly is needed in the Church. Laymen in this age have a
special vocation."[47] Daniel Callahan later concluded that "a viable
and significant lay movement depends upon the support and encouragement of the hierarchy," adding that the latter also needed a "sense
of confidence" and that "the more threatened the Church feels itself to

be, the more the hierarchy will tend to centralize all power and responsibility in its own hands."[48] It was such a failure of nerve on the part of high Church leaders that brought the "renaissance" to an end.

In 1899 Pope Leo XIII addressed to Cardinal Gibbons as leader of the American hierarchy a letter that condemned what he called "Americanism." By this term the pope did not mean legitimate love for one's country, its people, and its just political institutions. He did mean certain modifications, not only in the method of teaching Catholic doctrine, but also in Church discipline and even, he said, in the very "Deposit of Faith" itself. In response, the liberal bishops remained silent, or told each other they had always carefully distinguished between the *political* and the *ecclesiastical* implications of modernization. Indeed, the propositions the pope rejected had circulated among French Catholics enchanted with the American Catholic experience; Gibbons replied to the pope that such ideas had never been in vogue among his episcopal colleagues in the United States. Nevertheless, the conservatives among the hierarchy thanked the Holy Father for his efforts, and the next two decades of American Catholic affairs witnessed "the rejected Americanists hoping for changes that did not come," while their conservative opponents tried to win acceptance of Catholicism "without adopting the policies they had condemned."[49]

Within a decade other restrictive measures followed. In 1907 Pope Pius X climaxed decades of Church resistance to modern trends and ideas with two pronouncements condemning "the heresy of heresies," Modernism. A year later the resultant suppression of the *New York Review*, a journal edited by priests attempting to interpret Catholic faith in the light of contemporary scholarship, spread a *grand peur* throughout the ranks of those seeking an accommodation with democratic institutions.[50] That same year hierarchical bonds also tightened when the Holy See removed the American Church from the jurisdiction of the Congregation for the Propagation of the Faith, a recognition that Catholics in the United States lived no longer in "mission territory."[51] Bishops formerly had dealt with a single office in Rome; either liberals or conservatives might capture the ear of a lone official who wielded decisive power. Now, however, a maze of established curial channels received and disposed of communications from America. Bureaucracies, essential as they are for the functioning of large organizations, seldom radiate confidence.

The American Catholic landscape changed even more following the promulgation of the Code of Canon Law in 1917. In itself, the *Codex Juris Canonici* regularized administrative and religious matters and, when properly understood and applied, provided considerable latitude for adaptation and innovation. But only one canon of over 2,000 applied to the layman: Number 682 assured him the right to receive from the clergy, according to the rules of ecclesiastical discipline, the helps needed for salvation.[52] Legal experts in the typical American chancery reflected Anglo-Saxon attitudes and, sometimes, rigid Irish upbringing on the binding power of legislation. Furthermore, increasing numbers of them received their training, and in the process an ample portion of *Romanita*, at the American College in Rome.[53] It was true that the Federation of Catholic Societies, founded in 1901, attempted to keep the lay wing of the renewal alive; and the next largest organization of laymen, the German *Central Verein*, remained. But the Federation could not enlist participation from the single most active lay group of national importance, the Knights of Columbus, it lacked episcopal leadership, and it was eventually preempted by the bishops' National Catholic Welfare Council in 1919; and the *Central Verein* was too dedicated to German ideas to survive World War I.[54]

In the next three chapters we shall see how the Newman Movement came to life during these years of change on the secular campus and within the Church. The former was more ready to welcome Catholic participation than were the ebbing lay renewal and the no longer adventurous hierarchy to supply it. Such a situation would seem to preclude an optimistic outcome.

TWO

Strangers in a Strange Land

Like your great patron, be Christian gentlemen, allow-
ing the strength and sweetness of Christian charity to
mould and dominate your characters.

Archbishop Patrick John Ryan
Address to the Pennsylvania Newman Club,
March,1894

Young Catholics entered state universities around the turn of the century for many of the same reasons that attracted other believers of their age. Most were public high school graduates who found moving on to the university which capped their state's educational system quite natural. At the university these ambitious youngsters encountered a vast range of electives, specialized professional and occupational training, excellent libraries and laboratories, proximity to home, low tuition, and the possibility of forming beneficial business and professional connections. As Timothy Harrington, founder of the first Newman Club, put it: "We sought institutions of higher learning largely as a means of increasing our earning power, as a sure road to reasonably comfortable competence."[1] Financial considerations were usually paramount. Raymond V. Achatz, organizer in 1906 of the Newman Society at Purdue, claimed that "all of us would have preferred a Catholic school, but we could not have gotten the preparation we wanted, and even if we could, most of us could not afford to go there."[2] The "great majority" of Catholics must attend public colleges, concluded one chaplain, "or none at all."[3] Denis O'Connell, who became rector of The Catholic University of America in 1903, had to agree. Explaining to authorities in Rome why enrollments of Catholics in public colleges were rising faster than those in Church colleges, he noted in 1906 that the latter were "comparatively few in number, often situated in remote localities, and generally too expensive for the children of the people."[4]

THE TRESPASSERS

Whether they came by choice or by necessity, Catholics who entered non-Catholic universities after 1900 found they had encroached upon a kind of religious "free fire" zone where they could be raked by charges of disloyalty from their spiritual guardians and by assaults on their faith by campus figures. Pastors often accused these young men and women of giving bad example to their younger brothers and sisters because they were exposing their faith and morals to corruption while seeking worldly advancement; some college-town priests refused to permit college students to attend their services, others regularly condemned the campuses from the pulpit.[5] In 1906 the Archbishop of New York issued a widely quoted statement charging Catholics in public colleges with perpetrating "an act of unpardonable disloyalty and grossest ingratitude" to God Himself.[6]

Meanwhile on campus a number of pressures made difficult the task of living a faithful Catholic life. Atheistic tendencies among professors were often cited as one of these pressures, but the true picture is not so simply drawn. A pastor in Ann Arbor noted that five Catholics who fell away from the faith during their college years had never enrolled in any courses notorious for being antireligious. On the other hand, students who had enrolled in such courses but who had also shared their difficulties with him remained practicing Catholics.[7] Another priest believed that Catholics who were good athletes received a kind of quasi-official protection of their beliefs lest they withdraw.[8] In 1930, after sixteen years as a university chaplain, Father John W. Keogh of Philadelphia claimed he had "never met one Catholic student who lost the Faith from teaching." Usually the offending professor was "an odd one or ... young" and his offensive comments generally went "completely over the Catholic's head." Keogh estimated that a quarter of defections took place in high school, perhaps less than 20 percent in college.[9]

Far more serious than militant atheism, wrote John LaFarge of his days at Harvard, was the subtle kind, which at times tantalized young minds in the lectures of a "charming, half-Catholic" like George Santayana or a "fluent, imaginative" proponent like Josiah Royce. Usually, however, most dangers to faith arose from what LaFarge termed an "all pervading indifferentism" to religious questions, something "easily breathed in."[10] This nonchalance was not limited to the Ivy League. In 1901 President Cyrus Northrop of Minnesota in describing for a group of Baptists the university's atmospheric quality said that professors and students had three options regarding religion in higher learning. "One is to shut their eyes and believe what the Church declares that it believes," he explained; that was the "Catholic method." A second was "to think for one's self," the preferable Protestant method. The third and spreading response was the way of the agnostic; that is, simply to "drop the whole matter."[11] Down through the years most chaplains agreed that studied indifference constituted the most formidable opponent to their efforts at religious education.

Most challenging of all, however, at least during the opening years of the twentieth century, was the Protestant ascendancy among university students and administrators, a dominance that generally included some form of anti-Catholic bigotry. For example, President George A. Vincent of Minnesota seemed friendly toward all denominations, yet Catholics believed he approved of convocation preachers who openly attacked their beliefs.[12] At Michigan, President James B. Angell in 1905 advocated Bible study so that true scholarship might penetrate "medieval concealments" and thus liberate the "purity of the Gospels" from papal defilements.[13] Catholic priests believed the Christian Associations (YM and YWCAs) either positively sought or "unconsciously abetted" the subversion of Catholic faith.[14] Dormitories and Greek letter residences also became scenes of skirmishes. In some cases, as at Iowa City, Catholics besieged in boardinghouses organized discussion clubs based on Cardinal Gibbons' *Faith of Our Fathers* to keep themselves "upon the right track."[15] In some Bible Belt public colleges, Catholics had to take fundamentalist scripture study courses if they lived in halls erected by those denominations.[16] Dean Frederick Keppel of Columbia University noted that Catholic students were also usually indirect victims of off-campus anti-Catholic campaigns that swept in "from time to time."[17]

These were not the only influences that tested the Catholic commitment. Dogma stood open to question, Church laws on diet and Mass attendance to challenge, and the cult of the saints to ridicule. Nevertheless, a few facts or a grasp of history could usually dispel these harassments. Assaults on Catholic moral sensibility seemed to take the greatest toll of all. At least so Father Keogh believed. Falling away was almost always "due to laziness," he said; or to giving up daily prayer; or to skipping Mass and not receiving the Sacraments; or to "mental unbalance"; or to "sex curiosity and sex sin"; or, and he made this the primary nonintellectual cause, "from association with so many non-Catholics."[18]

Catholic professors in state universities were in a position to generalize about the fidelity of their young coreligionists. One professor at the University of Idaho noted that some of the youths were "shy in admitting" their religious affiliation, but he noted that many of this sort came from rural communities that only sporadically were graced with religious services and catechetical instructions.[19] A professor at Ohio State discerned three levels of commitment. "The great majority," he said, were "fairly well grounded" in their faith, able to "embarrass" teachers who attacked the Church, and exerted a "liberalizing" influence. "Comparatively few," he thought, were "nominal Catholics," and "very few" drifted from the faith. As a group, he concluded, Catholic students he met were "a pretty good class of men and women" who acted according to their Catholicism and earned the respect of their associates. Several priests familiar with the campuses agreed with him.[20]

Perhaps precisely because extracurricular situations proved to be more challenging to Catholic life on campus than did formal lectures, Catholics there regarded themselves as "a *distinct* minority,"[21] as "strangers in a strange land."[22] One way to remain true to their colors was to form defensive associations.

THE FIRST CLUBS

Reaction to supposed anti-Catholicism certainly accounted for the origin of the first Catholic student organization in secular higher education. This aspect of the Newman Movement began on Thanksgiving Day, 1883. John J. McAnaw, a pre-law student from Ohio, was celebrating the occasion at the home of Mr. and Mrs. John C. Melvin at 1000 University Avenue, just across from the University of Wisconsin, Madison. During the course of the festivities he told his hostess that one of his professors had slandered the Catholic Church. Other students on hand may have pointed out that the accused, William Francis Allen, was highly esteemed by scholars for employing original sources in his teaching: could one treat "Medieval Institutions" and not come across some scandals? McAnaw stood his ground. Allen was a Harvard graduate, class of 1851, the son of a Unitarian minister, one of a generation of scholars not famous for handling Roman Catholicism gently. At least, so it seemed to a young Irishman bent upon "self-defense." McAnaw declared that Allen's "persistent attacks against the Church" must be refuted.[23] But how?

Mrs. Melvin, who for several years had been opening her home to all Catholics at the university, suggested that if the students wanted to defend their Catholic faith and heritage, they first had better learn it. Why not form a society for the "study of Irish and Catholic history and literature?" she prompted. The idea caught on immediately. Before the night ended, young McAnaw found himself president of "The Melvin Club."[24] And for the next fifteen years the club earned a reputation as "one of the most prosperous" clubs on a campus bulging with extracurricular literary and scientific societies. Its meetings explored such topics as "The Temporal Power of the Pope," "American Converts," and "The Tendencies in Large Universities Toward Disbelief," discussions that earned it affection as the source of "most of the intellectual food on Catholic subjects."[25]

Still, we must not think that this oldest Catholic student club was narrowly Catholic. One of its members was Sidney Dean Townley, later an astronomer, who described himself as "an agnostic," prided himself on his "ability to hold a neutral position until all the facts were in," and wondered why the Bible could not "be studied from a purely nonsectarian standpoint in our state universities." Townley confided to his diary that his "mental alertness" did not develop in lecture halls; it was at extracurricular societies like the Melvin Club, where he shared views along with sleigh rides, oysters, lemonade, and cigars, that he experienced what he termed "a broadening" of his spirit.[26]

One with whom Townley frequently debated was Timothy L. Harrington, who was born in1866 on a farm near Bear Creek, Wisconsin, the sixth of seven children. Harrington worked his way to Madison by teaching for three years after preliminary studies, and worked his way to a B.S. in General Science by cutting firewood for President Thomas C. Chamberlain. During his student years he was praised as "an excellent writer and a clear, forceful speaker" and he graduated in 1890 with an "excellent record."[27] After he was denied the principal's job in a county high school because of his Roman Catholic faith,[28] Harrington taught literature and science at Pio Nono College in Milwaukee until he earned enough money to enroll as a medical student at the University of Pennsylvania in 1892.

Harrington carried the memory of the Melvin Club to the Ivy League and it stirred achingly within him during the Christmas holidays of his first year in the east. Lacking funds for the luxury of travel, he elected to spend the vacation in Philadelphia, said goodby to his new classmates, holed up in his modest rooms on Lancaster Street, and plunged into a second reading of Cardinal Newman's *Apologia Pro Vita Sua.* Fog sifted between the brownstone houses and rain trickled around the cobblestones as, hunched against the damp on his way down the lamp-lit street to Midnight Mass, the Midwesterner remembered the biting winds and heavy snows that bent the familiar trees back home. "I spent a dreary and lonesome, desperately lonesome, two weeks in Philadelphia," he later wrote. And when his classmates returned, he suggested to a few he met at St. James Church that they "organize a Catholic club on the pattern of the Melvin club"; he emphasized what it meant to the Catholic students" at Wisconsin.

Then the days grew longer, and the distractions of learning to be a doctor once again flooded his life. It was not until the following autumn that he gathered with eighteen or so fellow graduate students in his quarters to set up what he insisted should be called "The Newman Club." On accepting its presidency, Harrington noted that "no better name could be found" for an organization of young Catholics seeking to improve themselves socially, intellectually, and religiously in a university setting "than the name of the great English Cardinal who found his way into the Church during the stirring days of the Oxford Movement."[30]

During the two years that he remained at Pennsylvania, Harrington presided over the bimonthly meetings of the Newman Club at which members or invited guests presented topics ranging from "Evolution" and "Polar Exploration" to "The Nervous Mother" and "Newman as an Educator." He also arranged to have the Rector of The Catholic University, John J. Keane, address a university convocation in 1894. This event shattered the long-standing university ban against clerics of the Church of Rome ever speaking in the chapel. In 1895 the newly graduated M.D. returned to Wisconsin, opened practice in Antigo, and, so he thought, for all practical purposes withdrew from involvement in Catholic affairs on university campuses.[31]

Toward the end of the 1890s both the Melvin Club and the Newman Club were beginning to lapse from their original form as literary societies into purely social organizations.[32] The latter attempted to revive itself in 1902 by an unsuccessful try at organizing a national federation, and tried again a year later by sponsoring a gala reception in honor of Cardinal Gibbons, who attended but offered only the faintest of praise for its efforts at "safeguarding the spiritual interests of Catholics."[33] By 1904 the first Newman Club was virtually defunct. Melvin was making a comeback, but that story takes us into a second aspect of the Newman Movement, and must wait until the next chapter.

NEW MODELS

By 1905 Catholics had organized clubs similar to these proto-types on fifteen campuses as scattered and varied as Cornell (1888), Michigan (1889), Minnesota (1890), Brown (1892), Harvard (1893), Berkeley (1898), and, after 1900, Chicago, Columbia, and several other public universities in the Midwest. Though the records of these associations are usually quite incomplete, they nevertheless permit us to draw some conclusions regarding the purpose and forms these organizations adopted.[34]

Typically, the clubs arose either from an experience of supposed anti-Catholicism or from a sudden enthusiasm for some aspect of Catholic culture; they were mainly Irish in membership; they flourished for a few years as literary societies, but usually lapsed into dancing clubs upon graduation of their founders; clubs helped by professors or other adults more often remained true to their original aims than did those lacking such attention, and clubs aided by priests usually did best of all. These early societies adopted a variety of names. Some memorialized Catholic frontier history; Idaho, for example, had a "DeSmedt Club." Others honored famous Catholic personages: Tufts had a "Louis Pasteur Club." A few chose saints, as did "St. Melania's Club" at Wellesley, and one or two, like Michigan's "Foley Guild," commemorated the attention of an interested bishop. Several, such as the one at Harvard, were simply "The Catholic Club." The name of Cardinal Newman identified a few, like those at Berkeley or the University of Texas, but it did not become prominent until after the formation of federations began in 1908.

These associations also set out to achieve nearly identical purposes: to learn, defend, and spread the Catholic faith; to pursue cultural ideals generally; to offer mutual help to members. Officers scheduled dances, smokers, and teas to attract freshmen members. As for activities, some clubs sponsored hockey or basketball teams or organized whist tournaments; others mended clothes for parish bazaars or worked in settlement houses or taught catechism for the local pastor. Treasurers were seldom able to collect all the dues needed to mount programs that generally visionary committees planned. Furthermore, few clubs had their own meeting rooms. Quarters over stores, in Knights of Columbus halls, church basements, or, sometimes, classrooms filled this need. University presidents seldom denied requests for the latter. Wrestling with a "college problem" that included cheating, gambling, offensive language, drunkenness, some sexual indiscretions, and general misbehavior, these officials welcomed the moral influences religious clubs represented. Somewhat typical was President George A. MacLean's encomium of the Newman Society at Iowa in 1909. It was, he said, "a great club doing a great work for the greatest of all Churches."[35]

One fact deserves special mention: these clubs were truly pioneering ventures. At the turn of the century, apart from chapters of the YM and YWCAs, campus religious organizations were few in number. At Texas, for example, they numbered but four out of over two dozen extra-curricular societies; Minnesota and Illinois had only two each among a total at both places of almost sixty nonreligious clubs; Catholic clubs were nearly always a part of such counts. Furthermore, along with precursors of the present-day associations of student religious liberals, the Catholic clubs began to form during the last two decades of the nineteenth century and grew with rapidity during the first two decades of the present one. The fact that Protestants did not form denominational clubs in comparable numbers until after 1910 suggests how "at home" these students felt. It is also important to note that this Protestant effort followed upon the organization of denominational campus pastorates; Catholic organizations preceded such clerical innovations. For the latter, the Church truly *followed* its students.[36]

Clergymen leading the denominational chaplaincy movement seemed to prefer ministries that united students and townsfolk in a single congregation. According to The Reverend James C. Baker, Methodist Chaplain at Illinois, a "university church" tended to isolate students into "a class" and created problems of readjustment when they attempted to join local churches after graduation.[37] Although Catholic priests did not express any recorded opinion on this subject, a number of them provided a new model by admitting the student literary or social club into status as a parish society. The early history of the Spalding Guild at the University of Illinois illustrates this system.

Organized in 1902 after a convocation address by the brilliant orator and educator, John Lancaster Spalding, Bishop of Peoria, the guild stumbled along for three years until Father John H. Cannon of Urbana agreed to serve as its adviser. During Lent in 1905 Cannon filled the pews of St. Patrick's Church each week with his special lectures on student concerns. Encouraged by this response, local businessmen chipped in some funds and the students drew up a club constitution. "The religious motive was . . . to be the main purpose," they said, although "the social side could not well be forgotten."[38]

The reinvigorated Spalding Guild flourished for the next half decade. In imitation of the popular Starr Lecture Courses, its members engaged a number of outstanding Catholic speakers, including John Cavanaugh, C.S.C., President of Notre Dame, and William J. Bergin, C.S.V., Professor of Philosophy at St. Viator College, to discuss such topics as "Modernism," "Thoughts for Thinkers," and "The Eternal City." In 1908 a series of seven talks explaining Catholicism to non-Catholics climaxed with a Mass "celebrated in English."[39] The group also received a yearly $25 grant from the university library for the purchase of "Catholic references and literature;" and secured a special shelf to house donated books.[40] Such support of student religious enthusiasm apparently seemed appropriate on a campus that suspended classes on YMCA recruitment days and provided the Association with free stationery and use of the university chapel.[41]

As was the case at most other campuses, however, a strong adviser was necessary for the club to continue. After Father Cannon was reassigned to another parish in 1911, the Spalding Guild offered little evidence of activity until another chaplain appeared in 1917.

EARLY THEORIES

The founders of the Newman Movement did not approach the campuses with any well-thought-out, comprehensive ideology in mind. They developed features of a general theory in response to the various situations they encountered. These piecemeal formulations took in educational, social, and religious considerations.

Father Peter Edward Dietz, part-time chaplain at Oberlin College in 1907, addressed himself to the relationship between religious and secular learning. Convinced that openness to American scholarship was essential, he called the university "the battle ground of civilization" and scorned anyone who trembled at such names as "Princeton, Yale, Harvard, Cornell" and others. "If I did not firmly believe in the power of truth to conquer amiably," he declared, "I would throw aside my cassock as does a soldier a broken sword."[42] At Iowa City Father Edward S. Murphy apparently agreed; in 1911 he became the first Catholic priest of record to teach courses in religion accredited by the university.[43] Other chaplains felt that religious studies for club members would help to promote the reunion of Christians.[44] The sermon Monsignor Charles Ramm delivered at the dedication of Newman Hall at Berkeley in 1910 indicates the typical intent and scope of religious education among the clubs. The chaplains would not offer a "course in theology" because that was the specialty of the seminary. Nevertheless, he pointed out, the priests would impart "that measure of instruction" which the "condition and future" of the students required.[45]

Professors often joined clergy in lamenting how easily clubs squandered energies and time in often frivolous social pursuits. Yet a number of priests insisted that such activities were necessary to the preservation of Catholic faith and morals. As Father Edwin V. O'Hara of the University of Oregon put it, "religion itself creates a profound social bond, and in turn is reinforced by the social relation." He believed that leakage from Catholicism could be traced largely to "lack of social relationships."[46] Another chaplain saw social activities as "essential to the success of Newman Club work" and welcomed the clubs as a kind of "safe anchorage" amid "stormy seas of novelty and irresponsibility" upon which student life was "inevitably launched."[47] Parties and athletic leagues introduced non-Catholics to priests, helped to break down suspicion and prejudice toward the Church of Rome, and furthered one of the principal aims of these clubs, the avoidance of mixed marriages.[48] This social purpose, along with acceptance of coeducation, probably contributed to the rejection, about 1910, of the practice of organizing dual clubs for male and female students.[49]

After 1905, when bishops began to take a more positive interest in Catholics attending public universities, they began to prescribe the qualifications and tasks of chaplains. Archbishop Patrick W. Riordan of San Francisco did not think that "everyone would be at home in a university atmosphere." He believed that a chaplain had to "have a natural sympathy with intellectual pursuits" and at the same time be able to "interest and hold students of whom he is to have charge." The chaplain needed, in his estimation, "a patience and a perseverance exercised mainly in the work of personal contact with the individual student." Because such encounters were "apt to be uninteresting, and lacking in inspiration to a man of years," the archbishop wanted the priest in university work to be "a good, active, intelligent, young man."[50] Another archbishop cited specific duties for a chaplain to perform: find lodging for students in "representative Catholic homes"; demonstrate "by frequent and personal contact" that he was interested in their welfare; assist and advise students in historical and philosophical studies; "gladly correspond with parents and guardians ... also with Reverend Pastors"; conduct "special religious doctrine classes"; and invite "the best Catholic speakers, both laymen and clergymen," to visit the campus.[51]

One theoretical element was much discussed in these early years: Was it not contrary to Catholic church law to allow, much less to encourage, graduates of parish schools to attend non-Catholic colleges and universities? In 1875 the Vatican had denounced American public schools as an occasion of sin.[52] In 1904 John LaFarge addressed himself to this question as he drew up a proposal for a Jesuit chaplaincy at Harvard. Granted that "unwholesome influences to faith and morals" could be found in secular universities, he argued, the situation simply called for "all possible safeguards." He agreed that it was not reasonable to allow Catholic undergraduates to "suffer detriment to their faith, and exert a damaging influence on future generations, because we have failed to grasp that the question is one, not of theory, but of fact." Rather than condemn secular institutions of learning, Church leaders should instead revert to the "unchanging principle" of all pastoral care: "special treatment" for the "special and peculiar situation."[53]

In 1907 Father Dietz also took up what he termed the "Catholic college issue." Despite the fact that Church laws forbade attendance at "neutral schools" and implied that Catholics should enroll only in Church colleges, Dietz contended that there was "no one system in the Church"; that the Church did not exist "for societies, but societies for the Church." He did not think it made a "bit of difference whether the college was agnostic or Protestant or infidel." He believed "God's grace worked its wonders in ways that theologians had not yet ferreted out and mapped down in distinctions." He hoped that bishops would send more and more priests to assist the struggling Catholic student clubs. Picturing the Catholic college movement as a river, he predicted that under Providence the present trickle represented by clubs and chaplains would grow, and "the lay of the land will bring both . . . to meet in one mighty stream."[54]

In an effort to design a general theory for the Catholic student movement on non-Catholic campuses, Dietz' writings drew upon his knowledge of the sociology of religion. Man was "social by nature," and either explicit rules of tradition or implicit rules fashioned for the situation governed all efforts to form human groupings. "Given the Catholic students, an endangered faith, and the chaplain," he said, "we have social units and underlying principles." The clubs now blossoming in many states evidenced the working out of these principles. Because they were part of the university enterprise they would eventually achieve a clear identity, probably centered upon a library of Catholic authors and the discussion of papers relating Catholic thought to classwork; that is, the literary seminar rather than the parish society, appeared to be the most natural model to imitate. But because these societies existed to foster religious development as well as religious knowledge, "a deeper Sacramental life" would enrich their efforts and "crown" the structures and activities their members had fashioned. Finally, Dietz added with an optimistic flourish, these presently humble "social units" would contribute to "the influences already making America Catholic."[55]

Bolstered or not by such theorizing, the Catholic student club was to remain an essential phase of Roman Catholic involvement in American nonsectarian higher education for over three-quarters of a century. At times it would be the base for launching innovations and modifications in Catholic educational and liturgical discipline. At other times it would be able to serve only as a reminder of the neglected thousands of Catholics in secular schools. During the first decade of the twentieth century, some bishops attempted to develop the club movement into a fuller apostolate that would unite laymen, professors, priests, and students in religious, educational, and social programs centered in Catholic halls adjacent to the universities. The next chapter examines these efforts and explains why they temporarily faltered.

THREE

A New Link?

Is due care taken to instruct in their religion the legions of children who, for one reason or another, do not attend or will not attend Catholic schools and colleges?

Archbishop John Ireland,
Address, "The Church in America," 1901

The Catholic Citizen, the Milwaukee archdiocesan newspaper, noted shortly after the opening of the 1906–07 school year that the "Catholic student movement" was "growing wonderfully." Catholic religious-literary clubs now flourished on fifteen nondenominational campuses, six bishops had recently appointed chaplains to minister to the clubs, and four other bishops were inviting the Paulist Fathers to establish permanent "university missions." Such assignments projected club houses, chapels, libraries, and educational halls. Meanwhile, the archbishop of Boston encouraged the organization of a national association of priests serving on secular campuses.[1] Such initiatives had their inspiration in the 1905 encyclical of Pope Pius X, *Acerbo Nimis,* the papal charter for the Newman Movement. Bitterly lamenting the growth of religious illiteracy, the pope mandated the Confraternity of Christian Doctrine to bring religious instruction to pupils attending public primary and secondary schools. For the college level students he commanded:

> Let schools of religion be founded to instruct in truths of faith and in principles of Christian life youth who attend public Universities, Lycea, and Gymnasia wherein no mention is made of religious matters.[2]

In the face of such vigilant attention to pastoral and educational needs in higher education, George A. MacLean, President of the State University of Iowa, warned the Presbyterian Board of Education that "even the Roman Catholics are preceding us, and wisely, in care for college students."[3]

27

Catholics interested in religious education were divided on the wisdom of such measures, however. The progressive chaplain at Oberlin College, Father Peter Edward Dietz, expressed the positive opinion of Timothy Harrington, many other laymen, and the Paulists when he claimed that Catholic clubs and chaplains, chapels, and seminar rooms at state universities, would become "a lot of thin wedges" opening "the path of Christian empire."[4] On the other hand, another Americanist, Monsignor Denis J. O'Connell, Rector of Catholic University and President of the Catholic Educational Association [CEA], harbored doubts, saying that the spread of such arrangements meant that "the Catholic college was destined to disappear."[5] The Church's most prestigious religious order of teachers was also divided. Jesuits at the society's headquarters in Rome saw the university situation in Italy as "almost the same as that in America"; they credited the pope with realizing the sagacity of not doing battle "with conditions beyond our control, but in some manner providing for religious needs."[6] But the conservative Father John A. Conway of Georgetown University, President of the College Department of the CEA, tended to agree with O'Connell. "The quasi-recognition of the great non-Catholic universities" symbolized by episcopally appointed chaplains, he wrote to O'Connell, would be a "serious blow to Catholic education"; yet, he mused, perhaps the development would turn out to be "a new link in Catholic evolution."[7]

A year before Pius X issued his historic mandate for Catholic centers at public universities, Archbishop Sebastian Messmer of Milwaukee had attempted to organize a corporation for "educational, charitable, and benevolent purposes" to finance such a facility at the University of Wisconsin.[8] That same year a young Catholic in Cambridge, Massachusetts, had proposed a Jesuit chaplaincy for Harvard. To meet the educational and religious needs of Catholics at such places was a question, "not of theory, but of fact," the youthful John LaFarge explained.[9] It was this practical spirit in meeting evident needs that propelled the Catholic Hall movement—Conway's "new link"—into brief prominence between 1906 and 1908.

FACING THE FACTS

Messmer's 1904 plan for Catholic students at Wisconsin foundered principally because of "a general prejudice among priests against the University."[10] The appearance of *Acerbo Nimis* a year later encouraged Father Henry C. Hengell, curate at Madison's Holy Redeemer Parish, to answer student requests for Bible classes. The success of this endeavor led swiftly to a petition, signed by virtually all of the 300 Catholics then enrolled at Wisconsin, "humbly and respectfully" asking Messmer for "pastoral care" and "advancement in religious knowledge and the practice of Christian virtue commensurate with their advancement in worldly arts and sciences."[11] By January 1906 this petition supplied the archbishop with a flag to rally Catholic support from around the state and a shield to ward off charges that he was attempting to undermine the state's Catholic colleges. Messmer visited the campus on Washington's birthday to assure the students he would "most gladly grant" their request, and the following September 17 he assigned Father Hengell to the University of Wisconsin, making him the first full-time Catholic chaplain at a state university.[12]

Early the next year Hengell received Messmer's approval of the newly formed Catholic Students' Association, which had replaced the Melvin Club, and announced plans for a structure the archbishop described as a "Catholic college for the University of Wisconsin" to include a chapel, auditorium, and reading rooms.[13] Meanwhile, Messmer had also organized the Saint Paul's Chapel Corporation to advance "the religious and educational interests of the Catholic students."[14] As a founding member of the corporation board, Timothy Harrington set up a special alumni fund to secure lecturers for the "college."[15] Although the ambitious facility was never fully realized, a Tudor Gothic chapel seating 450 with an auditorium for 400 persons was dedicated in 1910,[16] and Hengell's vigorous ministry during three decades drew national attention from Catholics and Protestants alike. Most significant for the Newman Movement, perhaps, was the advice on how to organize and finance a student association that he offered Father John W. Keogh of Philadelphia in 1914 when this cofounder of the Newman Club Federation sought to arrange the "rebirth" of the original Newman Club.[17]

A second proposal for a "Catholic college" at a nondenominational school appeared at Cornell University in April 1907. The crusty Bernard J. McQuaid, Bishop of Rochester, New York, did not think Catholics should enroll in such schools. Nevertheless, since it was "never inopportune for a bishop to try to save souls," he projected a chapel, a residence for two priests, and a lecture hall where professors from his diocesan seminary would teach courses in psychology, scholastic philosophy, and medieval history to be accredited by the Cornell Faculty of Arts.[18] The plan ran into opposition from two sides. Cornell alumni damned the idea as a Romish plot to "subvert" American education "beginning with the university."[19] Catholic educators tried to rally the American Federation of Catholic Societies against the idea.[20] Claiming that publicity "stirred up the bigots of the country and made the university cautious," McQuaid in 1907 contented himself with appointing a chaplain, hoping that once the chaplaincy was "in full swing," accreditation of Catholic studies would follow "as a matter of course."[21] His death in January 1909 dashed the dream.

More successful was Newman Hall, which the Archbishop of San Francisco, Patrick William Riordan, set in motion in March 1907 when he appointed Paulist Father Thomas Verner Moore as full-time chaplain to the eight-year-old Newman Club at the University of California at Berkeley. Providing the chaplain with the $35,000 purse that laity of the archdiocese had raised for him on his silver episcopal jubilee, Riordan viewed the chapel and classroom complex as destined to "do more good for the great number of our Catholic boys and girls" than any institution he had been "instrumental in creating."[22] Although accredited courses were out of the question, the three-story timber and stucco structure topping a slope north of the campus was intended to offer California's Catholics "that religious instruction in things Catholic" which the university could not.[23] Dedicated in 1910, Newman Hall soon became the center for regular courses in ethics, church history, and Catholic social doctrine, along with more informal "tea and talk" sessions where students raised a variety of questions about religion.[24]

The most impressive example of the Catholic Hall movement rose next at the University of Texas in Austin. In May 1907 Bishop Nicholas A. Gallagher began to form a parish of fifty families and turned it over to the Paulist Fathers for the "special care and supervision of a very choice portion of our people, the Catholic young men and women who are students in the State University."[25] Upon completion in December 1908, St. Austin's Church became the first facility for Catholics on any public campus. It was followed in 1914 by a twenty-one-room brick center for the Newman Club, in which Father John Elliott Ross taught religion courses accredited by the university, and in 1918 by a four-story dormitory for girls administered by the Dominican Sisters of Galveston.[26] Ross saw the university as "the apex of the public school system" attracting "future legislators and lawyers and bankers and governors and congressmen" from all over the state. He urged members of the Newman Club to view themselves as missionaries,[27] and developed a liturgical-educational program that Dominican Superior Mother Paulinus Gannon evaluated as "in some ways the most encouraging and far-reaching movement that has taken place in Catholic educational circles for a generation."[28]

The final example of a Catholic hall, one which by its relative poverty became the prototype for most subsequent efforts, was Newman House, an eighteen-room residence near Harvard Yard which Archbishop William O'Connell purchased in 1907 for $10,000 when plans to open a Jesuit chapel had fallen through.[29]

The box score for the Newman Movement during the three years following the issuance of *Acerbo Nimis* was quite impressive: thirteen new clubs brought the total to twenty-eight; sixteen chaplains were now on the job, five of them full-time; eleven chapels and/or Catholic halls were proposed, the five under construction or completed representing an eventual total outlay in excess of $200,000. Bishops did not put up all this money, though the five mentioned in this chapter gave generously to start projects going. From then on chaplains and alumni were responsible for fund raising, in which their greatest ally proved to be the State Councils of the Knights of Columbus. Father Hengell was especially adroit in turning alms into profitable real estate investments; Father Keogh once claimed to have collected about $25,000 promoting his own and other Newman halls.[30]

Immeasurably more symbolic and significant than pecuniary assistance, however, was the role of the bishops as spokesmen and leaders of the young movement. And in this they enjoyed the advocacy of the bishop of Rome himself. Pius X "strictly commanded" that "schools of religion be founded" at public universities because he wanted to fulfill his supreme teaching office and wished "to introduce uniformity everywhere in so weighty a matter."[31] While opponents of the Newman Movement later insisted that the pope merely asked that "classes in religion be organized,"[32] examination of the original text suggests that this is a tendentious translation. The pope used "schola" only twice: once referring to "publicas scholas" (public schools); the other time to "scholae religionis" (schools of religion). Had he meant "classes," more appropriate words were at hand. Furthermore, the Latin verb "fundentur" signifies erection or establishment of something premanent, such as a stronghold or a city. Again, if the pope wanted to say "organize," he had more suitable words in his vocabulary. The Italian translation of the encyclical conveyed the same sense: the Holy Father was ordering the erection of permanent places for the study of Catholic doctrine and morals, not asking that arrangements be made for holding classes.[33]

The favorable response of some bishops to the pope's plan generated alarm among proponents of Catholic schools and colleges in the United States. Some laymen feared that such ideas, if "logically extended, would undercut the parish secondary and primary schools."[34] For the colleges, it was felt that while the Catholic Hall movement might indeed be a "new link" in Catholic American evolution, it might also be a predatory one. Monsignor O'Connell, for example, viewed Bishop McQuaid's Cornell plan as "detrimental to a very high degree" to Catholic colleges everywhere.[35] A survey of Catholics enrolled in institutions of higher education in 1907 had revealed that of 14,000 such students, two-thirds were on non-Catholic campuses.[36] In a letter to O'Connell, Father Conway noted that, save for religious instruction, these non-Catholic campuses were admittedly "better equipped than ours," and that now, by promoting chaplaincies, the bishops seemed to be saying that they were also "safe" for Catholics.[37] In other correspondence Conway said that in "this movement for Catholic chaplains" the bishops, without whom "we can do nothing [were] drifting away from us,"[38] and he wondered: "Can we stem the tide? Can we stand up against fate?"[39] He found a way.

FOR THE SAKE OF THE COLLEGES

We have seen that the cost of obtaining an education in Catholic colleges drove thousands of young Catholics to seek advanced training in state universities. Another factor contributing to the "shifting of the field" away from Church colleges was what might be termed their "ecclesiasticism." Emphasis on the papally endorsed Scholastic philosophy insulated students from leading modern scientific and philosophical thought. Moralism undercut and devotionalism diluted solid intellectual inquiry. Moreover, pride of order within sponsoring religious communities set their institutions into a competition for a very limited supply of funds. It was true that money came hard because more than two-thirds of the Catholic colleges operated outside the northeastern United States where all colleges were most prosperous and over one-third of the Catholic population lived. Even so, lay parsimony was but a symptom of ecclesiasticism. "The benefit of collegiate education has never been impressed upon the Catholic body," complained one alumnus, "except as a *sine qua non* for the priesthood.[40] Like many other lay intellectuals, he knew that only clerical voices would be heard in the policymaking and administration of what priests called "the compact system."[41] In 1905 Archbishop

John J. Glennon of St. Louis urged a move "to secularize our colleges" because they were "too ecclesiastical."[42]

Such episcopal prescriptions especially irritated that corps most prominently committed to moralism in learning, the Jesuits. Already convinced of a conspiracy between secular educators and philanthropic foundations to put Catholic schools out of existence, these ardent founders also perceived "a sort of organized opposition to the Society in the United States" on the part of "the clergy and hierarchy."[43] Had not bishops in 1904 attacked their academies? One diocesan spokesman had charged that they functioned as "a yoke ... holding back" the colleges that incorporated them as preparatory departments, and insisted that instead all secondary schools should enjoy an independent existence for both terminal as well as pre-college training and that they should operate within a national diocesan system. Even moderate Jesuits dreaded such an arrangement, fearing that it would destory their colleges.[44] And, had not Archbishop Farley a year later proposed that these institutions save themselves by submitting to control by the hierarchy?[45] It seemed clear at least to some Jesuits that the Catholic Hall movement was part of such an overall offensive against the managers of their colleges.

But the hierarchy had not given any national endorsement to the Catholic Hall movement. Asked to do so by McQuaid in 1906, the archbishops responded by saying that "as divers laws, sentiments and view-points" obtained in different parts of the country, no such general backing was possible.[46] Father Conway of Georgetown determined to lead a counteroffensive against the appointment of chaplains and the erection of centers for religious education at secular campuses. He hoped for a two-fold outcome: To win the hierarchy over to the colleges; and to rally Catholic college leaders around the flagging Catholic Educational Association as a potentially strong lobbyist with the bishops.

Conway's operation began at the January 24, 1907, meeting of the Standing Committee of the College Conference. Top on the agenda was "the alarming number of Catholic youth going to non-Catholic colleges" and "the patronage or encouragement lent that movement by the hierarchy by the appointment of chaplains." The members of the committee— Fathers Dennis J. Flynn of St. Mary's, Baltimore, Martin A. Hehir of Holy Ghost College, Pittsburgh, and Laurence A. Delurey of Villanova University, Philadelphia—felt that the bishops were dealing with a condition they could not control. But Conway pressed his argument and soon the college men discovered "the great abyss that for so long had kept them divided from the hierarchy and the hierarchy from them." The meeting concluded with a resolution instructing the committee to meet with the archbishops during their April gathering, for which Conway was to draft a memorial indicating how "the success of our Catholic colleges rested to a considerable part" with the bishops.[47]

By the end of March the brief was ready. It asked for the colleges the "same aid and encouragement" that the bishops had already given "to the parochial schools." It noted that "the [1893] compromise permitted Catholics in England" by which they could attend universities with Catholic chaplaincies, "did not appear to be justified" under conditions in the United States, nor to hold "the solution of the problem of Catholic education."[48] As a "strong ... temperate and respectful document" that set "responsibility for the future of the colleges" upon the bishops "insofar as" the responsibility belonged there,[49] Conway's work was approved by the committee.

On April 10 the archbishops gathered at Catholic University for their annual meeting, cordially received the memorial, and initiated a spirited discussion. The college men present—Conway, Delurey, and Hehir—insisted that parents would not view education in a Catholic college "as necessary and as sacred as the training of the primary school" until the bishops placed an outright ban upon Catholic attendance at non-Catholic universities, just as they had earlier done with respect to public elementary schools. The metropolitans noted that, unlike colleges, parochial schools were "under the,immediate management of the ordinary" in each diocese. Were the college men ready, as were principals in parish schools, to submit directly to episcopal jurisdiction? Here the conversation reached a dead end. Cardinal Gibbons suggested that the college men shape a consensus among their constituents on this point and meet with a select committee of bishops at the forthcoming Milwaukee CEA convention in July.[50] Conway felt this outcome represented an initial triumph; yet the future remained shrouded: "If we can only get the bishops with us," he sighed.[51]

Conway's counteraction now had to advance upon two fronts. One was the July general session on higher education at Marquette University, where, according to the wishes of Archbishop Messmer, a paper by a Catholic chaplain would be read. The other was in the private meeting between the college men and the select episcopal committee.

The paper, written by Father John J. Farrell, chaplain at Harvard University, was read on July 10 by Father Hengell. It cautiously advocated chaplaincies because of spiritual dangers to Catholics in secular institutions. Its author attempted to safeguard "fidelity to Catholic educational ideals" while thinking through the situation "as present conditions demanded"—the familiar "condition, not a theory" rubric.[52]

Conway led the attack on Farrell's paper. It was "clever," he said, to pass over the "main" question, which was: Was the appointment of a chaplain in accordance with "all the instructions of Popes and councils on Catholic education[?]" But the Georgetown professor preferred to allow a last-minute "addition to our program" lead the rebuttals. This addition was Father Rudolph G. Meyer, S.J., newly arrived from the Jesuit headquarters in Rome.[53]

Meyer's remarks, which passionately summarized all the objections we have already reviewed, dominated the rest of the session. While the appointed moderator, Father Francis Cassilly, S.J., praised Farrell's paper for its objective depiction of college trends, three other Jesuits took the floor to argue hotly for financial and moral support for the Catholic colleges, and Father Timothy Brosnahan, S.J., of Woodstock College added that any Catholics in secular schools "should be left to their own fate."[54] Timothy Harrington courteously questioned whether such an attitude could be termed Christian and argued for the foundation of centers of intellectual and pastoral activity in state universities as "the great work . . . to be done by the Catholic Church in the United States" if only because "a body of students backed by a chaplain who holds them together" could "have influence on the faculty and students of a University."[55]

The next day, during the general session, the convention endorsed "unity of principles of Catholic education," as Jesuit and other spokesmen had advocated. Citing the many Catholic young men and women in secular schools facing dangers to faith and morals "even greater than in non-Catholic elementary schools," this statement urged Catholics, as "a sacred duty," to support education in Catholic colleges "as they have so nobly done in building up and supporting their parochial schools."[56] Unlike resolutions at earlier meetings, however, this one did not make any reference to welcome support from the hierarchy for the colleges.

MASTERFUL INACTION

The reason for lack of tangible support probably lay in the shambles of Conway's second front—the closed meeting between the college men and Gibbons' special committee: Archbishops Farley,

James Hubert Blenk of New Orleans, and Messmer. The first two were
pro-college, and Conway's negotiators surely expected a favorable
outcome from the encounter. We still lack a full report of what
happened at the meeting; in fact, not even the exact time nor location
of the meeting is known. The only published account, Conway's,
attempts to dispel as "inaccurate to say the least," a report that the
special archepiscopal committee came to Milwaukee precisely to
support the college movement.[57] Private correspondence supplies a
more candid evaluation. Wrote Bishop Louis Walsh of Portland,
Maine, a former head of the CEA: "The conference between the
Archbishop of New York and the College Men did not end in harmony and good will."[58] James A. Burns, C.S.C., founder and vice
president of the CEA, said the parley was "a failure."[59]

What happened was this. A week before the Milwaukee convention opened, Cardinal Gibbons mailed his personal instructions regarding the private session to the chairman of the episcopal committee, Archbishop Farley. "The wisest course" for the representatives of
the hierarchy to pursue in Milwaukee would be to "listen to what the
Heads of the Colleges have to say," and then "pursue rather a passive
attitude." Gibbons noted that the college men "would be very glad if
the Episcopate would conformably and officially denounce the practice of Catholic parents sending their children to secular colleges," as
they had done with respect to the public elementary schools. However, the cardinal concluded, "denunciation in the present condition of
things would be untimely and fruitless."[60] The following May the
hierarchy dissolved Farley's committee without issuing any statement
regarding either chaplaincies or the colleges.[61]

But Conway had achieved one of his objectives. Those who hoped
that airing the issue of episcopal support for chaplaincies would
strengthen the Catholic Educational Association felt that the organization was now growing strongly—in July 1908 it held its "largest and
most representative session" ever.[62] The college men worked so assid-
uously to upgrade their programs and expand their institutions that
in 1912 a prominent observer warned Protestant college leaders that
Catholic educators were men who "never slumber and seldom blunder."[63]

Meanwhile the spectre of the Catholic hall idea seemed laid to
rest. Nevertheless, during the next dozen years new Catholic clubs
opened on about two dozen campuses. Officials at the University of
Chicago and at Yale were ready to welcome the erection of "Catholic
colleges," such as Messmer and McQuaid had proposed, and the Johns
Hopkins University wanted to hire a priest to hold a permanent chair

in philosophy.[64] However, the only significant fresh attempt to provide facilities for Catholics at these schools after 1908 was the men's residence hall the Knights of Columbus opened in 1920 at the University of Missouri.[65] Father Dietz tartly summed up the fate of the Newman Movement following the Milwaukee meeting of 1907 by saying that chaplains had as much likelihood of influencing "such interests as were represented" there as a herring trying "to push an iceberg out of its way."[66]

We have seen how Father Dietz attempted to work out a theory for the early Newman Movement.[67] A few bishops shared his optimism for the Catholicizing of America and his confidence in doing so by confronting and triumphing over modern thought. For example, Archbishop John Ireland of St. Paul warned: "This is an intellectual age," one that would "not take kindly to religious knowledge separated from secular knowledge."[68] Such leaders were the spiritual kin of the Paulist, Isaac Hecker, who believed that "intelligence and liberty" were "not a hindrance but a help to religious life."[69] These men were also known as "Americanists," the proponents of an accommodation to modern life whom Pope Leo XIII had condemned in 1899. It would indeed be convenient to think that the Newman Movement, usually regarded as *avant garde,* was a spawn of the Americanizing wing of the Catholic hierarchy. The interest of such prelates as Spalding of Peoria and Ryan of Philadelphia, as well as Riordan and Ireland, might suggest this.

The truth is quite otherwise. The Catholic Hall movement was led by one prelate seemingly indifferent to the whole issue, Gallagher of Texas; and by three others hostile to the Americanizers, O'Connell, McQuaid, and Messmer. Indeed, the last two of these launched their campus projects partly to protest liberalism in Catholic higher education. Messmer applied the yearly collection for the Catholic University to help build St. Paul's Chapel.[70] The efforts of conservative ordinaries on behalf of Catholics in secular colleges was primarily neither educational nor missionary, but, rather, pastoral and custodial. These bishops may have reassured themselves that, for the most part, their beneficiaries enrolled in technical courses and would not later wield the kind of intellectual influence their counterparts from Church-sponsored, traditionally organized liberal arts colleges would. At the same time, Americanizers had a stake in Catholic colleges: the best of them were evidence that the Church did not fear the new thought.[71] Thus, it was not surprising that when the time for vigorous prochaplaincy effort came at the Milwaukee CEA meeting, it was the shining knight of the liberals, James Gibbons, who struck a gentleman's agreement favoring the colleges by advising vigilant and masterful inaction.

WHAT MIGHT HAVE BEEN

Thus what Father Conway had seen as possibly "a new link in Catholic evolution"—chaplaincies and Catholic halls as a mutation of the Church's pastoral and educational life in the environment of the non-Catholic campus—was arrested in its earliest development. Had Catholic educational leaders supported this movement would things have gone differently in higher education? The answer to such a question can only be speculative, but the question is worth pondering.

In the first place, these were the formative years of the American public college and university. Even bishops like Messmer and McQuaid, who believed that Catholics belonged in conservative Church colleges, nevertheless promoted Catholic chapels and educational centers precisely because they recognized the importance of trained lay leaders and wanted to maintain a Catholic influence on their formation. And university presidents welcomed this influence, something they found more difficult to do a generation later. Prominent figures like Harvard's Charles W. Eliot, Pennsylvania's William Pepper, Michigan's Angell, Chicago's William Rainey Harper, Wisconsin's Charles Van Hise, and California's Benjamin Ide Wheeler positively encouraged the appointment of priests and the work of Newman clubs.[72]

Also, during these years the ecumenical movement was just getting under way in the United States, and Catholic chaplaincies at state universities might have made a significant contribution to its advance. It does not seem likely, as Father Dietz claimed, that Catholic halls would abet "the influences already making America Catholic."[73] Yet President MacLean insisted in 1909 that "a larger Americanism" was taking shape, one rooted in confidence that "religion and morality in the schools" would no longer "trench upon liberty of conscience and degenerate into sectarianism."[74] Chaplains found that the social activities of the clubs brought priests into contact with non-Catholics who otherwise might never have met Catholic clergymen, and who usually had their misunderstandings of Catholic attitudes and doctrines corrected. The Dominican Sisters' dormitory at Texas provided an additional means for fostering such interfaith understanding.[75] Such a flowering of tolerance Van Hise hoped would eliminate church-state problems in higher education.[76] Interfaith activity would probably have moved from the social to the academic level, and eventually engaged the secular disciplines of the university in mutually beneficial dialogue. Indeed, this was primarily why former President Andrew Dickson White called McQuaid's efforts to win accreditation for Catholic studies at Cornell "a happy omen."[77] And this from the author of *The Warfare of Science with Religion*! Also, halls for religious education at state universities might well have helped to reverse trends isolating seminaries from the centers of American higher learning, a condition that presidents like Angell and Wheeler lamented and tried to correct.[78]

Without doubt, young Catholics preparing for leadership in American society would have benefited on a much wider scale than they did. The Irish constituency of most of these early clubs tended to make them seem narrowly clannish. The appointment of a full-time chaplain attracted students from all national backgrounds and helped to replace an ethnic Catholic self-image with a more "truly Catholic" identity.[79] Pastoral ministry decidedly improved when a priest was released from general parish work to serve the campus full-time. Under these conditions, noted Father Farrell of Harvard, "the good Catholic became . . . more bold in the profession of his faith, and the practice of his religion," while the timid Catholic "frequently took courage," and the bad one "in very many instances, became much better."[80] Recalling the early days of Newman Hall at Berkeley, an alumna described its chapel as "an oasis in a desert of loneliness" where "the Silent Friend was always at home when tired and often discouraged students came for a visit."[81] Priests were also able to help interested professors transform the often defensive clubs into more self-assured communities for positive counseling, instruction, and even evangelical activity. A graduate of Minnesota found help in thinking through the conflict between evolutionary theory and Catholic belief, and later was able "to help many other students as time marched on."[82] A student at Texas, who learned in the Newman Club program how to become a catechist in rural areas, believed St. Austin's parish accomplished "as much for the Catholic students of the university as any Catholic school or Catholic college."[83]

This comment raises the ultimate might-have-been: if the Newman Movement had received early approval and substantial financing, would it have put Catholic colleges out of business as their proponents gloomily forecast? No one ever produced convincing evidence that Newman chaplaincies lured Catholics from attendance at Church colleges. As a matter of fact, in 1906, when the "shifting of the field" led many college men to fear their institutions would run out of students, the vice president of a midwestern Jesuit institution urged appointment of "vigorous and scholarly" chaplains to serve Catholics enrolling in state universities; his statistical projections led him to conclude that "there will be as many students in Catholic colleges and universities as we shall be able to take care of."[84] Two decades later, near the climax of a second, broader, and much more bitterly conducted debate on the issue, an official at Notre Dame believed his counterparts around the country had "really little to fear from the multiplication of Newman halls."[85] What these and like-minded Catholic educators meant was that good Catholic colleges would succeed, and that bishops should feel free to develop the "new link" for the benefit of those in their flocks who could not find or afford superior Catholic education.[86]

Without strong chaplaincies and schools of religion at state universities to compete with them, weak Catholic colleges probably were enabled to survive when they otherwise would have failed. For example, in 1916 a professor at St. Viator College, Bourbonnais, Illinois, castigated what he termed the "three great evils" that kept Catholic colleges from achieving excellence: "excessive multiplication . . . extreme autonomy . . . [and] erroneous and inadequate financial methods." He believed the existence of fourteen Catholic colleges in his state with a total enrollment of only 1,000, a ratio he claimed was better than in most states, helped to explain not only why these colleges were inferior, but also why they resisted efforts to standardize their programs. He wished for a pope who would "suppress the vast majority of them."[87] Not until the 1950s did leaders of the college movement begin to regard over-expansion as a serious problem.[88] Meanwhile the continual appearance of new and comparatively weak institutions only reinforced the protectionist policy that made them possible.

Defenders of the colleges claimed that any national planning for Catholic higher education awaited "more cooperation and more unity of effort in the higher episcopal quarters."[89] For their part, the bishops seemed convinced around 1906 that no unified policy regarding either colleges or chaplaincies was possible because of differing laws, opinions, and outlooks in the several states and among the several sponsoring religious orders.[90] Yet when the hierarchy concluded that they could not support the demands of the colleges, they offered a reason that might have worked in favor of the Catholic Hall movement. The bishops could not back the colleges as they had the parish schools, they said, because only for the latter could they "give some guarantee to Catholic parent[s] concerning the studies and progress made in these schools."[91] But according to *Acerbo Nimis* the bishops were ordered to establish at secular campuses precisely the kind of schools of religion for which they could provide parents a guarantee of "studies and progress." The Catholic Hall movement was presumably the kind of diocesan venture accountable to the local ordinary, as were parochial schools.

Why, then, did the bishops not erect such halls and appoint chaplain/teachers to them? Partly because of a shortage of qualified priests. But partly, also, if we are to believe comments by chaplains, because the bishops were too involved in paying for schools, rectories, convents, and churches.[92] At mid-decade, according to one report, sixteen dioceses were expending $15,000,000 on cathedrals.[93] Father Felix Thomas Seroczynski, chaplain at Purdue University, most trenchantly attacked this policy. He agreed with Archbishop Riordan that "if we neglect the Catholic young men at our state universities, we shall lose many of our educated laymen."[94] Yet the bishops were pouring millions into the erection of what the chaplain termed "expensive cheap imitations of European Cathedrals" for the benefit of the "ready-made Catholics of Europe, many of them poorly made." By neglecting the potential of the educated young lay person, this policy seemed designed to keep the Church "forever at the starting point."[95]

But among these young Catholics were a few determined to avoid such a calamity. If the "new link" could not become dominant, they would have to search for an alternative way to fulfill their hope of permeating their secular education with their Catholic faith.

FOUR

The Only Alternative

"Should Catholic higher education ever break down,
it would be upon our Newman Clubs and the Federa-
tion that the burden of keeping the faith strong in
students would rest."

Father Charles Briehl,
Address to The Federation of College Catholic
Clubs, July, 1920

Raymond V. Achatz thought the story of his family was "pretty much the history of thousands" of American Catholics. Born and raised among German shopkeepers, baptized and catechized by Irish priests, and educated in public schools, Achatz decided at seventeen to become an electrical engineer. He attended Iowa State and Purdue, taught electrical engineering at the latter institution for ten years, then began his own business in southeastern Indiana in 1918, after marrying a girl he had met at a meeting of the Newman Society in Iowa City years earlier.

The Newman Movement was important in Achatz' life for many reasons. During his undergraduate and graduate years he believed strongly that his coreligionists in state universities needed some common bond, a way of identifying themselves to each other as Catholics without attracting the hostility of often anti-Catholic college-town populations. He felt that belonging to associations under the name of John Henry Newman fulfilled this requirement perfectly. When a 1907 YMCA census at Purdue revealed several Catholics whom the Newman Society did not know about, Achatz said in an interview, "the old missionary spirit began to boil, and we set out to enroll every Catholic, not only at Purdue but all over the United States."[1] The outcome, the first national federation of Catholic student clubs on non-Catholic campuses, served as more than an attempt to unify and give an identity to these struggling societies. It represented the first appearance of a kind of lobby dedicated to regaining for the Newman Movement the official status and assistance discussed in chapter 3. It took over fifty years, and a second national body, before such efforts won their reward.

BRANCHING OUT

Back at the Newman Society in Iowa, Daniel Sheehan was thinking thoughts similar to those of Achatz. In December 1907 he shared them with Father Henry C. Hengell, chaplain at the University of Wisconsin, and the following March he met with Achatz to draft a constitution for the federation and to plan a founding convention.[2] Early in April 1908 Hengell's delegates journeyed to Purdue to join representatives from nine other midwestern, four Ivy League, and one West Coast university. After debate lasting into the wee hours of the second day, the Wisconsin delegation succeeded in having the group reject "The Newman Club Federation" as its title, and instead adopt "The Catholic Student Association of America" (CSAA). Being Catholic was nothing to be ashamed of! The meeting agreed upon six purposes for the new national body:

(1) To bring the Catholic students of America into closer relationship with one another through their local organization. (2) To effect the establishment of local organizations at non-Catholic universities and colleges where they do not now exist. (3) To make a concentrated effort to secure special spiritual direction from the clergy. (4) To further the good will already existing between the Catholics and non-Catholics. (5) To endeavor to correct occasional misconceptions of Catholicism. (6) To promote among the members unswerving loyalty to the Catholic faith.[3]

The founders made a special point of their need to seek out a bishop who would serve as a "national spiritual director" to be "elected for life."[4] After electing Achatz as their first president, the founders of the CSAA adjourned amid great jubilation and optimism.[5]

The organization led a shaky existence over the next seven years. To begin with, it was never able to find a bishop able to supply vigorous guidance.[6] Apart from generous and far-seeing men like Father Felix Thomas Seroczynski, chaplain at Purdue, most parish priests ignored pleas for encouragement and help. Moreover, the distances separating the schools proved to be an insurmountable obstacle to unity and growth.[7] In 1915, with only three of its sixteen affiliated clubs operating outside the Midwest, the "national" association went into a fatal decline. The most serious blow was Hengell's withdrawal. He charged that the CSAA held interest only for its own officers, a complaint to be heard about such organizations many times in the years that followed. In the opinion of the "Dean of Catholic Chaplains," as the outspoken priest liked to term himself, it was more important to "concentrate on efforts in achieving a local success before we should branch out and dissipate energies all over the United States."[8] Although the Paulist Fathers in Chicago and the Knights of Columbus in Milwaukee tried to save the association, a convention called for Boulder, Colorado, in 1918 never met.[9]

Significant as a symbol, however faltering, of student desire for Catholic religious leadership in higher education, the CSAA remains important also for the few surviving copies of its journal, *The Catholic Student*, which appeared irregularly between 1909 and 1916. These give us the flavor of Catholic life in both the Protestant twilight of the state university, and the Catholic penumbra of official indifference; they also echo the vigor of the lay renaissance of the 1890s.[10] Its articles on woman's suffrage were strong and favorable: "Catholic women can best prepare themselves by working for its arrival." Those on Protestantism were strong and unfavorable: "Born in disobedience," it would soon "crumble by its own internal discord." So also were articles criticizing college text books for ignoring "the omnipotent Power behind every science." On the mission of Catholics in secular higher education, the *Student* was often eloquent. The Church was an expeditionary force "waging war against social and educational corruption"; Catholic students, "obedient to the high command of bishops and priests," marched as "non-commissioned officers at the head of the ranks of the laity." Their mission, Father Seroczynski told students in 1910, was to show forth the Church as "the truest democracy" in existence: he instructed them to "permit no Greek letter snobbishness," to repel "bigotry with organized protest," to live as "sermons on modesty, temperance, obedience, and reverence for all authority," and to be "a laity intelligently self-assertive."

In 1914 leadership of the Newman Movement began to pass to the East Coast as the result of a reenactment, in some notable ways, of events that had begun to unfold in Wisconsin thirty years earlier: a woman supplied the initial impetus; a prominent archbishop approved; a fulltime chaplain appeared upon the scene. But the Federation of College Catholic Clubs of Greater New York, as the organization was known during its first year (the last four words left the title when it went national in 1915), added one important new factor: concerted guidance from Catholic professors in metropolitan colleges. These adults cooperated with energetic students to develop the second, and the successful, interstate association of Catholics on the secular campus, the direct ancestor of the Newman Club Federation. They also debated the issue of lay versus clerical influence, an argument which, after some bitter internal squabbles early in the 1920s, the latter won.

OUT IN THE EAST

Mary F. Higgins was a member of a unique order of women religious. Although she had taken vows of poverty, chastity, and obedience, she did not wear a distinctive garb nor did she live in cloister. Her order, the Society of the Daughters of the Heart of Mary, was dedicated to penetrating everyday life with the message of the Gospel by working in some profession. Miss Higgins taught education at Hunter College in New York, where she also served as adviser to the Catholic students' society, The Barat Club.[11] In 1914 she decided to share her club's well-developed social and educational program with those on nearby campuses. A wealthy friend and Jewish convert, Mrs. Jacob L. Phillips, used her influence with Cardinal John Farley to arrange for Father Terrence Sheely, S.J., to address the clubs invited to a "lecture-dance" at Delmonico's Restaurant. Sheely's talk, "Catholic Doctrine," was enthusiatically received, the scheme was repeated, and within a year the program was drawing up to 1,000 students from all the college Catholic clubs in the city.[12]

Encouraged by Cardinal Farley's praise, the two women, together with leaders and faculty advisers of clubs at Hunter, City College of New York, Barnard, Teachers' College, New York University, and Adelphi formed at Mrs. Phillips' home on October 28, 1915, a "federation" which they intended to expand into a national organization. Cardinal Farley agreed to serve as its "episcopal patron," and John Michael Kieran, Dean of Hunter College, was elected its first president. "The knowledge of Catholic doctrines and deepening the spirit of faith" was to be the most important work of the federation, Kieran said in an inaugural statement.[13] Contact with clubs in Massachusetts, New Jersey, and Pennsylvania encouraged the leaders to design and announce a conference at Cliff Haven, near Plattsburg, New York, in the summer of 1916.[14] Here, surrounded by natural beauty and enveloped in a Catholic summer village and seasonal school that Cardinal Gibbons had once said pulsed with the "spirit of the primitive Church,"[15] the Newman Movement received what was to be its basic shape for the next half-century.

The fifty student delegates and adult advisers who gathered at Cliff Haven in August of 1916 and 1917 had plenty of time for classes at the Catholic Summer School, as well as for hiking, swimming, and boating. But they also met together to pray, and to hammer out the following principles for their national association.

First, the Catholic Church in the United States stood in danger of losing "those of her sons and daughters most thoroughly equipped for life's journey." Since "in union there is strength," the first line of defense against loss of faith came "from the students themselves" when they formed into clubs "to be fortified against all doubts." Second, since these societies tended to be small, weak, and isolated, the Federation of College Catholic Clubs arose as "a logical consequence" to enroll them in a national movement to "secure the highest possible development and efficiency" for each club while at the same time respecting and guarding its "legitimate independence." Third, because of distances separating the clubs to be federated, a mediating provincial structure would carry the national program, modified according to regional circumstances, to each club.[16]

Three additional measures set up guides for the functioning of these structures. The first of these required that before being accepted into the federation, each club must receive the approval of the bishop in whose diocese it would function. To earn this approval, the members had to eschew all Greek letter social and Protestant religious activities and pledge "unswerving loyalty to the teachings and authority of Holy Mother Church." Such stringent requirements were designed to assure bishops that Catholics in state universities were not, as they had so often been portrayed, traitors to the Church.[17]

The two other far-reaching resolutions established the *Newman Quarterly* and the office of chaplain general. The journal was intended by its chief proponent, Alexis Irénée duPont Coleman, Professor of English at City College of New York, "to hasten growth and expansion . . . inter-club cooperation and national unity" and "to be the expression of intellectual Catholicism."[18] The office of chaplain general was filled by Father John W, Keogh of Philadelphia, whose two decades of service would prove him to be the staunchest friend and the bravest promoter of the Newman Movement and would win for him the soubriquet "Mr. Newman."[19] We shall examine the contribution of these two men in the next section.

By the time America entered World War I, then, the Federation of College Catholic Clubs benefiting from adult leadership and favorable circumstances in the Northeast, had formulated its goals, secured episcopal sanction and priestly guidance, and worked out a plan for expansion on national, provincial, and local levels. During the next several years the federation accomplished little beyond holding its annual conference and encouraging member clubs to adopt the name of John Henry Newman, but little more could have been done. Enlistments and influenza disrupted the campuses. In 1920, of the 40,000 Catholics attending non-Catholic universities, fewer than one-fourth belonged to the seventy clubs, and only twenty-two clubs were in the federation. Of fifty-one known chaplains, a mere six served on a full-time basis. Well-organized provinces like those around New York City and Boston were becoming strong bastions of the Catholic student movement, but beyond the mountains conditions remained in disarray.[20] Even so, the Paulist chaplain at the University of Toronto, speaking at the convention that year, urged the clubs to "assume a missionary role at all universities," and not "be content with simply taking care of Catholic students." "Newman Clubs," he said, "ought to be a dynamo of Catholicism, radiating the principles of the Church in all directions."[21]

FEDERATION AND ITS DISCONTENTS

Notwithstanding such aggressive assertions, the federation in 1920 was entering some very tricky waters. Within a year it nearly foundered when Professor Coleman, its president from 1918 to 1921, differed with Chaplain General Koegh over the degree of lay control to be allowed in the national movement. Within another four years Father Keogh's policy of rapid expansion led to another moment of tension that also threatened to wreck the fragile union. Both conflicts were symptoms of the larger struggle within the Church in the United States to maintain what was becoming a quite conservative ecclesiastical supervision over a renascent lay initiative—the latter epitomized in A. I. duPont Coleman.

Born in 1864, the son of the bishop of the Protestant Episcopal Diocese of Delaware, Coleman received his higher education at Keble College, Oxford, and returned to serve as an Episcopal rector in Delaware until his conversion to Roman Catholicism in the mid-1890s. For several years he lived something of a bohemian life before joining the faculty of City College of 1909. His colleagues thought of him as an expansive scholar of wide interests whose love of life radiated through the philosophical calm of his discussions on English literature or anything else. His students could not forget his massive frame, the heavy mouth that could boom with laughter, the quick, piercing eyes that flashed behind rimless spectacles, and the massive, balding head wreathed in smoke from a huge pipe. A person of Olympian proportions, yes, and also one divinely freed, it seemed, from "the constant urge for self-aggrandizement."[22] The Newman Club for which he was adviser, upon his sudden death in 1926 appropriately set up a yearly communion breakfast in tribute to his "services and sacrifices."[23]

Keogh differed from Coleman in many respects. Born in "Fishertown," a shabby section of North Philadelphia, on November 29, 1877, Keogh attended local Catholic primary and secondary schools, and matriculated for two years at night classes in Temple University, supporting himself by managing his father's cigar store. His friends claimed these humble beginnings made him "a scrapper," and some, amused by the jaunty tilt of his derby, dubbed him the "Iron Duke."[24] By background and temperament, Keogh was suspicious of elitism in any form. He entered St. Charles Seminary in 1900, and was ordained nine years later, after which he served as a rather intractable curate in three parishes before being sent to the University of Pennsylvania as chaplain in September 1913.[25]

At the university he gradually rebuilt the defunct Newman Club into a model for the nation by furnishing it with a Catholic hall consisting of two adjacent brownstones on Chestnut Street, and by setting up, as Pius X had mandated, a school of religion. He insisted that the greatest thing Pennsylvania had was "Jesus Christ, present in the Sacrifice and Sacrament of His love."[26] This conviction rallied thousands of Catholic students whom the seemingly tireless chaplain instructed at worship, supervised in the teaching of catechism at seven center city missions, and cajoled into attending theology courses he put together with the help of former seminary professors.[27]

All this, and chaplain general too! In his capacity as chaplain general Keogh crossed the country on four major tours and dozens of minor trips, addressing national and regional conventions, founding clubs, studying trends, cheering up chaplains, writing reports, pointing to Newman's intellectual honesty and devout humility as a model for all scholars, and pleading everywhere with bishops for help, help, help. In return he was "abused, ridiculed, criticized, scolded, and harangued from coast to coast and border to border for being so 'radical' as to suggest that the Church give a so-called approbation to nonsectarian education," remembered his coworker and successor at Pennsylvania, Father John Donnelly. But Keogh received merited, if belated, recognition: In 1949 he was awarded an honorary Doctor of Letters from Villanova University, and a decade later he received both the Cardinal Newman Award from the federation and a monsignorate from Pope John XXIII. Very likely, however, the spunky advocate who hoped against hope to improve the lot of young Catholics in secular higher education was most gratified because of the many Newman clubs in existence at the time of his death, on October 15, 1960, which proudly boasted that they owed their origin to him.[28]

The Newman Movement almost foundered early in the 1920s because Coleman and Keogh differed on one crucial point: Was it to be primarily a lay apostolate cooperating with the newly formed National Catholic Welfare Conference, or was it to be a student operation dominated by clergy who secured aid from individual bishops and other benefactors while, at the same time, free of ties with the newly formed national secretariat in Washington, a central agency suspect in conservative quarters such as Philadelphia?

Coleman favored the former vision. His contacts with A. C. Monahan, Director of the Bureau of Education within the NCWC Department of Education, convinced him that the bishops' secretariat stood ready to promote the work of Newman clubs all over the country. In Coleman's scheme, the federation would work closely in some kind of liaison with Monahan's bureau; Keogh could possibly fill such a role.[29] Also, although the federation would continue to exist at national, provincial, and local levels, its makeup at the top would be drastically altered. Only volunteering graduates of proven ability could hold positions of national leadership, rather than, as at present, elected undergraduates, in whom the sixty-year-old academic found "so little to be depended upon."[30] Finally, each local club would develop counterparts in public high schools to provide religious education and groom members for the collegiate Newman clubs. Coleman was convinced this arrangement would render the Federation of College Catholic clubs more efficient, supply it with guidance from the bishops, and help it to become financially independent from what he termed "benevolent outsiders."[31] By this last remark he apparently meant Mrs. Phillips, to whom Keogh turned for a dole whenever federation dues could not support a needed program. For example, in 1921 she agreed to pay the salary for a field secretary, even though the NCWC was willing to take responsibility for such an officer.[32]

Nor did Coleman's plan exist only inside his own fertile mind. Early in 1920 he organized twelve alumni from several clubs into what he titled "The Tenth Legion," naming it after Caesar's most trusted cadre. The legion was dedicated to furthering "the work of the federation and any other good works which the Church" had in hand.[33] Within a year the organization included sixty members and had eight committees busy on apostolic activities as varied as teaching catechism in several parishes, carrying on settlement work among Italian and Spanish immigrants, and helping foreign students to find lodging and friends. Furthermore, by 1921 the "splendid organization of the chosen," as Coleman termed it,[34] had helped finance Newman Hall at Columbia University and organized a number of junior Newman clubs.[35]

Another major project for this elite corps was the securing of articles for the *Newman Quarterly*. Determined that the journal should follow the lead set forth in the Bishops' Pastoral Letter of 1919, Coleman saw to it that a substantial number of these pieces expounded Catholic social and economic doctrine written by such qualified thinkers as Michael Williams and Fathers John A. Ryan and Charles A. Briehl. Other contributions examined the compatibility between Catholicism and the findings of scholars in medieval studies, art, biological science, and psychoanalysis.[36] Each issue of the *Quarterly* also carried items highlighting the Catholic contribution to various American institutions, e.g., religious freedom, the advance of science, politics, and military victory. Naturally, the issues also carried regular reports of club and province happenings. Through such literate and forceful presentations of the Catholic heritage, the federation, linked to the national apostolate of the Church, could not fail to achieve its aim of surrounding students with "a Catholic environment" by securing "Catholic faculty members to teach the truths of the Catechism, of the Bible, of sacred history, of Catholic philosophy and Catholic sociology."[37]

Keogh harbored doubts about the whole thing. He interpreted collaboration between Coleman and Monahan as an attempt by the NCWC Department of Education "to absorb" the movement, something he viewed quite negatively.[38] Personal considerations also played a role. Keogh was very upset when members of the New York province, presumably at Coleman's behest, voted their foundress, Miss Higgins, out of the chairmanship; this action alienated Mrs. Phillips, something the chaplain general regarded as a calamity.[39] Finally, Keogh resented proposals that the elite Tenth Legion should direct the executive committee of the federation rather than serve it as an auxiliary group under orders from that committee to "do the work of the Federation, nothing else."[40]

The showdown came at the 1921 conference. Coleman went to Cliff Haven confident that he had enough votes to put his plan across; but Keogh had been working carefully among the delegates and had gradually built a majority ready to break the legion into alumni councils attached to the clubs.[41] So well had the chaplain general lobbied that even the CCNY delegate voted against Coleman. The president, Keogh recalled, "stepped back from the rostrum in amazement," and conceded defeat.[42] Coleman's version differs slightly—because of the "bitter attack" on the Tenth Legion that some of Keogh's spokesmen mounted, its advocate elected to withdraw his scheme and "go on exactly as we were."[43] In the confusion, more harsh words were exchanged, including the professor's charge that the chaplain could not understand the English language,[44] and as late as October 1922 Coleman continued to press his cause.[45] The matter was not finally settled until 1924, when the Tenth Legion dissolved itself into the Newman Alumni of New York City.[46] Asked about the whole affair some time later, Keogh replied that Coleman had been a great pioneer, that nothing could be achieved without enthusiasm, and that the FCCC's second president had been "an enthusiast."[47]

Keogh's victory over Coleman, and thus over what the priest saw as excessive lay initiative, seemed to be secured at the conference of 1921. There, the federation elected as its new president one whom the chaplain general found to be much more tractable, David A. Gibson, a graduate of the University of Pennsylvania.[48]

Enjoying a new sense of confidence, Keogh addressed himself to solving the ever-present financial problems of the federation. Each member of an affiliated club was expected to pay a ten-cent tax in support of the national work. Yet publishing 2,000 copies of each issue of the *Quarterly* consumed half this budget even when its own meagre income was figured in, and student dues covered less than a fourth of all expenses. Officers had to meet their own costs of traveling and sometimes even pay for their own stationery and stamps. Two massive fund drives were attempted, but neither succeeded; indeed, the second collapsed when it could not finance its own mailings. By 1929 Keogh figured he had donated $8,000 of his own to keep the federation in business.[49]

Keogh insisted that a continually broadening base for taxation would automatically result from expanding the federation, something that would also further the great work that all were committed to accomplishing. To promote expansion, he hired William F. Starsinic of the University of Pennsylvania as full-time field secretary in the fall of 1921.[50] During the next two years Starsinic crisscrossed the country, speaking to Catholic student groups, organizing them into clubs, and encouraging them to affiliate with the national federation. His first year's effort brought in twelve new member clubs, raising the total number to sixty-four. But soon a debate over "extension versus intension" broke out. Applications for affiliation were coming in from Oregon, Arizona, Utah, Florida, and other distant regions. Part-time provincial and national officers began to complain that they could not handle the mounting business of mailing out membership cards, Newman emblems, pins, and other paraphernalia; moreover, they did not have enough resources to visit all the new places.

In 1924 the Newman Club of Toronto, regarded as one of the largest and strongest in the federation, withdrew because the Keogh-Starsinic program was draining away money to affiliate infant clubs without returning proportionate amounts to finance the educational helps an advanced club needed. Other local officers joined in this complaint.[51] At that summer's conference Keogh once again faced restive students. The federation "was approaching a state of decadence," claimed the students' spokesman, because it had become "the shadow of Father Keogh." Admitting that the priest had generously taken upon himself "the enormous burden" of leading the movement, he was now acting like a man with "so many trees around him" he could not "see the forest." Keogh defended his policy by pointing out that "this federation has no money," and reiterated his strategy. Father John Elliott Ross, now chaplain at Columbia University, defended the chaplain general. "Extension and concentration" should advance hand in hand, he said, because a long-range view, one that students admittedly could not have, assured eventual mutual assistance as well as increased national publicity for the cause. The session nevertheless came very close to being a disaster. In addition to voting against continued expansion,[52] some students started a short-lived campaign to replace Keogh with Ross.[53]

Keogh went to the 1925 conference armed with a streamlined constitution to govern the enlarged organization. It increased dues, added another officer at the national level, made the development of new provinces as important as founding new clubs, created an alumni section, and replaced the Newman emblem that Coleman had designed with one of his own. All this was drawn up on an elaborate chart to illustrate how the refashioned structure would set the federation surely "on its way to the goal it has long been striving for." Apparently forgetful of the previous year's resolution against expansion, or perhaps having no alternative, the delegates adopted Keogh's proposal. He thanked them for making this tenth annual meeting "the most remarkable in Federation's history."[54]

LOOKING BACK OVER THIRTY YEARS

In the mid-1920s, having beaten back an attempt to place alumni in charge of the Federation of College Catholic Clubs, ostensibly in the interest of permitting undergraduates to develop as leaders of their own organization; and then having surmounted objections from this quarter to his own dominance over their affairs, especially with regard to what he saw as the interrelated issues of finance and expansion, the pugnacious chaplain general appeared to be in full control of the national phase of the Newman Movement. Keogh's prominence at yearly conferences, his control over its publications, and his zeal in organizing local chapters more or less assured him of a strong voice at the local level as well. A student recounting one of the priest's convention addresses offered this tantalizing bit of evidence of the latter: "Father Keogh expressed his belief that the first duty of every club should be religious and to know what the Catholic Church presents," he noted, and then added, "therefore, this should be the aim of our clubs."[55]

Father Keogh's assertion of clerical prerogative is evident in much of his behavior as a leader of the Newman Movement. In 1915 he attended the first federation convention because he feared "talk against the Church" might break out; he was satisfied that his presence averted this.[56] He apparently advanced Newman as patron, not chiefly because of the convert's probing intellectuality or advocacy of laymen becoming leaders in the Church, but more because his "high position ... as Cardinal" and "his ideal life as priest and prelate" supplied "propaganda for Catholicity and the Catholic priesthood."[57] The chaplain general repeatedly warned students that "Newman Clubs may come and go but the Archbishops and Bishops remain";[58] he was always fearful lest some liberal opinion or questionable activity (such as an interfaith conference) threaten "that general approbation we have been looking for."[59] It may well be that the cleric's humble origins and precarious position as leader-protector of a movement denied full Catholic respectability made such outbursts inevitable. But the fact that he was remembered as "always obedient to the voice of authority"[60] suggests that special pressures were upon him. We shall examine this possibility in the next chapter. Now it is time to review how the first aspects of the idea of a Newman Movement emerged.

We have seen that these elements are five in number—club, adult advisor (often a professor), chaplain, center, and federation. Between 1883, when the Melvin Club appeared at the University of

Wisconsin, and 1908, when St. Austin's Parish opened at the University of Texas, the incipient Newman Movement showed a logical development. Responding to dangers, at times even hostility, to their faith and morals, some Catholic students in secular colleges and universities organized into literary societies to study their heritage and reinforce their commitments. But these associations usually found the going rough. Only those served by chaplains seemed able to surmount both ethnic differences among members and the normal turnover among leaders so as to develop strong religious and educational programs. At the turn of the century these struggling groups already appeared to be in the vanguard of those lay societies of two decades later of which it has been said: "In the United States . . . for the first time in the Christian era, the faithful preceded the priests and cried for them to come out to them; not to evangelize, but to keep alive their faith."[61]

Fortified by a papal decree commanding in 1905 that "schools of religion" be established at public institutions of higher education, some bishops transformed these lay-initiated local efforts into centers for worship and religious education. As did the early clubs, this response to "conditions, not a theory" represented a miniscule effort. Yet, had the normal laws of development been in command, as Father Dietz outlined in 1907, the provisions made at Madison, Berkeley, and Austin would soon have become the prototypes of similar adaptations in nearly every diocese in the land; as indeed they finally did, especially as pastoral centers or "Newman parishes," but only after the Vatican Council sixty years later.

What arrested the growth of chaplaincies and Catholic halls at state universities as "a new link in Catholic evolution" in the United States was a shortage of capable priests, a scarcity of funds, and the general failure of Catholic clerical and lay leaders to envision their Church playing a significant role *within* American secular higher education as a coming dominant influence in national life. In this perception, the Catholic college exercised a commanding position, not only for conservatives as a "safe" place, but also for some progressives as an acceptable expression of intellectual Catholicism. This did not mean that the bishops gave these struggling institutions much more financial help than they directed toward the early Newman Movement. It did mean, however, that as a national leadership body they withheld moral support and encouragement from the latter.

Then, with the logical implementation of the fragile Catholic hall idea aborted, the fifth aspect of the Newman Movement, the federation, emerged as "the only alternative" to both campus threats and ecclesiastical rejection. First in 1908 as the Catholic Student Association of America, then after 1914 as the Federation of College Catholic Clubs, the idea of a national association served several functions. It set up clubs among the ever-mounting numbers of Catholics in secular institutions. It lobbied with bishops for financial and moral support. Most important of all, perhaps, for five decades it became the principal expression of unity, expansion, and travail for thousands of young Catholic men and women; in many ways it was their truest alma mater. At first led mainly by students and professors, the federation after the mid-1920s became much more subject to governance by the lower clergy in the interest of winning approbation by the higher. The memory of Cardinal Newman, first celebrated in the club founded at the University of Pennsylvania in 1893, became a central factor in this effort.

Because these events took place within an American Catholicism that was becoming increasingly conservative and ingrown, and because the Newman Movement represented a hopeful attempt to integrate Catholic piety and doctrine with the process of learning worldly disciplines, the movement's history would be one of poverty, struggle, even censure. For this reason, its modest accomplishments, announced by Father Keogh in 1926, seemed all the more noteworthy: Of 134 Catholic clubs then in existence, eighty-three (comprising about 25,000 Catholics) belonged to the FCCC; twenty-seven of these clubs had Newman halls, twenty-three of which provided some form of religious education; more than thirty chaplains were assigned to Newman work, of whom at least six were full-time.[62]

The five basic elements of the Newman Movement—club, faculty advisor, chaplain, diocesan-sponsored center, and national federation with its provincial infra-structure—were all in existence prior to America's entry into World War I. Their commitment to pastoral care and religious education within the context of American secular higher education was also established. With the numbers of young Catholics entering state and nondenominational institutions increasing from 40,000 in 1920 to 140,000 two decades later, these aspects of the Newman Movement entered upon a time of testing and refinement. The story of these developments constitutes Part Two of this study. However, because during these years secular higher education and Catholic life were also undergoing transformations, we must first examine the new setting in which Newman's apostles of hope labored.

PART TWO

DEVELOPMENTS

... By which the aspects of an idea are brought into consistency and form ... in the busy scene of human life ... modifying and incorporating with itself existing modes of thinking and operation.

John Henry Newman,
An Essay on the Development of Christian Doctrine

FIVE

Religion Suffered in College

*The elementary proposition of this new philosophy
which is now so threatening is this — that in all things
we must go by reason, in nothing by faith.*

John Henry Newman,
"The Infidelity of the Future,"
The Olton Sermon, 1873

In 1955 Joseph T. Karcher, a popular Catholic lecturer, bore witness to his brand of Americanist faith before a New Jersey assembly of the Catholic War Veterans. "And *never, never* lose faith in the great destiny of America," he urged. "When we have said our prayers, let us get up, roll up our sleeves like strong and perfect Christians and soldiers of Jesus Christ, ready to pledge our lives, our fortunes, and our sacred honor for the preservation and protection of our hearths and our homes, our country and its institutions."[1] If fifty years earlier Pope Leo XIII warned American Catholics not to place greater emphasis on their national loyalties than on their religion, this devout layman could see no conflict between the two; indeed, by linking in one sentence excerpts from Pope Pius XI, Archbishop John Ireland, and the Declaration of Independence his peroration symbolized the harmony. And millions of his coreligionists shared his feelings.

From World War I to about the middle of the 1960s American Catholics felt increasingly at home in their chosen land. In fact, they tended to think of themselves as being more American than Protestants and others; they denounced certain features of American society precisely because they saw them as departures from the original soundness and goodness of the national experiment.[2] One perversion of the pristine dream came in the form of secularism spreading throughout nondenominational higher education. Such worldly ideology clearly subverted the normative philosphies set forth in founding documents like the Declaration of Independence, the Northwest Ordinance, and Washington's Farewell Address. Catholic spokesmen censured manifestations of this ideology and with them, at times, leaders of the Newman Movement, who, as one influential archbishop put it, were attempting "to make the best of a bad job."[3]

Yet public colleges and universities were among the most powerful centers for assimilating the descendants of immigrants, including Catholic ones, into the American mainstream. Reluctance of clerical leaders to provide the latter with adequate spiritual care and religious training called into question the long-held assertion that the Church of Rome was "one of the most effective of all agencies for democracy and Americanization."[4] In these matters students in Catholic colleges were served quite well. Left to themselves, however, their counterparts in secularistic institutions largely had to go it alone.

THE GLOOM OF GHETTOISM

The spiritual leaders of the Roman Catholic Church in the United States emerged from the First World War with an urgent sense of mission, and on September 26, 1919, they signed their first national pastoral letter in thirty-five years. Reflecting the Americanist spirit that had flourished during the closing years of the nineteenth century, the bishops wrote that because the Church maintained "inviolate the deposit of Christian faith and the law of Christian morality," it could "profit by every item of truth and every means for the betterment of man which genuine progress" uncovered. They welcomed breakthroughs in science and technology, the growth of political freedom, and the expansion of American education. The bishops also felt that since Catholic believers retained a "firm hold on the principles of reasonable liberty and of Christian civilization," they were "destined to have the chief role in the restoration of peace and order." Much of what was "best in modern civilization," they said, was "due to the Catholic spirit." The bishops commissioned their flocks to perfect and spiritualize American life, just as their forefathers had labored to transform earlier cultures.[5]

Yet, according to one Church leader, this mission faced a serious obstacle. About 1920 Catholics encountered "the adverse public opinion of the majority." Either they had to change this climate, an all but impossible task, or create a public opinion of their own "without isolating our people and increasing the volume of prejudice."[6] During the 1920s many exclusively lay organizations and other groups uniting Catholic clergy and laity in various endeavors came into existence: *The Commonweal,* a lay-edited weekly on politics, religion, and the arts; associations of Catholic historians, philosophers, anthropoligists, writers, doctors, and lawyers; the Knights of Columbus night schools; the Lay Retreat Movement; the Catholic Association for International Peace; and the American Federation of Catholic Alumni.

In most instances such organizations did not set out to insulate their members from their social, intellectual, or professional surroundings; things just turned out that way. One reason lay in the recent immigrant status of so many Catholics, something that the restrictive immigration laws of the first half of the 1920s helped to alleviate as the years went on. Another explanation was the bigotry, especially active at mid-decade, that tended to drive Catholics together. But we must also explore a factor that was critically influential for the Newman Movement. This was an intensification of the process, already under way since the turn of the century, of centralizing control over Catholic affairs in the hands of the hierarchy. Although it seemed to some that a Catholic cultural revival was "at the flood" during these years, a contemporary believed that Catholicism was actually "less modern and more medieval in both doctrine and discipline" than it had been a generation earlier. "The liberalizing movements," he claimed, had been "either crushed out or driven under cover."[7]

The emergence of Catholic Action in Italy early in the 1920s and its arrival in the United States at the end of the decade assured clerical control of lay movements. "Official" groups, generally moderated by a representative of the National Catholic Welfare Council, defined themselves as collaborators "in the apostolate of the hierarchy,"[8] an implicit assertion that laymen in the Church did not have their own unique responsibilities for evangelizing the world. Increasingly alienated by this paternalistic and legalistic perspective, key laymen rallied to organizations which had minimal, if any, official sponsorship, such as the Catholic Worker Movement, the Association of Catholic Trade Unionists, the Jesuit-sponsored Sodality Movement, the Young Christian Workers, the Liturgical Movement, the Catholic Youth Organization, the Childerly Farms Retreats, the Calvert Associates, the Christian Front, and *Pax Romana.* Although such relatively independent efforts prepared the way for broader lay responsibility and autonomy after World War II, they often drew heavily upon European experiments and lacked official theological or canonical sanction.[9]

Many progressively minded Catholics believed that as members of a pluralistic society they should participate with Protestants in most civic and some religious matters; here, too, papal centralization wielded a balkanizing power. For example, early in the 1920s Catholic educators committed themselves to furthering interdenominational efforts to bring religion to public schools and universities. The NCWC Department of Education strongly supported Ora D. Foster's American Association on Religion in State Universities and Colleges and hosted the first conference of that organization in its quarters on November 13, 1923.[10] The success of this meeting moved Foster to remark that Catholics manifested a truly liberal spirit; his major obstacles arose among suspicious Protestants. By 1926, however, incidents at several universities with active Catholic chaplains made official Catholic participation in the affairs of the association difficult. Though Father James H. Ryan, Chairman of the Department of Education, and his episcopal adviser, Archbishop Austin Dowling of St. Paul, promised to continue to help Foster in private ways,[11] the papal encyclical of 1928, warning against religious indifferentism,[12] thwarted effective interfaith cooperation toward developing religious life and learning at state campuses. Local priests supported such movements as Foster's at Iowa and UCLA.[13] But between 1930 and 1936 the Davenport chancery refused to reappoint a Catholic instructor in the School of Religion at the Iowa campus after the retiring teacher contributed articles to the Jesuit weekly, *America*, contending that the "Iowa Plan" did not serve the best interests of Catholic undergraduates.[14]

Of course, Vatican policies do not go into effect simply because an official decrees them. They must be implemented in greatly divergent situations by clerical and lay leaders who are often widely dissimilar in temperament, training, and responsiveness. Key figures in such a potentially chaotic setting are the papal representatives in each country. As supervisors of Church affairs, they may not interfere with a bishop in the administration of his diocese; but they do exercise what is known as "vigilance" over ordinaries and their charges, and they send back pertinent information to the Holy See. One would not want to attribute too much influence to such men, even though for each country they are normally the sole means of communicating with the pope. Also, because bishops are reluctant to talk freely about how they are supervised, it is not easy to discover the many ways in which these overseers wield their power.[15] Nevertheless, a few scraps of evidence suggest that the Apostolic Delegate to the United States from 1922 to 1933, Archbishop Pietro Fumasoni-Biondi, contributed greatly to the climate of caution and conservatism that dominated American Catholicism during these years.

For example, the prestigious Archdiocese of New York came into Fumasoni-Biondi's purview in 1924 because the Holy See was concerned about priests not wearing the accepted black clerical garb. The delegate directed Cardinal Hayes to make an inquiry and consult with him so that he, in turn, could inform the pope. His Eminence sent assurances that no such grave abuse disfigured his presbyterate, and added that "priests from Canada receive more respect and reverence when they come to New York garbed as the American priest is garbed, than they do in Canada in cassock and in clerical hat."[16] More obscure dioceses were also watched. Bishop Thomas Welch of Duluth was regarded as a most reserved and prudent administrator, utterly loyal to his metropolitan in St. Paul and to the Holy Father himself. Yet older priests of that diocese recall how Fumasoni-Biondi visited Duluth and placed a number of its pastors under a perpetual promise of silence before interrogating them about their ordinary's behavior; and then paid his respects to the good man.[17]

Nor did the formidable delegate remain indifferent to affairs in secular higher education. He told Hayes that the pope wanted special watch kept over the Czecho-Slovak Institute at Columbia in the interest of protecting the faith of its students. Hayes once again sent off a reassuring reply which carefully added that the "very efficient chaplain," Father John Elliott Ross, C.S.P., was "not identified in any way with the University."[18]

We have no evidence clearly demonstrating direct impact upon the Newman Movement from such vigilance. However, we do have a reference in Father John W. Keogh's letters to "some big men in the hierarchy" who pressured conservative bishops into criticizing aspects of it.[19] It is the constantly depressed temperature, rather than its specific origin, that is important for our understanding. Pressures constricting American Catholicism during the 1920s and 1930s took their source in a narrowing of apostolic initiative to "official" movements authorized by nervous bishops acting either individually or as a national body. This was the policy, and it was not an optimistic one.

We have seen in the previous chapter how Father Keogh manipulated himself into control of the Federation of College Catholic Clubs. In doing so, he may merely have been satisfying requirements of his own insecure temperament. It is clear, however, that he was responding to the general drift of American Catholicism and to the specific orientation of its hierarchy. A. I. duPont Coleman represented the learned and concerned Catholic layman who believed that professionals had something to say about ministry in public secondary and higher education, who believed that character emerged from the interaction of natural virtue with supernatural grace, who was confident that undergraduates and alumni could join forces in a common effort to develop a Catholic influence among students. Once in the ascendent, the chaplain general considerably revised the professor's orientation. He saw to it that the constitution of 1925 delegated alumni to units defined by and subordinated to the appropriate Newman clubs of the federation. His preachments and pamphlets placed primary stress upon sacramental participation as the way to fully developed character. Finally, under Coleman the *Newman Quarterly* had been a challenging journal of opinion presenting some of the best liberal and scholarly Catholic thinking for its day; under Keogh's watchful, and sometimes censorious eye, its successor, *Newman News,* deliberately eschewed overly "intellectual" pieces and catered mostly to often trivial student matters.[20]

In brief, a priest from the ghetto attempted to lead the Newman Movement into a kind of student-centered isolation, away from the broader trends and their leaders in both Church and secular higher education. Two things characterized this transformed national organization: a strong urge to appear as "respectable" in the eyes of the hierarchy and a tendency to profess loyalty to things Catholic by vigorous attack against perceived enemies of the Church. As we shall see in subsequent chapters, Father Keogh adamantly rejected communism, the Christian Associations, and any moves toward "interfaith" cooperation, and was also a determined opponent of various liberal Catholic efforts.[21]

Before we examine these reactions, however, we must review the emergence of secularism within American higher education during the 1920s and 1930s. These were very trying years for a reformer like Keogh; it could well be that the only way he could reassure his superiors of the validity of his cause was to insist upon a tightly knit, closely controlled Newman Movement. How else could he and his co-workers, with their growing thousands of followers, ever hope to turn the hierarchy around? The bishops believed that "education provided at the public expense" was potentially "the strongest means of attacking the public weal."[22] Not only was secular education inimical to Catholic principles; it might turn out to be not even American at all.

PROFESSORS IN WONDERLAND

In chapter 1 we saw how problems of sectarianism and legal interpretations complicated the lives of university presidents who

wanted to maintain or reintroduce religious elements in nondenominational higher education prior to World War I. Before and between
the wars students remained basically interested in and loyal to religious commitments despite the secularistic philosophy the professoriate imposed upon them. Now we shall try to see how secularism
came to dominate American public and independent higher education between the wars.

Early in the 1920s, President David Kinley of Illinois warned his
faculty that they should not "destroy existing standards in the domain
of thought or life without putting something better in their place."[23]
Surveys of professorial attitudes indicated that instructors who were
not timid about relating their subject matter to religious teachings or
traditional moral standards were able to rekindle fervor in the lives of
doubtful or confused students. Commenting in 1933 upon the responses of 200 professors at thirteen western universities, sociologist
Phillip A. Parsons claimed that the professor who was "interested in
religion" made it "interesting to his students" and was not uneasy
when the topic came up in class.[24] Some professors tried to keep the
state university a beneficial institution by cooperating with local
church groups in developing accredited courses in religion that
combined the presumed scientific objectivity of other subjects with
sympathetic treatment for denominational traditions. These arrangements assumed various forms according to state laws, broadness of
cooperation, and the availability of funds and competent teachers.
Roughly, they took two forms: the "transfer-of-credit" method and the
"in-house" method.

The first imitated the system pioneered at the universities of
Michigan and Missouri by the Disciples of Christ "Bible chairs" of the
1890s and such chairs at Iowa City, Greeley, Colorado, and Grand
Forks, North Dakota, prior to 1910. By the early 1920s these chairs had
become interdenominational and were regarded as autonomous, cooperating educational institutions. Those at the universities of Missouri, Virginia, Texas, Indiana, Illinois, and Kansas received accreditation because their courses reached "university grade on subjects
suitable for university instruction" and were taught by clergy and
others whose training, methods, and time commitment corresponded
"to those of the university."[25] Another form of the transfer-of-credit
arrangement sprang from the fertile brain of Charles Foster Kent of
Yale. He hoped to replace these independent off-campus centers with
the "union schools of religion" he proposed in 1921. Each cooperating
campus would become the site of a privately financed center, housing
a refectory and seminar rooms. University professors would join
chaplains, YMCA instructors, and other qualified persons to teach

students, rural and urban pastors, and lay leaders, and would eventually prepare "professors of Biblical literature for colleges, universities, and secondary schools."[26]

The second, or in-house, approach made the school of religion established by cooperating denominations an integral part of the campus. It first appeared at Iowa State College, Ames, in 1922. Several Protestant denominations used college classrooms, office space, and libraries to teach religion with the same recognition accorded any other department within the institution. After five years of investigation led by the indefatigable Ora D. Foster, the legislature chartered the Iowa School of Religion at Iowa City in 1927. Elected trustees from all the major faiths governed the school and procured denominational funding for its faculty. It was financed at first by grants from the Rockefeller Foundation and the Davison Fund, but after 1935 the director, M. Willard Lampe, received his salary and administrative budget from state funds.[27]

By 1932 twenty-one state universities seeking to guarantee some form of religious instruction had adapted some form of these approaches, but no unified national pattern emerged. Some programs could not maintain high standards and disappeared. Only Idaho, Alabama, and North Dakota accredited courses taught off-campus in denominational student centers. Kent's union school plan enjoyed only a brief life at Michigan from 1923 to 1927; insecure funding, the deaths of several key leaders, neglect of denominational interests essential to success, and Catholic opposition caused its demise. Efforts to spread Foster's durable Iowa Idea to Oregon faltered when Lutherans could not in conscience join it; similar plans for Oklahoma ended in an independent school of religion, and those for UCLA ended in an off-campus center more concerned with pastoral than academic matters.[28]

Nearly everywhere presidents harbored expectations for schools of religion different from those of faculty review committees. At Minnesota George E. Vincent was willing to allow the proposed school of religion to enjoy the modest beginning usual for any new academic venture; the faculty rigorously insisted that "*all* teachers" had to be "equal to the *best* in the University."[29] Burton of Michigan wanted the Union School "to fight organized vice and to develop citizens of high moral character."[30] Such conflicts between religion as academic pursuit and promoter of morality thwarted many proposals.

But if secularists rejected the scholar's claim that religion was a respectable field of study, they welcomed the ideologist's claim that any remnant of traditional faith was detrimental to an intelligent citizenry and a fulfilled humanity. In some instances this assumption was not advertised. "Since social phenomena are natural phenomena," wrote George A. Lundberg of the imperatives shaping his discipline, "sociology is a natural science."[31] Said the director of a program in business education, "scientific method," by which he meant that of the natural sciences, had become "the first article in the creed" of commercial training.[32] Similar quantification infiltrated programs in education, psychology, salesmanship, public health, social work, and the law during these years. But some professors did not fear to flaunt the deeper meaning of this narrow empiricism. "The attitudes of mind required by every religious faith," wrote one, rendered "impossible the most thoroughgoing type of humanitarianism."[33]

These professors were secure in their positivism. When they bothered to follow them, they found amusing as well as reassuring the fundamentalist-liberal controversies in theology because in them they found support for their own cool conviction that "sincere and earnest men" could not agree upon the "general meaning and ends of human existence."[34] On almost every public campus could be heard psychologists denying personal immortality, anthropologists the possibility of religious faith, biologists the spiritual nature of humankind, sociologists free will; all while the philosophers argued that such teachers and their students would not be fully unbiased until they became atheists. Textbooks designedly eschewed mention of the role of religion, a silence that often amounted to denunciation. Concluded one liberal churchman well acquainted with the scene in 1927: Many professors seemed to consider themselves "commissioned by High Heaven itself to instruct the 'credulous and previously misguided' youth to view with contempt the moral standards and teachings given them in their homes and churches."[35]

Some observers cited personal considerations to explain the appearance of these crusaders of secularism. Professors had become specialists, "bees, each storing up honey in a narrow cell, unobserving and unobserved," wrote Daniel Coit Gilman of the Johns Hopkins faculty.[36] Wrote another, "Germanization" of the academy eroded traditional professorial concern for "pastoral work."[37] William Rainey Harper of Chicago was less gentle. Irreligious teachers, he thundered, revealed "that cowardly spirit which too frequently characterizes even good men and good institutions."[38] The social pressures exerted by the profane spirit especially threatened the younger professors. Pioneering an unpopular field such as religious study, or relating newly departmentalized sciences to religious meaning, won neither budgetary support nor scholarly rewards in state universities after 1920. Friendships and blood ties with senior professors and department heads seemed to be "more potent" for advancement than one's quality as a teacher; original research and publication counted for even less.[39]

Still, specialization and sycophancy could not have secularized the professoriate unless its members were also wrestling with problems of intellectual honesty posed by conflicts stemming from the confrontation of their childhood faith with their own higher learning. The vast majority of university teachers in the 1920s appeared unable to reconcile their Sunday school memory of the God of Vengeance with the findings of quiet inquiry into nature and man. Over half of them had been born in the last quarter of the nineteenth century, and their childhood and early adolescent religious convictions could not stand up to the questions that college lectures and reading raised; doctoral studies widened the chasm even further. As one professor put it, "the teaching of the Christian churches was either a matter to be taken very seriously or a monstrous system of delusion." His pursuit of psychology finally inclined him to become "very skeptical."[40]

A handful of surveys illustrated the decline of traditional belief and practice among professors. Whereas prior to 1910 nearly three-quarters of all college teachers attended services in local churches and many were also prominent in Sunday school programs or as church officers, after 1920 only about half belonged to local churches, with many in this group admitting their ties were merely nominal. The intellectual world they inhabited appeared to be more conducive to Unitarianism than to the traditional faiths that students still held. Twice as many professors as students claimed to have no religious preference; nearly 90 percent of sociologists, biologists, and psychologists doubted the existence of God, and three-fourths of them did not accept the personal immortality of the soul.[41]

Should we therefore conclude that professors had "lost religion"? Perhaps they had found a new one. The "patient, uncompromising search for truth," wrote one professor in 1937, "is essentially 'religious' in its motivation."[42] The sciences offered a methodology, an intellectual fascination, an absorbing commitment, status, power, and a new perspective and moral responsibility for humanity. Applied research seemed to be precipitating a new unification of learning and to be synthesizing a new sense of social responsibility. One professor hailed the penetration of empirical psychology into the ranks of natural scientists as a signal that their "isolation from other departments of human study and interest was at an end."[43] Business educators believed that the magical light of science was attracting board directors, managers, and proprietors "from acquisition to production and service."[44] More significantly, science gave the professors a new world view. "It is beginning to be evident," wrote Gerald B. Smith in 1927, "that modern science is creating a type of culture which stands on its own feet, asking and needing no support from religion."[45]

Prophets of a wondrous new world to be informed by a new humanistic religion, could the professors be blamed for showing scant interest in preserving the sectarian traditions that students brought to them from their pious hearthsides?

SOULLESS ENGINEERS

Preoccupied with their administrative duties, increasingly deprived of the help of the Christian Associations, and unable to depend upon the understaffed and underfunded developing denominational campus pastorates, college presidents began to appoint, and to expect, deans of students to take on the pastoral role that they and the professors no longer could fulfill. It is not surprising to note that, just as it had among teachers, scientism between the wars secularized the emerging profession of student personnel work.

Folklore traces the origin of the deanship of men to an afternoon in 1901 when President Draper of Illinois summoned English professor Thomas Arkle Clark to his office, introduced a rowdy student, and said something about shaping the boy up or having to ship him out. As a matter of fact, Iowa had established something like a dean of men in 1895 and Harvard had a nonacademic counselor in 1870; perhaps Oberlin was first with its "lady principal" in 1833.[46] Of more importance, until the 1920s "Matriarchal, Patriarchal Thomas Arkle Clark" (as the students dubbed him; he preferred to be known as the "Dean of Deans") and his counterparts believed that they could best build character and raise grades through inspirational motivation and moralistic talks. Thus at Texas Ruby Terrill sought to instill "wise social standards and high ethical principles" while ferreting out undergraduates "jeopardizing the standards, morals, and reputation of the University."[47] At Iowa, Robert Rienow pictured himself as "the father of a large family."[48] Clark himself told undergraduates in one of his many Sunday morning exhortations that "the privilege of earning his bread by the sweat of his brow" was "the greatest blessing that God ever bestowed on fallen man"; for him, as probably for most of the other deans appointed at the time, "low scholastic work and low moral ideals went together."[49]

Motivated by a desire to help graduates find rewarding careers, and inspired by the corporate efficiency of American business structures with their reliance upon psychological testing and social manipulation, student personnel workers of the 1920s began to replace moralizing individualists with teams of scientific specialists. Medical doctors, psychologists, physical education directors, psychiatrists, remedial reading instructors, employment agents, and social workers linked up with deans of men and women, dormitory supervisors, YMCA workers, counselors, and faculty discipline committees. Together they tried to engineer a wholesome extracurriculum which would foster the intimacy they thought should characterize education and preserve the intimacy and moral influence of the old-time collegiate model. By the 1930s the American College Personnel Association had formed and these campus architects of a better humanity were concentrating their efforts on "the development of human individuality."[50]

The trouble was that their reliance upon rationalism of plan and behavioralism in application shouldered out traditional religious and moralistic impulses. For example, procedures for dealing with misconduct seldom included referrals to local clergy or campus pastors. Such practices did go on "unofficially," most often when extreme cases turned up at the president's office; then the president, not the student affairs professional, turned to the church. The explanation Joseph Geiger offered for this situation seemed plausible enough, since he based it upon a careful inquiry: Campus psychologists "had it in" for religion because they felt it contributed to maladjustment.[51]

What one faculty committee termed the "officialism" of the newly emerging profession also frustrated attention to the deepest needs of many students. Students' files got lost among scattered offices, departments, and committees. An extensive study of personnel practices concluded that "despite much fervent protestation, students remain the forgotten item when organization and administration are considered."[52] If the young person felt alienated from his local church, noted one counselor, neither did he "care to advertise his tangles by going to the official 'psychologist' as to a kind of secular confessional."[53] Asked to comment upon her sexual anxieties, a student in 1928 quipped, "Were I a Catholic and this a confessional, I should perhaps be able to answer";[54] she could bear to be silent, or to look elsewhere than to the personnel office for help. As a case in point, of upper classmen dissatisfied with the adviser system at one leading midwestern university in 1940, only 14 percent turned to deans of men and women, and only 7 percent visited the Student Health Service to talk over worries. Another 14 percent consulted their parents, while 28 percent sought out their classmates.[55]

Reticence about appealing to traditional ethical and moral values and dependence upon presumably efficient bureaucratic patterns reflected the growing popularity of the "scientific approach" to human problems. Both exercises were in fashion on all public campuses. For this reason they may have appealed especially to practitioners of an infant profession lowest on the academic pecking order and sometimes in conflict with administrators who demanded discipline, not tolerance of student "experimentation." But as it tried to restore the expanding campus to older collegiate standards by the methods of the new social sciences, this new and vitally important sector of the higher educational enterprise lost its soul. Looking back in 1959, a leading proponent of the student-centered approach acknowledged that literature of the personnel movement lacked both "generally accepted value-oriented aims" and "scientifically based understandings of human nature." Its "philosophical and psychological foundations," he continued, were "only haltingly developed and ... disturbingly incomplete."[56]

By then, of course, administrators and professors had already had second thoughts about the profane spirit pervading the "best embodiment of the uplifting forces of the modern time."[57] "During the past two decades," said Charles Seymour of Yale in 1940, American universities "analyzed issues and balanced factors [and] exposed the follies and the vices of historical figures and movements," but failed to generate "a positive philosophy to which students ... might attach themselves."[58] One "cannot build a program of education on the right to doubt," commented professor Frederick S. Breed of the University of Chicago; "one must also believe."[59] The "agnostic campus" worriedly foreseen by Cyrus Northrup four decades earlier was flunking out.[60]

SIX

All the Way to Rome

The mind of man is created for truth; an open-minded quest for truth, such as the university promotes, is ideal for sowing the seeds of Christianity.

Father John A. O'Brien,
The Newman Quarterly, Winter 1921-22

In May 1922 leaders of the Federation of College Catholic Clubs received some good news. Pope Pius XI congratulated the organization on "the good work" it was doing "for Catholic youth at the various Newman halls situated near large secular universities."[1] Two years later, Father John A. O'Brien, chaplain at the University of Illinois, returned from the Vatican with a special blessing which he said signaled the pope's "approval" for the educational program of his Newman Foundation.[2] It seemed that authorities in Rome were beginning to appreciate how the Newman Movement was attempting to fulfill the mandate of an earlier pope, Pius X, who in 1905 had commanded that "schools of religion be founded" at public universities. Denied official approval of the American hierarchy, could the movement expect the pope himself to become its ecclesiastical patron? For something like this, Father John W. Keogh, chaplain general of the Federation of College Catholic Clubs, devoutly hoped.

But many roads led to Rome. Some of them carried opponents to the notion that priests be assigned to teach religion and conduct pastoral ministry in nonsectarian universities. Those opponents succeeded before the 1920s ended in placing the Newman Movement under a cloud, and the pope issued an encyclical supporting the cause of Catholic colleges.

PART OF THE SYSTEM

In January 1920 the National Catholic Welfare Council opened in its Department of Education a special Bureau of Education headed

72

by Arthur C. Monahan, a former public school teacher, administrator, and researcher with the United States Bureau of Education. The bishops gave Monahan a double commission: (1) "cooperate in all desirable movements for the improvement of the public schools," provided this cooperation did not prejudice parental rights "to maintain private and parochial schools"; (2) "join with other church organizations in their endeavors to provide religious education" for children attending public schools.[3]

Almost at once Monahan's bureau showed an interest in the condition of Catholics attending secular colleges and universities. It sponsored a survey which revealed that these institutions enrolled over 40,000 Catholics compared with only 19,000 students in Church colleges.[4] These figures served as the basis for discussions between Monahan, Keogh, FCCC president Professor A. I. duPont Coleman, and bishops serving on the NCWC Administrative Committee. The participants agreed that "the most practical plan of furnishing religious instruction to these students" was through the FCCC. In early April 1921 the Administrative Committee stood "unanimous in deciding to support Newman Club work all over the country," and promotional efforts began without delay.[5]

The Council's Bureau of Education issued 3,000 copies of a brochure explaining the role of the Newman club. Once "a defensive movement," it claimed, these clubs now recruited "loyal Catholic men and women walking shoulder to shoulder in promoting the interests of religion and morals as well as culture." Such societies also assured Catholics on the public campuses that they were "not away from home because the Church" followed them.[6] Other publications described Newman clubs as "thriving and fruitful home missions"; noted that Pope Pius X had ordered classes in religion organized at public institutions; urged the clubs "so to ground every student in Catholic principles that his religious education may develop together with that which he is receiving in secular fields"; predicted that, if well provided for, Catholic graduates of state universities would become "all the more eager to work for the fullest possible development of Catholic education in all its branches." Far from being "prejudicial to the future of Catholic higher education," said the Council, Newman clubs were potentially "one of its most powerful aids."[7]

Monahan also hired as organizer a graduate of Fordham and the University of Pennsylvania, John A. Kennedy. Kennedy wrote about Catholics on the secular campus for the NCWC press service, visited schools, lectured to Newman clubs, and set them up; in July 1921 he reported on this work to the FCCC's annual conference.[8] Monahan began to receive many letters from places where students wanted help from the Welfare Council. These efforts, along with those by the federation itself, accounted for the growth of the Newman Movement during the early 1920s reviewed in Chapter 4. Moreover they furthered the objective of organizing "programs of religious instruction . . . and material of Catholic interest for discussions and debates"[9] to be coordinated by a proposed NCWC "section for Catholic students in non-Catholic institutions."[10] In 1923 Monahan's representative assured the FCCC that "the NCWC considers Newman Clubs a part of the Catholic Educational System."[11]

Nevertheless, these same encouraging months witnessed developments that profoundly changed this hopeful outlook. Surveys suggested that only about 5 percent of Catholic high school graduates intended to enroll in Catholic colleges.[12] Advocates of the latter concluded that the Church in the United States had "to get the wandering sheep away from the influence of pagan culture" and to awaken the Catholic laity to "the necessity of building up the Catholic college so that nobody need be ashamed of it."[13] As they had in 1907, the college men once again turned to the bishops for help. "Our American miracle of the parochial school system," flourished, one spokesman said, "because in season and out of season the hierarchy and the clergy" insisted upon its "necessity and aroused the laity to think and act with them"; what the colleges needed, he concluded, was "a propaganda campaign."[14] And that is exactly what they got.

In January 1922 the college men received approval from the bishops for "Catholic College Week," a promotion to run from April 30 through May 6. This publicity advanced two lines of argumentation to convince parents of the advantages of Catholic campuses. The first centered on the preservation of faith and morals. "The atmosphere" in Catholic colleges was "religious and therefore wholesome" said the literature; since the instructors were "religious," offspring would have their home-learned values reinforced; such "safeguards" defended against "moral contamination." The second proof appealed to the church's traditional stance on education. The Catholic college was not "a modern invention," wrote James H. Ryan, head of the NCWC Department of Education; it represented, rather, "a definite policy of the Church, consecrated by centuries of acceptance" and constituting "the keystone in the arch of Catholic education."[15]

The dissemination of this philosophy took several forms. One was the series of seven daily advertisements placed in Catholic publications. The first told parents in bold type that college graduation meant "LEADERSHIP AND SUCCESS." Another offered short biographies of such alumni as Cardinal Gibbons, Archbishop Ireland, and Chief Justice of the Supreme Court Edward Douglass White to demonstrate "Catholic Colleges Promote American Ideals." A third notice listed other American Catholic leaders who had graduated from church colleges. The fourth day's broadside asked "What Does American Business Need Most Today?" and answered "more morality, justice and plain everyday honesty," all of which Catholic graduates would bring to the halls of commerce. A fifth ad proclaimed the need for more Catholic lawyers, physicians, editors, and engineers. That on the sixth day cited advantages women gained from college graduation and urged "Send Your Daughter To A Catholic College." Nor did the college men rest on the seventh day. In the final advertisement, the head of the Continental and Commercial Bank of Chicago warned parents not to let their children enter the marketplace under the handicap he had endured as he made his way to the top without a college diploma to help him![16]

As another way to propagandize for Catholic institutions, Ryan urged each campus to schedule its own "Catholic College Day." This fiesta should combine music with "short addresses by the college president, prominent alumni and leaders of the student body" calculated to "impress" the undergraduates "and increase their devotion and respect for the advantages" they were receiving. High schools should also join in. They should have their students prepare essays on such topics as "Why Go to a Catholic College?," award a prize, and read the winning paper at a general assembly where posters and displays illustrating the advantages of church colleges covered the walls.[17]

Seventy-nine colleges joined in celebrating the first Catholic College Week. Priests in hundreds of churches delivered motivational sermons. Many leading metropolitan dailies took favorable note of the promotion; Ryan received some 3,000 news items and over 300 supporting editorials from his clipping services. The college men believed they had attracted "more widespread attention, both inside and outside of Catholic educational circles" than any similar promotion in recent years.[18]

What was happening, of course, was quite contradictory. In simultaneously promoting the development of Newman clubs and Catholic colleges, the NCWC was not propelling Catholic education forward on a set of freshly laid rails; it was working at cross-purposes to what college leaders, who were well represented in the Department of Education, and a growing number of bishops perceived as the total good of Catholic schooling in the United States. Several situations conspired to brake the growing momentum of the Newman Movement.

Settlement of questions about the legal status of the NCWC itself generated the first of these crises. From February to June 1922 the principle of corporate episcopal action, which the American bishops were pioneering, underwent a severe testing. Some ordinaries suspected the national secretariat would assume the function of a law-making body and preempt their authority in their own dioceses. Without discussing these doubts with representatives of both sides, Pope Pius XI responded to expressions of these anxieties on February 25 by suppressing the council. After considerable difficulty, bishops favoring it succeeded in having the NCWC, with the word "Council" changed to "Conference," reinstated. Guidelines for its activity indicated that any decisions the bishops came to as a body had "nothing in common with conciliar legislation" but only expressed "a common public interest for the safeguarding of the Church's work." Furthermore, any committee or "agent" of the NCWC which interfered in the internal management of a diocese would be "summarily dismissed."[19]

In the outcome, this accommodation tended to give the Catholic colleges an advantage over the Newman Movement. The former enjoyed status in canon law; the Catholic halls and Newman clubs of the latter had no such official recognition. In such a context the ruling about any "agent" of the NCWC meddling in a diocese severely crippled Monahan's efforts to set up Newman clubs and draw them into a national union; his field representative presumably fit the description of the forbidden intruder. Indeed, in September 1922 the bishops made their policy quite clear. Reaffirming their collective support for the Catholic colleges, they ruled that "inasmuch as no two dioceses present the same conditions in regard to student attendance at secular institutions of learning, each ordinary should handle the problem in his own way according to the particular needs of his diocese."[20] This restatement of their 1906 policy was logical enough. But it was harmful to the Newman Movement, since it deprived chaplains and students of the morale, protection, guidance, and support that they desperately needed and opened the way for allegations, often repeated in the years following, that priests who promoted Newman work were somehow not loyal to the church.

A leg up in canon law was not enough to win the day for the colleges, however. What brought them increasing support from clergy and laity alike were efforts by persons opposed to a public school monopoly in education to undo the Oregon Compulsory Education

Act which, after two years of maneuvering, became law on November 7, 1922.

Bigots argued against private and denominational schools by appealing to the need for "Americanism" and by stirring up anti-Catholic prejudice. The Catholic bishops found themselves in a constricted situation. They dreaded what they termed "a federalized monopoly of general education" of which the Oregon law seemed a harbinger.[21] Spokesmen for the NCWC claimed that "a titanic struggle" was under way, "one of the most momentous crises in the history of our country and . . . of the Church." The "continued welfare, if not the existence, of the Church" depended upon the outcome of the battle to preserve freedom of choice in schooling.[22] The bishops knew that an open show of Catholic power against the bill would play into Nativist hands. Their safest and strongest tactic lay in capitalizing upon the new unanimity for Catholic education that was emerging among the laity fearful for the future of their parish schools. And, since the official philosophy of their national department of education had already produced the conclusion that "Catholic education itself would end in disaster" if the colleges failed,[23] these institutions became beneficiaries of the tendency to unite solidly against what Catholic leaders called totalitarian efforts to destroy freedom of religious schooling in America.[24]

The NCWC backed off from the Newman Movement almost as rapidly as its advocacy had built up. In March 1923 Monahan resigned, and the Department of Education suppressed a follow-up on its 1920 survey of Catholics in state universities.[25] By February 1925 the NCWC no longer regarded the Newman Movement as "a part of the Catholic educational system." That month the agency's *Bulletin* initiated a regular series surveying the history and outlining the educational opportunities of American Catholic universities and colleges.[26] Never again did any favorable mention of Newman clubs appear. Quite the opposite. During the second Catholic College Week, observed in May 1926, the Department of Education issued a booklet stating that "the presence of a Newman Club does not warrant a Catholic parent thinking for a moment that the religious needs of his child will be as well cared for as in a Catholic college." Officials in Washington evaluated this brochure "as effective a piece of propaganda for the Catholic college as has ever been published."[27]

Meanwhile the NCWC advertising campaign delivered handsomely. By 1930 Catholic colleges and universities were educating two-thirds of the 158,000 Catholics in higher education; some administrators were actually thinking about limiting admissions![28]

JESUIT BUSINESS

When Arthur Monahan left the NCWC he became the editor of *Catholic School Interests,* a monthly devoted to school administration, which was published in Chicago and co-founded by Father John A. O'Brien, Newman chaplain at the University of Illinois. From his new vantage point in the heartland of the country, Monahan witnessed the bitterest of all assaults against attempts to secure religious education for Catholics in state universities.

Johnny O'Brien, as his friends called him, was a stocky red head equally at home on a tennis court, in the pulpit, or behind the wall of books topping the desk in his jealously guarded study. He was the first diocesan priest to earn a doctorate in an American public university, and he became both pastor of St. John's Church, Champaign, Illinois, and Newman chaplain at the university in 1917, the year after his ordination by the bishop of Peoria. He was a 1913 graduate of a Catholic college, St. Viator, and had done part of his advanced training at The Catholic University of America. Because of his work on speed reading, he was a frequent lecturer before groups of Catholic teachers. He also served as superintendent of Peoria's parochial schools and contributed regularly to the pages of the journal he had helped start; during the Oregon school crisis his was one of the most lucid and forceful voices raised to defend the Americanism of Catholic education. Yet in 1925 the thirty-two-year-old scholar-chaplain found himself in the path of a Jesuit counterassault that enlisted the services of one of the most powerful archbishops in the American hierarchy.[29]

The center of the controversy was O'Brien's Newman Foundation. In 1919 the priest had joined with chaplains of other faiths at Illinois to secure accreditation of courses in religion to be taught in what the university senate stipulated as a "physical plant adequate to instruction of University grade."[30] Since O'Brien had no such facility, he set out to build one, meanwhile holding classes in a dilapidated house. With the "unqualified sanction and approval" in writing from his ordinary, Edward M. Dunne, who hoped for "a Catholic students' hall rivaling all others of its kind,"[31] O'Brien had plans drawn up projecting lecture halls, library, seminar rooms, dining facilities, and dormitories for men and women. A "million dollar campaign" got under way in 1922 to fund what some friends of the scheme, including Monahan, termed "a Catholic college" for the University of Illinois.[32]

O'Brien rested his foundation and its accredited courses in Catholicism upon a somewhat simplistic concept of religious education. He held that the Church was not "primarily interested in the teaching of engineering, ceramics, physics, or agriculture"; its true mission was "to teach religion." He insisted that if one removed religious instruction from the Catholic college, "little but secular education" would remain; on the other hand, if one introduced Catholic theology into secular education, "the essential feature of Catholic education was preserved." In O'Brien's view, set forth in a 1925 pamphlet, the Newman Foundation constituted "*the heart of Catholic education,* shooting its throbbing life blood through the whole body of the curriculum and vivifying it from head to foot."[33]

Not until 1925 did his foundation plan begin to face severe opposition from the proponents of Catholic schooling. Father Herbert C. Noonan, S.J., former president of Marquette University, opened the attack in August. He termed the scheme "a half-baked substitute" for the moral influence of Catholic higher education and charged that "flattery deftly used by a university president" had transformed O'Brien into a huckster for schools that "give scant courtesy to religion and morality."[34] That same month Claude Heithaus, a Jesuit scholastic teaching classics at St. Louis University who had supplied Noonan with material for his address, began publishing in the Jesuit weekly, *America,* a series of eight articles charging that the foundation plan was opposed to Catholic educational ideals and canon law. He also suggested that O'Brien was guilty of misrepresenting the intentions of his bishop.[35] Later that year *America's* Roman counterpart, the *Civiltà Cattolicà,* armed with materials forwarded by Noonan, took up the battle by reprinting what he and Heithaus had said.[36]

Early in 1926 an associate editor at *America,* Father John LaFarge, S.J., who as a student had wanted Jesuits to set up a chaplaincy at Harvard, added four more articles to the barrage. These articles claimed that the foundation plan was "of doubtful benefit to students," clearly harmful to all of Catholic education, and would probably end up as a kind of Catholic ghetto. He did not think it wise to "pour our millions into the social coddling of Catholics at non-Catholic universities." If needed at all, the acceptable measure would be "a Newman Club, *precisely that and no more.* "[37] Later that year *America's* editor-in-chief, Father Wilfrid Parsons, S.J., summarized what these protagonists said in three long essays later widely circulated as a pamphlet. He made two points very damaging to the Newman Movement. The first concerned its educational mission: since canon law did not incorporate the *Acerbo Nimis* directive about setting up schools of religion at public colleges, this mandate of Pius X was no longer in force. The second concerned pastoral ministry: the "prior right" of

Catholics in Catholic colleges to receive spiritual care precluded "any extensive program" of that sort among Newman clubs.[38]

Meanwhile, Michael J. Curley, Archbishop of Baltimore, began denouncing the plan when it appeared to threaten the expansion of his parochial school system. In March 1926 he termed O'Brien's efforts a form of "secret, hypocritical warfare against the best interests of the Church in America," and said that the priest stood among "the Modernists who were bent on destroying the Church from within."[39] That August the College and University Department of the National Catholic Educational Association passed a resolution which directly rejected O'Brien's educational philosophy and insisted that attendance of Catholics at secular colleges was "at most tolerated."[40]

Fearing that public debate would endanger completion of his project, O'Brien at first asked his friends to remain silent[41] and answered his opponents quietly. In February 1926 he mailed an article to *America* in hopes of clarifying that journal's "misrepresentation"; it was never published.[42] In April he issued his avowal that "a Catholic foundation can never be logically identified or confused with a Catholic school,"[43] and in June he published a 2,000-word profession of faith in Catholic education that ended with the formula "for a full-staffed Catholic college there can be no adequate substitute, and nothing can supplant or replace it";[44] these were ignored by the NCEA resolvers later that summer. The embattled chaplain also sent Archbishop Curley several long letters denying that he held "an educational philosophy other than that of our Holy Catholic Church."[45] Curley replied that O'Brien "said one thing in public and another in private,"[46] and began his public denunciations.

O'Brien refused to reply in kind so long as Curley went after the foundation. But in March 1927 when the prelate told a gathering of the Catholic Alumnae of America that O'Brien's cooperation with Jews and Protestants in Illinois amounted to "a sheer denial of Catholic teaching," the chaplain came out swinging. His news release explained how the interfaith effort tried to rebuff KKK activities; noted that Curley had in hand "my signed rejection" of educational views "as alien to me as to him"; and concluded the archbishop had violated "the most elementary principles of the moral law" by attacking him in public "instead of filing his charges with the proper ecclesiastical superiors."[47] At this, Curley sent documentation of the affair to the Holy Office in Rome, where he presumed curial officials commissioned to watch over the purity of Catholic doctrine would settle the matter.[48]

No such conclusion to the affair was immediately forthcoming, but all the appropriate signals were going up. The *Civiltà Cattolicà* pieces were serialized in three issues of the quasi-official Vatican daily, *L'Osservatore Romano;*[49] from here they were translated into English and published in *Woodstock Letters,* a house organ of the Jesuits in the eastern United States;[50] finally, this article, preceded by an introduction claiming that the Illinois foundation plan was a model for twenty-five such centers, appeared as a pamphlet that ran to over 3,000 copies and was circulated among all the Catholic bishops of the United States.[51]

Despite this protracted and sometimes virulent opposition, accredited courses in Catholicism continued to be taught at Illinois, where O'Brien, fearing some kind of order to stay the project, speeded up construction and saw the Newman Foundation dedicated in 1928.

ACERBO REDIVIVUS

Father Keogh watched these developments with great apprehension. He somewhat resented O'Brien's unwillingness to participate in federation affairs and in general harbored suspicions of his liberalism.[52] If the Illinois chaplain was trying to "set up something contrary to Canon Law," he told Newman Club leaders in July 1926, it was "most unjust" to attach the name of their patron to the project and bring the entire movement into disrepute with the bishops.[53] Nevertheless, when Parsons' articles appeared in the fall of that year, the chaplain general tried unsuccessfully to have *America* publish his own refutation of them.[54] Believing that his dual lack of academic degrees and status as a pastor made him "a little fish," Keogh turned finally to a sympathetic young professor of canon law at St. Charles Seminary in Overbrook, Pennsylvania, Father James Ryan Hughes. Hughes agreed to write a counter-broadside to be entitled "School of Religion in *Acerbo Nimis* of Pius X."[55]

This four-page pamphlet attempted to show that in 1905 the pope had commanded exactly what the Jesuits were now trying to thwart. In a section on the interpretation of canon law, the author insisted that only a positive statement of revocation, not silence, annulled the force of a papal decree. He also defended the idea of erecting centers for religious education at state universities by appeal to precedents set by European Catholics as well as to the supreme law of the Church, the good of souls.[56] Though this little publication received the approval of ecclesiastical authorities in the Philadelphia chancery, who even termed its subject "a new mode of education in

America,"[57] and was circulated among all the bishops, it seemed not to have had any great impact. Indeed, its author later said he performed his assignment in the most cursory fashion and was rather surprised at the importance that Keogh ascribed to it when it was published in June 1929.[58]

But Father Keogh appears to have been fully justified in his urgent wish to keep the earlier papal teaching in the forefront. During these months officials at the Vatican were drafting a new encyclical on Christian education. Among the consultants was Father Parsons, who had been summoned to Rome by the General of the Society, Father Vladimir Ledochowski, S.J. At one point in the deliberations Parsons closeted with the Secretary of the Holy Office, Cardinal Raphael Merry del Val, who had earlier received Archbishop Curley's delation of O'Brien. To illustrate where the American Catholic population and its colleges were concentrated, Parsons produced a map of the United States upon which he drew a line from Milwaukee south to St. Louis and east to Washington, D.C., adding circles around New Orleans, San Francisco, and Los Angeles.[59] Parsons' intervention seems to have been hugely successful. The final text of the letter, entitled *Divini Illius Magistri* and published on the last day of 1929, asserted "the right and mission of the Church" to establish "universities spread over every country and always by the initiative and under the protection of the Holy See."[60] Furthermore, in a departure from the usual practice of locating a new encyclical within the line of earlier papal documents treating the same subject, this one cited works of Leo XIII and Pius XI, but ignored the interposed *Acerbo Nimis* of Pius X.

In a sporadic way, *America* continued to snipe at the Newman Movement. In 1931 it urged Catholics to boycott the School of Religion at the State University of Iowa, with which the local Newman chaplain was cooperating, as a poor substitute for the kind of instruction in religion to be gained under strictly Catholic auspices.[61] A year later the journal descended to what appears to have been a shabby trick. It published an article about a prominent eastern preparatory school for boys whose headmaster wanted religious instruction offered by the local parish priest, but half the Catholic parents had not supported this idea. The author made perfectly clear his intention of criticizing the apathy of certain parents, not the effectiveness of Newman clubs; indeed, nowhere did he use this name or refer to such collegiate organizations. Nevertheless, the editors published his report as a "Clinical Study of a Newman Club."[62] Shortly after it appeared, Father Ledochowski commanded *America* to cease such attacks. "Newman Club work," he said, "was a work of the Society of Jesus."[63] Although the journal never again attacked Newman clubs,

Jesuits continued to speak out against the movement as a vehicle for religious education; for example, in 1934 one of them claimed that Pius XI had, in fact, "vigorously" condemned O'Brien's foundation plan.[64]

Looking back upon the 1920s, leaders of the Newman Movement have claimed that proponents of Catholic higher education, especially the Jesuits, most effectively blocked their efforts to develop Catholic pastoral and educational programs in secular colleges and universities. Although not all Jesuits opposed O'Brien's plan, the undermining role of these college advocates cannot be minimized. For example, in 1925 Francis P. Garvin, a Yale graduate, was at the point of erecting a half-million dollar Catholic foundation in New Haven but gave up the idea when the Jesuits refused to staff it, since they saw it as a threat to their own eastern campuses.[65] As one Jesuit later acknowledged, the society simply had too much money and emotion invested in its institutions to tolerate such schemes.[66] Furthermore, the pro-college crusade also effectively subverted the bishops' 1922 policy of allowing each ordinary to develop the Newman Movement "according to the particular needs of his diocese." What business did the Archbishop of Baltimore, an "outside agent," have in meddling into the affairs of the Diocese of Peoria?

The answer lies in the fact that the Newman Movement, not only in the persons of its students seeking entrance into the mainstream, but in its institutionalized response to their religious needs, represented a rejection of the kind of security a ghettoized Catholicism sought. It was no longer possible for bishops to provide for the local needs of their dioceses without sometimes having a broader influence. Throughout the first quarter of the twentieth century a kind of educational domino theory controlled the thinking of most Catholic leaders. This point of view claimed that the Catholic college supported the "whole fabric of the Catholic system," and that if the college failed, the parochial school "could not continue to exist."[67] The reaction of the hierarchy to the Oregon school controversy most dramatically illustrated this conviction. So it came down to this: the Newman Movement was almost done in, not by the Jesuits, not by the Catholic college, but by the parish school. The protectionist attitude was so strong that the *Civiltà Cattolicà* even claimed that O'Brien's project endangered the existence of Catholic schools in Italy![68] Not until 1938 did a pope again acknowledge with appreciation the existence of Newman clubs.[69] It seemed that what in 1907 had been a lone herring trying to find its way past an iceberg, by 1930 had become an endangered species.

SEVEN

Educational Apostolate or Youth Movement?

You appeal for Catholic Action by the laity. Here are about 600 or more lay Newmanites. Reach out your arms and gather these in.

Father John W. Keogh
appealing to NCWC spokesmen, 1938

In 1907 the Newman threat had forced Catholic college leaders to define their objectives so as to earn respectability among the hierarchy. Now, reeling under the impact of the college counteroffensive of the mid-1920s, leaders of the Newman Movement had to accomplish a similar task.

First, they had to shape an easily understood identity for their undertaking. They had always thought of theirs as a pastoral-educational mission within non-Catholic higher education. Given the accepted policy of restricting religious education to Catholic colleges, even of limiting any pastoral activity outside of these schools, could Father Keogh and his colleagues maintain this image? Second, to be an authentic expression of concern on the part of the Catholic Church for its young members in secular institutions, the Newman Movement must be both accountable and acceptable to an increasingly reactionary hierarchy. It was not enough never to seem "too liberal"; the movement had to attach itself to some respectable Catholic enterprise.

Father Keogh was able to accomplish both of these objectives before his retirement from the national chaplaincy in 1934. He developed the "Newman Idea" as a focus of identity and made it part of the papally sanctioned Catholic Action movement to ensure orthodoxy. This restatement of essential principles and accommodation to current church fashion permitted the Newman Movement to become part of the Confraternity of Christian Doctrine in 1937, and helped to achieve its re-entry into the National Catholic Welfare Conference in 1940.

FROM IDEA TO ACTION

The ferocity of the Jesuit attack in 1925–26, the complexity of issues facing all Catholic leaders, and the emotionalism churning throughout what have been termed the "tribal twenties"[1] threw proponents of the Newman Movement into confusion. Timothy Harrington, founder of the first Newman Club, remained silent; he was convinced that the Jesuits were the best teachers in the world.[2] James J. Walsh, a member of the first Newman Club, and now famous as the author of *The Thirteenth: The Greatest of Centuries,* had contributed to the 1926 promotion of Catholic College Week.[3] On the other side, Father Henry C. Hengell, the first priest appointed full-time to a state university chaplaincy, documented how pious members of his congregation at Madison "lost their faith when they transferred to Marquette."[4] Other chaplains insisted that Catholics attended public colleges only because they were too poor to attend such colleges as Loyola for Fordham. A few college leaders took their side if only in private correspondence. For example, Father James A. Burns, C.S.C., of Notre Dame, wrote of Father John A. O'Brien's Newman Foundation plan at Illinois: "It is simply a question of meeting an existing emergency."[5]

But all these responses fell short of what Father Keogh, almost single-handedly, accomplished for young Catholics seeking to make their way by getting an education in non-Catholic institutions. What was needed, and what Keogh produced between 1926 and 1930, was a blueprint for a pastoral-educational apostolate. Sometimes calling his concept the "Newman Idea," sometimes "Newmanism," he defined it as "the philosophy" of Catholic student work "based on Newman's idea of a gentleman, his idea of a university, and his concept of Catholic education."[6] The Newman Idea included three basic elements, one pastoral, one instructional, one related to the leadership the bishop of each diocese should provide. In some ways, it forecast the present shape of Catholic campus ministry.

During the FCCC conference of 1926 the chaplain general rallied the movement around the central mission of developing spirituality among students. For the first time chaplains met in a private session. Here they discussed a survey that had been conducted among their charges, and concluded that these young people hungered for religion and piety and tended to get lost in mere social activities chiefly because of a frequent "lack of keen interest" on the part of priests themselves.[7] As a result, the Newman Movement began to place greater emphasis on communion breakfasts, the discussion of religious and moral problems, and inaugurated the Newman Club Liturgical Movement. This latter ambitious endeavor put students to work studying and using Sunday missals, forming choirs, and reading summaries of articles by the Benedictine monks of St. John's Abbey at Collegeville, Minnesota, a center for the development of the Catholic liturgical tradition.[8]

Of course pastoral ministry was both an expected function of priests and one of the major reasons why students formed Newman clubs; development of a rationale for the instructional phase of the Newman Idea required more time.

Father Keogh had been thinking on this point since 1916. That year John Elliott Ross, Paulist chaplain at the University of Texas, had explained how Catholics were forbidden to attend the English universities and how in 1858 some laymen had asked Newman to establish a center at Oxford in hopes that their sons would then be permitted to enroll there. The hierarchy rejected the idea, however, and the first "Newman Center" never saw the light.[9] Now Keogh found in an article by Father Hengell a link between Newman's aborted plan and the encyclical on Christian education by Pope Pius X, *Acerbo Nimis*. The article told how Pope Leo XIII in 1893, three years after Newman's death, had permitted Catholics to enter English universities so long as their bishops provided the very kind of moral and doctrinal safeguards Newman had proposed, and how the Roman canonist, Adolpho Giobbio, had carried the idea to Pius X and successfully urged him to include it in his 1905 encyclical.[10] The feisty Philadelphian must have chuckled when he learned that Giobbio was a Jesuit. Such information spurred him to secure the commentary, "School of Religion in *Acerbo Nimis* of Pius X," which we reviewed in the previous chapter.

Armed with this commentary, Keogh asked the 1928 conference of the federation at Toronto to answer the question, "Why does a Newman Club exist?" Two hundred delegates and fourteen chaplains representing 120 clubs, over 75 percent of the total, were on hand. They unanimously resolved: "Newman Clubs are based upon the Encyclical, *Acerbo Nimis*, in which Pius X strictly commanded that 'Schools of Religion' be established at all secular institutions of higher learning." The resolution directed the delegates "to carry back to their respective organizations the need of emphasizing systematic religious instruction."[11]

With the pastoral and instructional aspects of the Newman Idea developed and accepted by the movement, Keogh next turned to the third essential component, episcopal leadership. He set down his thoughts on this aspect in a report to Cardinal Denis Dougherty, his Philadelphia superior, in 1930. Every bishop should consider the Newman Movement "his personal responsibility," Keogh wrote. Every ordinary should appoint at least one full-time chaplain to each college, fortifying him with "a pastor's salary and parochial rights" over the student body; a part-time chaplain should receive extra pay for his campus work, thus "obligating him to do it"; in each place these priests should "represent the Church and the Bishop . . . in all matters of policy"; finally, the bishops in every state should unite behind their archbishop to promote at each public university "a state-chartered Newman Hall as a school of religion," something presidents and trustees would welcome as a remedy to "college rowdyism and immorality" that would "recreate a new spirit of student living."[12]

By the end of the 1920s, then, Father Keogh had successfully refashioned the Newman Movement. In 1925 he purged it of professorial leadership and turned it into an exclusively student-chaplain led endeavor. In 1926 and 1927 he reinvigorated the pastoral commitments of the movement. In 1928 he justified its involvement in religious education by demonstrating unity of thought between Cardinal Newman, the English hierarchy, Pope Leo XIII, and Pope Pius X. He completed his blueprint with a clear guide to how American bishops could further this apostolate. Keogh's effort unknowingly confirmed the earlier sociological insights of Father Peter E. Dietz regarding the emergence and shape of the movement. The Philadelphian did not share the Oberlin chaplain's optimism regarding the university nor his confidence in the ability of lay persons to take the lead in religious education and interfaith affairs. But he did offer a significant development of Dietz' insistence that a "deeper Sacramental life" must "crown" the endeavor.[13]

With the identity and mission of the Newman Movement so clearly drawn, Father Keogh was ready to address himself to the second great task: the achievement of respectability with the bishops. For those bishops who thought "Newmanism" smacked of heresy,[14] Keogh had an answer: The same pope who had ordered schools of religion to be established at non-Catholic universities had also coined the phrase "Catholic Action." This was a call to laymen, especially educated ones, to use their talents and status to "labor for the restoration of the human race in Christ."[15] Now Pius XI had made this engagement a central effort of his pontificate. The American hierarchy were speaking of the 1930s as "the Catholic Action Decade."[16] Keogh was quick to show how local Newman Club programs and those of the national federation were "all along the line of Catholic Action."[17]

The chaplain general and his co-workers viewed the non-Catholic university as a microcosm of the laicized world of which the popes spoke. Pius XI identified the "first and greatest end" of Catholic Action to be "the pursuit of personal Christian perfection" in the modern world; the FCCC placed the spiritual life of students first among its concerns. The pope described Catholic Action as an apostolate uniting "Catholics of every social class in thought and action around sound doctrine"; the Newman Idea made religious education and the formation of truly Catholic social groupings central to its mission. The Holy Father defined Catholic Action as "the participation of the laity in the Apostolate of the hierarchy"; Newman leaders consistently tried to work hand-in-hand with the bishops, and Keogh was utterly obedient to whatever Church authorities prescribed.[18] Accordingly, in June 1929 delegates attending the Cincinnati convention, noting how the pope had summoned the laity "to service through Catholic Action," resolved "that clubs invoke their members to adhere to the call to personal perfection and to dedicate themselves to secure volunteers for service in this lay apostolate."[19]

To promote these commitments, leaders of the Newman Movement began to organize their yearly conferences and intervening activities around Catholic Action themes. For example, in 1932 the federation centered upon "Catholic Action" itself; in 1934 it was "The Church and the New Social Order"; 1938 witnessed efforts in "A Program of Human Betterment for the Individual and Human Society." Yet Pius XI also insisted that "the fundamental law of Catholic action" imposed "abstention from every political activity" and "pan-Christian" interfaith movements.[20] This meant that by hewing to Catholic Action, the movement limited its scope for significant action.

Federation officers viewed most forms of campus activism as rebellion against parental authority, piety, the Church, and Christian sexual norms. Their response at the 1933 Atlantic City convention to Hitler's emerging persecution of liberals, intellectuals, and Jews typified the aloof position they adopted on nearly all campus political issues. The delegates were told by their president that censure of Nazism was "not . . . pertinent to the function of our organization" and they voted a "hands-off policy."[21] For similar reasons, Newman leaders refused to affiliate with the Vatican-approved international student movement, *Pax Romana*. Keogh claimed that it was a "political" organization, that it got involved in "certain peace movements," and might even be "tinged with socialism."[22]

The Communist threat, however, had to be confronted. When some Newman clubs supported the signing of the Oxford Peace Oath that the American Student Union was circulating at mid-decade, the federation denounced the activity as Communist inspired.[23] The president of Vassar's Newman Club replied to this charge that it was wrong to "discourage Catholic young people from cooperation with other young people on such vital and immediate issues as war prevention."[24] The 1936 convention silenced this kind of protest. Its theme was "The Rise, the Extent, the Remedy for Communism in Our Secular Colleges and Universities." Delegates heard arch-conservative Judge Harry S. McDevitt of Philadelphia charge that Communism was "rife" in the public schools and the private, nondenominational colleges of that city;[25] Franciscan economist Peter B. Duffee described students as "human guinea pigs for crackbrained professors" and Communism as a "false front" for international capitalism;[26] Keogh himself denounced the YMCA for endorsing "creedless Christianity" and selling out to the American Student Union.[27] The delegates voted against Communist tendencies, peace strikes, and campus infiltrators, and then went home. But some delegates wrote expressing their dissatisfaction with the one-sidedness of the meetings. Feelings ran so high that the minutes were never circulated among the officers nor reprinted in *Newman News.*[28] Keogh probably felt the greatest victory came with the NCWC publication of his address in its 1937 survey, "Communists in the United States,"[29] which reminded the bishops that the Newman Movement was fighting on their side.

Other students were upset with the ban Catholic Action placed on interfaith cooperation. During the January 1938 meeting of the New York Province, one undergraduate won considerable support for his argument that "the Protestant is not . . . a heretic trying to prove his contention; he is, supposedly, a person quite sincerely seeking salvation, faced with the same difficulties and temptations as we." Since Protestantism was "a force tending in the same ultimate direction" and "pitted against the same evils" that threatened Catholicism, he urged cooperation on the basis of "pragmatic validity."[30] A number of other students chimed in with attacks on the intransigence of certain Catholic bishops and added their support to "the unity movement." Keogh tried to keep the account of this meeting out of *Newman News,* and when it appeared he lamented that the hierarchy would surely think "these non-Catholic institutions must be infernal despoilers of the Faith."[31]

Such heavy-handed attempts to keep Newman Club activism

domesticated as "official" Catholic Action contrasted sharply with a contemporary midwestern development. During the 1930s at the University of Chicago, Professor Jerome Kerwin, sometimes called "The Pope of the Midway,"[32] became the central mover in confronting Marxism with Thomistic philosophy; providing opportunity for liturgical experimentation; and utilizing spiritual retreats at Childerly Farms as the well-spring for intellectual search and engagement in social justice, as well as personal piety. In this he had the help of many concerned persons, including a group of Catholic lay intellectuals promoting *The Commonweal*, the Dominican priests of St. Thomas the Apostle Parish, enthusiastic lay women like artist Johanna Doniat, graduate students like Father George Dunne, S.J., countless itinerant scholar and activist priests, such as J. W. R. Maguire, C.S.V., Edward Mangan, C.S.S.R., and James Rigney, S.V.D., and such visiting personalities as Louis Budenz, then a leading Communist, and Waldemar Gurian, a leading Communist specialist. None of the enlightenment, prayer, or conversions to Catholicism that took place among this company could be classed as "Catholic Action." Accordingly, Archbishop Mundelein of Chicago ordered the nearby pastor not to let Kerwin and his Calvert Club hold a meeting in his parish "under any conditions."[33]

THE CONFRATERNITY EXPERIMENT

At least one bishop, however, was a former Newman chaplain now in a position to help implement the Newman Idea by promoting religious instruction among Newman clubs. He was Edwin V. O'Hara of Great Falls, Montana, chairman of the National Confraternity of Christian Doctrine, which the American bishops had recently established as part of the NCWC. O'Hara was delighted when Keogh's successor as national chaplain, Paul A. Deery of Indiana University, approached him in 1936 about linking the Newman Movement and the Confraternity. It was quite fitting. The *Acerbo Nimis* of Pope Pius X authorized both apostolates.[34]

Bishop O'Hara at once set up a committee to explore the idea, and in 1937 the first phase of the operation began. That year the federation convention took "The Problem of Imparting Religious Instruction to Catholic Students in Secular Colleges and Universities" as its theme. Speaking to this point, Bishop John Mark Gannon of Erie, Pennsylvania, declared: "A Newman Club is the best vehicle in the secular institutions of higher learning for the introduction of the

Confraternity of Christian Doctrine."[35] The delegates roared their agreement.

The next year they received even more encouragement. Archbishop John T. McNicholas of Cincinnati had distinguished himself in 1929 by setting up a school of religion at the metropolitan university of that city. Despite the rumpus at that time over Father O'Brien's foundation at the University of Illinois,[36] McNicholas consistently referred to his center for "research . . . Biblical lectures, [and] scholastic philosophy and history" as the "Newman Foundation," and attempted to have its courses accredited by the university.[37] Now he uttered a challenge to the hierarchy that some Newman leaders regarded as "the turning point" in their difficult migration toward acceptability and effectiveness.[38] "Assuming that Catholic students attending secular colleges and universities in the United States today number one hundred thousand," the archbishop eloquently trumpeted, "we have one hundred thousand reasons to care for their spiritual well-being."[39] The delegates roared their approval even louder.

Although annual CCD congresses devoted a special session to the issue of religious education on the public campus,[40] these auspicious beginnings failed to fulfill the hopes they raised. The CCD approach to religious education focused on discussion clubs using a specially prepared manual, but after two years leaders concluded that this method was not adequate. The students preferred lectures; they also thought the texts read like "elementary school matter" and lacked notable authors. Indeed, as one confraternity official put it, "secular college students are accustomed to judge the authority of a book by its author—he must be known and accepted in college circles."[41] As a remedy, the CCD issued a special "Christendom Series" edited by the famous Carlton J. H. Hayes of Columbia University and authored by Catholic specialists in several fields.[42] By then, however, only one club in twenty was using CCD materials, and the federation reassigned Confraternity matters to the "Club Programs Aid" committee.[43] In 1941 Bishop O'Hara sadly concluded that "no one acquainted with the question of religious instruction in secular colleges can be satisfied with present achievements in that field."[44]

The deflation associated with the brief partnership between the CCD and the Newman Movement was part of the latter's general decline throughout the Catholic Action decade. In 1930 Keogh recorded that about half the 70,000 Catholics he knew of in secular institutions belonged to 164 Newman clubs, 111 of which were affiliates of the eight fully organized provinces of the federation. About thirty of these clubs had chaplains, only ten of whom were serving one a full-time basis. The figure for Newman halls stood at thirty-three: seventeen had chapels and twenty-eight had "schools of religion" regularly offering classes that in nine places received university accreditation.[45] The 1940 summary was incomplete, itself evidence of how the movement was faltering. That year the total of affiliated clubs stood at 140, that of provinces at seventeen; no figures for priests and centers were at hand. Meanwhile, leaders had set up the John Henry Cardinal Newman Honorary Society in 1936 and in 1938 had adopted a new constitution and name, The National Newman Club Federation. If the records were at all accurate, however, these developments did not reflect growth among the ranks. Membership of federated clubs hovered in the 20,000 range, while the yearly budget fluctuated between $1,000 and $1,500. Indeed, the treasurers' reports suggested that the number of members had peaked at around 25,000 in 1938 and was thereafter in decline.[46] As for religious activities, these were generally minimal, and the educational purposes set forth so boldly a decade earlier all but nonexistent. The leadership brooded among themselves about being "in a slump."[47]

Father Keogh tried to explain why to his Washington correspondents. "Large arid tracts of the country," he said, separated Newman leaders, while less tangible, but nevertheless real, barriers blocked efforts that churchmen working within provincial and national organizations might otherwise have put forth. Prominent diocesan priests like Hengell and O'Brien, he charged, too often preferred "independence and exclusiveness" and virtually boycotted the federation phase of the movement; at the same time, chaplains from the various religious communities tended to place "glory for the Order" ahead of cooperation with the FCCC. And the bishops? In Keogh's tested opinion, the vast majority of bishops remained ignorant of what he called "the splendid piece of work that the Federation has been so quietly and effectively carrying on."[48] Thus, around 1940, the Newman Movement was a national enterprise without permanent headquarters, secretary, or treasurer. It existed as an apostolate needing priests, an educational movement lacking teachers, and a student welfare project seeking inspiration and supervision. This depression stemmed from more than the perennially anemic financial state of its coffers. It was related to the very quality of its leadership.

Although after Keogh's retirement from the national chaplaincy in 1934 the office circulated among Fathers Paul A. Deery at Indiana University and John J. Collins of New York State Teachers' College (1938–40), what power there was remained with East Coast clubs.

These clubs supplied seventy of the ninety national officers elected between 1930 and 1940, all but one of whom came from schools in Boston, New York, or Philadelphia, which could also take credit for contributing three of the six presidents who served during the decade. These officers tended to depend heavily upon alumni for monetary assistance and guidance. Given the absence of hierarchical leadership and finance, where else could they turn? Ironically, it seemed that Father Keogh's efforts in the early 1920s to eliminate "The Tenth Legion" as a carefully selected corps of elite, apostolic alumni leaders was now having unforeseen and undesired consequences. Some observers asserted that the alumni "played around" with the movement, did so with "smug complacency," and "consistently limited its outlook to the Atlantic seaboard." Such an appraisal may have seemed unfair to businessmen who volunteered to help Father Keogh keep his dream alive. But it led one spokesman working closely with the bishops to say that the Newman Federation should "die a natural death" so his bosses could start all over "from scratch."[49]

WHEN THE SYSTEM WAS IN NEED

The Newman Movement did not re-enter the National Catholic Welfare Conference intact. It is more correct to say that its wardens snared it, and in the process almost suffocated it. The authorities finally granted the movement national recognition and direction, not primarily to promote religious education in secular universities, but to accomplish their own aim of uniting all Catholic youth organizations under a central office. On two occasions they tried and failed; without cooperation from leaders of the Newman Movement, they might have failed again.

Worried by juvenile radicalism such as that found within the American Youth Congress, the bishops early in 1934 joined with the National Council of Catholic Men to set up an official Catholic Youth Movement. After seven months of indecisive effort, however, the program ran out of funds and ended.[50] Pope Pius XI reopened the question in the fall of 1935 when he urged Catholic youth groups in all nations to "cooperate with each other" under Catholic Action and warned that failure to do so would "be seriously out of place and harmful"; no such organization should operate "in miserable rivalry" to his program.[51] The Apostolic Delegate in Washington tactfully hinted that this was precisely the situation in the United States.[52]

For example, the Catholic Scouting Movement, boasting 3,000

troops in sixty-six dioceses, offered stiff resistance to attempts at national coordination.[53] Youth clubs in dozens of ethnic parishes also posed a problem, and efforts by *Pax Romana* to link these with youth federations in Europe complicated the matter all the more.[54] In addition, the two most powerful and successful Catholic youth organizations flatly withheld cooperation. One of these was the Sodality Movement begun by the Jesuits of the Missouri Province in 1913. By the 1930s, it enrolled 1,500,000 young people in 2,500 Catholic high schools and 200 Catholic colleges, a growth credited principally to the dynamic leadership of Father Daniel A. Lord, S.J. Leaders of the second group, the Catholic Youth Organization, which Bishop Bernard Sheil, Auxiliary of Chicago, started in 1930, were active in fourteen dioceses.[55] Both groups expressed fears that NCWC coordination would lead to duplication and loss of autonomy.

Antipathy toward NCWC efforts to centralize youth work broke into the open in January 1939, when one hundred CYO leaders met with Sodality officials in Chicago. Lord and Sheil put their heads together. The Jesuit thought the "secret enemy, against whom we have often been warned," had at last become visible. Sheil assured him that "the establishment of a real CYO center" would protect the Sodality movement "as nothing else" and asked him to move for the adoption of a report favoring a national Catholic youth organization that would reflect grass-roots sentiment. Lord did so, and even recommended that Sheil, "the logical leader," serve as its episcopal chairman and act as liaison with the rest of the hierarchy. Though Father Vincent Mooney, C.S.C., head of the Catholic Youth Bureau in the NCWC had not been invited to this meeting, he came anyhow as "the appointed representative of the bishops" and vigorously rebutted Lord's proposal,[56] a performance that got him invited out of the conclave. But one CYO director took up Mooney's cause and wrote afterwards of "the urgent necessity of the Bishops' Committee taking over the guidance and control of Diocesan youth meetings" lest undesirable "agencies" do so first.[57]

Frustrated at making no inroads at the parish and high school level, officials at the Youth Bureau turned to the colleges. In December 1937 representatives from eighteen Catholic institutions had formed the National Federation of Catholic College Students (NFCCS), chiefly to counteract Communist-inspired student clubs by making "authentic Catholic Action" a force among national and international student organizations.[58] The prospect of using the NFCCS as a core for centralizing all Catholic youth work enchanted Washington. But would this group also turn down their invitation?

And, if not, could a handful of clubs started by Catholic girls in upper middle-class schools attract ethnic and athletic clubs into the fold?

Father John W. Keogh suggested the answer. During the 1938 Newman Club Federation convention, the former chaplain general closeted with Monsignor Michael J. Ready, General Secretary of the NCWC. "Why not bring the Newman Federation and the NFCCS together as a section of the proposed Youth Department?" he asked. This would provide the NCWC with a creditable array of 20,000 affiliated young men and women of the highest type from all corners of college life. It would also give the Newman Movement identity at the national level as "official Catholic Action."[59] Father Mooney welcomed the prospect as a "tremendous impetus" to his as yet inert program. More than a year passed, however, and nothing was done; indeed, nothing happened until the Vatican once again indicated its displeasure with the plethora of independent Catholic youth organizations in the United States and singled out for special mention Catholic clubs in non-Catholic colleges.[60]

Quickly responding, the bishops' National Catholic Youth Committee met in July 1940 at Niagara University to work out a plan of unification. The Newman Club Federation and the NFCCS were to comprise the College and University Section of what would become the NCWC Youth Department. Bishop John A. Duffy, the newly appointed ordinary of Buffalo, accepted chairmanship of the department with Father Mooney as director.[61] When Bishop Duffy addressed the first annual conference of Diocesan Youth Directors that December, he reaffirmed the bishops' goal of coordinating "all youth groups" under Catholic Action because this was "the mind of the Popes"; all Catholic youth efforts should follow the good example given by the college federations.[62]

Newman leaders greeted the announcement that their movement was back in the NCWC with joy. "Those who have suffered and toiled in giving of themselves, their time, and their money for the past twenty-five years," wrote National Chaplain Donald M. Cleary of Cornell University, knew that the federation's years "as a stepchild" were now over; the movement had finally won acceptance because the Church, "with that characteristic ability of adapting her disciplinary legislation to circumstances, without compromising one whit her dogmatic teaching," was at last taking the necessary steps to protect, "insofar as she can," the faith and morals of Catholic young men and women in secular colleges. Cleary also credited Keogh with being "the one man above all others" who charted the federation course that was now bringing it into "the harbor which it enjoys today."[63]

Federation officers soon learned that being in harbor also meant being penned. For example, in July 1941 they agreed that their clubs could benefit from some leadership seminars and welcomed an offer from the Marian Sodalities to conduct the desired training programs. When Mooney learned that the minions of his 1939 antagonist seemed about to infilitrate the Newman Movement, he warned Cleary about collaborating with "a set up which opposed the development of" the Youth Department; Newman clubs did not need the help of any "agency outside the N.C.W.C." he insisted.[64] And they did not get it.

A year later more evidence of NCWC possessiveness came to light. Mooney's travels about the country convinced him that students wanted eastern alumni out of control of the federation and that bishops desired a new constitution so that the movement would conform more perfectly to the ideals of Catholic Action. Accordingly, Bishop Duffy and Mooney drafted a new constitution that the executive committee of the federation unanimously adopted in June 1942. Since wartime restrictions canceled the yearly national meeting, the general membership was unable to vote, and this situation caused some rumblings about "clericalism." Yet Bishop Duffy's work proved to be immensely popular and profitable. The elections of 1943 swept in a truly regional slate of undergraduate candidates, and widely based student representation remained the rule in every subsequent election except that of 1957, when eastern clubs took over the majority of offices for one year.[65]

Nevertheless, progressive as the NCWC reform was, it hardly achieved its aim of getting "the federation from top to bottom into the hands of students."[66] A comparison of key passages of the 1938 constitution with the new constitution revealed this. In 1938 the federation was "to organize Catholic students"; in 1942 it was "to assist, when invited by the local ordinary." Formerly, the national chaplain was elected to serve as "spiritual advisor"; now he would be "appointed by the Episcopal Moderator." Again, in 1938 "the executive committee" enjoyed "complete jurisdiction over all matters relating to the business and management" of the federation, with its decisions subject to review by delegates at the annual meeting; under the new regime all matters of policy and execution were "subject to the review of the Episcopal Moderator . . . as supreme authority of this organization."[67] The philosophy underlying Catholic Action required this kind of accountability. "The laity can most truly be instruments of priestly work," explained the Apostolic Delegate, when the instruments are "coordinated with the principal cause, and yet subordinate to it."[68]

The most glaring example of how NCWC direction tended to reorient the Newman Movement came to light when the Youth Department issued its *Manual for Newman Leaders* in May 1942. This forty-eight-page booklet contained a history of the federation; discussed the complementary functions of chaplains, officers, and members; described the procedure necessary to start a Newman club; offered a model club constitution; and listed works members might wish to take up. It also included six pages headed "Religious Courses at Secular Universities" that featured prominently those for credit at the University of Illinois. For the first time, such basic and comprehensive information on the identity, mission, and methods of the Newman Movement appeared between a single set of covers to be transmitted to hundreds of clubs with the full sponsorship and authorization of the bishops.[69]

But there was a catch. The unsigned preface to the *Manual* indicated that the Newman Movement no longer adhered to the Newman Idea that Father Keogh had developed a decade earlier. Rather, the primacy of the Catholic college was to be affirmed, and its priority in matters both pastoral as well as educational, protected. "No one thinks that the Newman Club, or its equivalent, can in any way equal the work and results of the Catholic college," said the preface. Indeed, "all Newman Chaplains" agreed "it would be far better if all Catholic students were enrolled in Catholic colleges." Furthermore, the Washington leadership of the Newman Movement concurred "heartily with the conclusion reached by Father Wilfrid Parsons, S.J., in his articles in *America*." The preface then quoted from the September 18, 1926, issue of that journal: "Admitting the necessity of pastoral work for Catholics at secular colleges," one must also admit that "the prior right of Catholics at Catholic colleges, and the prior duty of others to be in Catholic colleges, preclude any extensive program of expansion of that pastoral work until the Catholic colleges have been fully provided for."[70]

It is difficult to believe that this is what John W. Keogh had in mind when he offered to help the NCWC launch its Youth Department by having the Newman Club Federation join it. It is even more difficult to believe that Father Cleary wrote this preface, although his is the only name appearing in the *Manual* as editor; only six months earlier he had told students "the Jesuits have been our greatest stumbling block."[71] Yet such was the price the movement had to pay to gain respectability by becoming Catholic Action "all along the line." That line lay securely in the grasp of those who believed that "the

Catholic college is in the very heart of the Church's apostolate,"[72] and gathered Newman clubs into the world of boy scouts and parish basketball teams.

Still, although students and chaplains leading the movement often chafed under such compartmentalization, they nevertheless remained hopeful. In the long run they were sure that NCWC recognition, and the power of episcopal encouragement it however so cautiously represented, would be more helpful than otherwise. Once again part of the system, they could stop working toward it and start working on it.

EIGHT

Federation Running Strong

The entire Newman Movement is passing through a highly important transition. Now the Newman Club holds almost limitless possibilities.

Father Edward Duncan
"Newmanism Comes of Age,"
National Chaplain's Address, 1951

Many veterans of World War II would never have darkened a registrar's door but for the war and the magnanimity of Congress; most of them proved they could make the grade. Catholic enrollments in non-Catholic institutions, which had stood slightly over 100,000 early in the 1940s, trebled by the end of that decade and exceeded half a million in 1960.[1] According to one bishop, "all of a sudden the large number of Catholics going to secular colleges stood up and hit us between the eyes"; he believed this shock did more than anything else to awaken the hierarchy to the religious challenge out there on the secular campus.[2] Admission of the Newman Movement to the Youth Department of the National Catholic Welfare Conference provided the bishops with a ready means of addressing themselves to the long-neglected work. And even though a strict interpretation of Catholic Action required a distinction to be drawn between "official" and "unofficial" Newman clubs, the hierarchy now defined them as "the mutual program of chaplains and students."[3] As such, the movement entered a period of remarkable expansion: 385 clubs with an estimated 32,000 members in 1950 grew to 496 clubs enrolling close to 45,000 Newmanites a decade later. Furthermore, by the latter date over 500 chaplains, 150 of them appointed full-time, were serving the campuses, and nearly 100 of them had Newman centers of one kind or another. The federation budget, up from a record $3,000 in 1945 to $15,000 at mid-century, reflected this growth;[4] with help from the chaplains, the budget doubled during the 1950s. We shall review that part of the story in the next chapter. Now we want to watch how the students helped their still-cautious Church to revitalize religious life on the post-war campus.

THE SPIRITUAL LIFE OF THE NEWMAN CLUBS

"In theory, Newman clubs are established to give a Christian integration to the life of the Catholic students on the secular campus," wrote a graduate in 1950; in practice, however, they were "often directed not to the Christianization of the Catholic, but rather to the secularization of Catholicism so the students will be attracted."[5] Such an observation may have correctly depicted the condition in some clubs. One knowledgeable chaplain once termed the old Newman house everywhere in the United States as "a place and provision for Catholic ping-pong."[6]

Even if these were totally accurate assessments, they must be placed in context. Catholics enrolling in secular higher education tended to differ significantly on measures of religiosity from their counterparts entering Catholic colleges; the latter appeared to be "more" Catholic.[7] Since Newman clubs tended to attract the more religiously inclined among Catholic students in secular institutions,[8] any generalization would more than likely be correct in accentuating the positive, however minimal, than in concluding the negative. Above all, since any religious group on campus seemed to appeal primarily to the more passive, dependent student,[9] the intensity of religious activism would vary according to the attention and motivation its pastor or chaplain could provide, and also according to the character of the student generation on hand in any given year: a comparatively activist group of students in the late 1940s gave way to a much more easily domesticated corps in the 1950s. Given their unbenignly neglected condition, the inevitable inexperience of youthful leaders, and the rapid turnover among the older ones, Newman clubs seemed to do relatively well in making Catholic faith and heritage significant in the lives of their members, admittedly a minority of Catholics on the secular campus.

True to the mandates of Catholic Action and the ideals of their patron, regular club members placed great emphasis on the fulfillment of religious duties. Members were admitted to the clubs through a ritual that included hymns and prayers, were encouraged to receive the Sacrament of Penance and the Eucharist frequently, and to make a retreat and mission annually. They received holy cards bearing the short prayers by Cardinal Newman which opened and closed their business meetings. Where they did not have a full-time chaplain or chapel, they gathered at least once a year, and in most places once a month, for a "Club Mass" followed by breakfast; on these occasions they generally also heard a talk by a well-known parishioner on the practice of the faith or conducted a lively inquiry into the theme of the sermon. Their clubs also scheduled special group services at various times during the year, such as First Friday devotions in honor of the Sacred Heart of Jesus, the daily rosary and litany at some shrine of the Virgin during October and May, and Stations of the Cross and Benediction of the Blessed Sacrament during Lent; and they sometimes set up car pools to help members get to these services as well as to Sunday Mass. When members became officers, they were often invested in a chapel or parish church and received their insignia and commissions from the chaplain or the bishop. Members also faithfully sought permission to read works assigned in class that were on the *Index of Prohibited Books*.[10] An official from Notre Dame who attended the 1950 federation conference provided a resounding reply to critics who maintained that Newman clubs indulged too much in social affairs and scanted apostolic formation. He was "favorably impressed" with the Newmanites he met and claimed it was "somewhat mortifying to me to find that these Catholic students from non-Catholic schools are so much more apostolic in their zeal than students I encounter on Catholic campuses."[11]

The Holy Sacrifice of the Mass was, of course, the central act of worship and the indispensable fount of the apostolic spirit for Catholics; students at places with chapels and full-time priests participated in Sunday and weekday services in numbers that impressed observers who had formerly viewed them as "lax" Catholics or "lost souls." Though it was never an easy task, many clubs developed choirs that sang at High Masses on Sundays. The students' venturesomeness led them to adapt the ritual of the Mass according to ideas they read in *Orate Fratres,* the journal of liturgical studies published by the Benedictines of St. John's Abbey in Minnesota, and proposals by such leaders in the movement for the reform of Church worship as Fathers Martin Hellriegel and H. A. Reinhold. Long before parish congregations were singing hymns or listening to homilies at weekday Low Masses, conducting "dialogue" Masses in Latin and English, setting up demonstrations of the ceremonies, replacing the abbreviated and often overly ornate "Roman" vestments with the full and simple Gothic chasubles, or presenting the bread and wine in offertory processions, such practices were common among some Newman clubs.[12]

The religious revival on the campuses of the 1950s converged with the appointment of a large number of priests to campus posts to produce a gratifying surge of liturgically centered activity. God was at last worshipped among them daily, sometimes at several hours throughout the day, in what their patron had called the "great Action," and they were able to arrange their lives around the lead idea of offering themselves, their hopes, and their works to Him through Christ "in its consummation."[13] Active participation in the Mass helped students to view classes and club socials, meetings of province and national officers, and the programs and labors of the many federation committees no longer as "the participation of the laity in the apostolate of the hierarchy," but as the works of Christ Who adored the Father and transformed the world in and through the members of His Mystical Body, the Church. Such perspectives emerged most clearly where the liturgy was richest and most dynamic. A campus chapel often visited for private prayer and meditation bore fruit in the rising number of students who consecrated themselves in religious life. During the twenty years leading up to 1957, fifty-four Catholics attending Louisiana State University answered the call of the Spirit to become priests, sisters, and brothers;[14] between 1951 and 1956, twenty-five students affiliated with the Newman Center at Illinois enrolled in seminaries and thirty-one girls at UCLA entered the convent. During the same period, reports from 302 Newman clubs revealed a total of 550 vocations to the religious life and nearly 6,000 "converts" to Catholicism.[15]

Apart from suggesting that Newman clubs were, in one way or another, doing apostolic things, it is difficult to know just how impressed we should be by such figures. Federation officials cited them to sway both their critics and their bishops, and they did not offer comparative statistics drawn from Catholic colleges, military bases, or parishes with comparable populations. Perhaps the best assessment of the religious value of Newman clubs was, and remains, the lives of former Newmanites who today cheerfully practice and transmit their faith and remember their campus associations as helpful.

TUGGING ON THE LINE

Catholics who returned from the war to enroll in college were older than the typical undergraduate, more restive, doubtful, probing, tempered. They had little time for student organizations or structured extracurricular "monkey business," and not much more for

clerical fussiness.[16] The leadership of the movement had to accommodate its ways to become meaningful to these thousands of tough-
minded young men who, as one told a chaplain, believed the bishops
now wanted the federation to develop *"student responsibility,* even at the
risk of mistakes."[17] Such assertiveness began to carry the movement, if
only a little and only temporarily, beyond the ghetto.

The resulting new burst of student initiative made the National
Executive Committee of the federation more important in policymaking than were either the national chaplain or the annual conventions.[18] By 1950 several dozen top-flight leaders, priests, and interested bishops were attending the committee's quarterly two-day meetings where they worked out ideas critically important for the
expanded work of the Newman Movement. Prominent among these
was the affirmation that concepts like "Newmanism" and "Newmanite"
did not reflect the breadth of perspective the federation ought to foster
because, as one student argued, "all of us are Catholics, not just
Newmanites."[19] The students determined to participate fully in "the
world of the secular campus . . . in its mind, in its life, in its environment." "We have a mission," they said, "not just to our Catholic
students, but to every student and to every faculty member and
administrator . . . to the institution itself."[20]

Educational materials that federation leaders developed reflected this new determination to be more outgoing. "The Responsible Catholic Program," originated by the New York Province in 1947
and adopted nationally three years later, attempted to form "mature,
prayerful, and socially conscientious" Catholic graduates of secular
colleges. The monthly units included carefully worked out class
outlines, bibliographies, and action projects, and explored a theme
for each year the student was in college: "The Courageous Catholic"
(personal morality); "The Informed Catholic" (history, philosophy,
theology, psychology, the arts); "The Prayerful Catholic" (ascetical
theology and liturgy); and "The Apostolic Catholic" (papal ency-
clicles on social questions).[21] Unlike earlier times, when "isolated
groups of Catholic students exhausted themselves in beating off
attacks on the Church,"[22] the new approach to religious education
sought "personal sanctification and the ultimate re-Christianization of
the college world."[23] Other programs developed out of this one, and
when the 1954 convention delegated forty-two educational, administrative, and religious projects to the executive committee, its hard-
driving members had thirty-four on the way to completion within four
months.[24] A year later a master's thesis completed in a Jesuit institu-

tion described the Newman Club as "undoubtedly the largest organized force for good and for the promotion of the ideals of Christian education on the secular campus."[25]

Journalistic effort among the clubs also evidenced the new seriousness about penetrating the college milieu on its own terms. As we have seen, *The Newman News* replaced the *Newman Quarterly* in 1926 to supply the clubs each month with articles and items more attuned to their immediate interests.[26] After the Depression reduced *The News* to a quarterly and World War II cut it back to a semiannual publication, the convention of 1949 replaced it with *Newman News Notes*, which the federation executive secretary in Washington compiled, mimeographed, and distributed monthly.[27] That year, however, the Newman Club at the University of Minnesota decided to inaugurate and edit *Newman World*, "The Paper for Club Members," which for three years served as the national organ for federation news. Students at Iowa State College, Ames, continued the program between 1952 and 1954 with *Contact*, which next became *The New Contact* when Chicago's Calvert Club took up the task, and was transformed into *Newman* when clubs in the Boston Province won the bid for editorship in 1956.[28] Meanwhile, club mimeographs or job printers produced a plethora of local campus sheets: *Newmanweal* at the University of Cincinnati, *Impact* at Louisiana State, *The Newman Log* at West Virginia University, for example. One count indicated that seventy-five club papers and twelve province organs were in production during a single year.[29]

Interestingly, the succession of club-edited national papers followed a trend opposite to the trend of the 1920's. *Newman World* began at the opening of the 1950s largely as a vehicle to build up club membership through motivational articles and a generous sprinkling of pieces of the what's-going-on-where variety. Shortly after 1956, however, *Newman* advertised itself as a magazine "geared to those who have the time and ability to study the faith on their own," and each issue "centered around one of the great themes of the Church," incorporating articles written by leading Catholic spokesmen and scholars and featuring original student drawings, editorials, and poetry. By 1958 its efforts to supplement the educational programs of individual clubs earned it 2,800 subscriptions, the high point. Simultaneously, other quality publications, generally managed by graduate students and helped by professors and alumni, maintained a lofty level of philosophical and theological discussion.[30] Examples are the *Harvard Currant*, Wayne State's *Newman: A Review* and Minnesota's *Newman Annual.* These publications were able to keep themselves solvent through paid advertisements or funding from a center budget. By 1960 *Newman* was costing the federation over $2,000 each year and a plunging subscription rate closed a decade of rewarding local journalistic effort, leading, once again, to a duplication of the popularizing trend of the late 1920s.[31] The television generation had arrived on campus.

The internationalism that swept college ranks after the Fribourg-Prague student assemblies of 1946 and the pronouncements of Pope Pius XII on the need for world order "in harmony with the principles of social and political justice so firmly founded and sustained by the Church,"[32] helped to shatter the pre-war isolationism of the federation. A year later it set up an external affairs department to provide representation "in various national and international organizations of either secular or religious nature." These organizations included the National Council of Catholic Youth, the North American Commission of *Pax Romana*, World University Service, the Young Adult Council, the Joint Committee for Social Action, and the World Assembly of Youth.[33] The federation also developed "Newmanmission," a recruiting agency "to utilize the tremendous resources represented by the Catholic young men and women in secular colleges around the country for the work of the Papal Volunteers for Latin America, the U.S. Home Mission, Aid for International Development, the Grail, South Mission, and their own campus chapels and centers.[34]

Federation leaders were more than ever opposed to Communism. Upon affiliating with the National Student Association (NSA), which was organized in Chicago in 1946, they looked with caution upon the participating International Union of Students, and felt justified when its Communist leadership failed to censure an illegal suppression of the liberties of Czech students twelve months later. Against the inclination of delegates from some Catholic colleges, the federation also opposed participation in a cultural exchange program with the Soviet bloc; in addition, it maintained surveillance of Communists administering funds collected for International Student Relief and the World Student Service Funds.[35] However, a philosophy of responsible engagement had now replaced the aloof criticism of the 1930s. "No Catholic student should become active ... simply for the purpose of combating Communism," explained a federation spokesman. "Catholic students," he said, "should support or oppose measures solely on the basis of merit" while keeping "a check on minority group members to prevent them from exerting influence" out of proportion to their numbers.[36]

Some members of the hierarchy expressed concern, however, over the possibility of Newman clubs becoming tainted with Communist propaganda, especially when their members got involved in European youth rallies, a special target of the Red "soft sell."[37] The poor performance of Catholic students at some of these gatherings confirmed these fears—the meeting held in Vienna in 1959 being a notable example. Yet Father Thomas A. Carlin, Assistant Director of the NCWC Youth Department, was able to assure inquirers that federation members were receiving "consistent and well-documented orientation" on Communist tactics and objectives at youth meetings, and cited this as "another case of where the students are ahead of the chaplains!" As a matter of fact, the most informed, capable, articulate, and politically astute participants in the Vienna Congress came from those schools where the federation had been closely involved.[38]

Determined to respond in positive ways to the stirrings of the new internationalism, the external affairs department participated in sponsoring a wide range of overseas financial aid and literature exchange programs. At home it attempted to educate Newman clubs on the dimensions of world problems, and the U.S. Congress on the need for more liberal legislation on behalf of displaced persons and other immigrants. Its correspondence program attracted return mail from Latin America, Africa, the Philippines, and Australia, where Catholic students were attempting to form campus organizations similar to Newman clubs and wanted federation manuals and educational publications as guides. Educators from abroad, especially those concerned for the development of Catholic life on the campuses of emerging national universities, indicated their desire to visit Newman clubs while touring American universities.[39]

The federation also renewed its concern for foreign students studying in the United States. Ever since the 1920s, its officers had felt that missionary effort among these students would yield more results than work carried out in Asia, Africa, or Latin America. American campuses did not merely train leaders for other societies. It initiated them into a new way of life, one whose qualities impressed them with the depth, or lack of it, of American religious convictions and values.[40] Early in the 1940s, with Pan-Americanism running high, the federation began to look with special interest at students from south of the border, partly from fear that front organizations were "getting the jump" on them.[41] A federation survey revealed that of 18,000 foreign students in American universities, nearly one-third were Latins and less than 800 of them were in Catholic colleges. Another study showed that the Foreign Students Committee of the Newman Club at Austin,

Texas, provided a good model for the coordination of hemispheric efforts and that Catholic clubs at Columbia, Michigan, Pennsylvania, and Temple universities had developed useful intercultural and religious programs. In 1949 the federation set up a Committee for Aid to Foreign Students.[42]

Almost from the start, however, efforts to place foreign students in American universities ran into trouble. Episcopal Moderator James E. Kearney objected to directing these students to secular colleges because he thought it inconsistent to have an "official Catholic organization helping coreligionists attend secular colleges," something he regarded as violating canon law. At their national meeting in 1949, the bishops worked out a compromise. The federation was not to advocate "placement," but rather was to have "Newman Clubs throughout the nation try to interest other clubs on the campus in sponsoring" students, while directing Catholics to the chaplain and the Newman Club. In the mid-1950s, however, with 35,000 foreign students on American campuses, 30 percent of whom were presumed to be of Catholic background, the clubs finally received episcopal approval for a broader program. In 1956 the federation adopted the Voluntary International Student Association plan worked out by Catholics at New York University to link students and families in a cooperative effort. A year later it collected funds for the relief and placement of refugee students from Hungary.[43]

While the federation adopted a broader world view in the post-war years, its leaders also attempted to deepen Catholic involvement in campus affairs. From 1948 conventions began consistently to oppose all campus discrimination based on race. By 1956, when the civil rights movement was starting to take hold among students, Newman clubs, "even in the Deep South," opposed with encouraging success "racial barriers to membership, office, and acceptance in our organization." The Southeastern Province did not hold a convention that year because the host university wanted the housing arrangements to be segregated by color. Yet the federation remained reluctant to become directly involved in political action. Half a dozen years later, when the civil rights movement was agitating the broader society, most southern clubs "urged caution," and only one was prepared to take up the cause even though the federation had adopted a policy of pursuing no forms of civil rights activity the hierarchy would disavow. As late as 1962 the executive committee tabled a motion to cooperate with "organizations interested in racial and religious equality."[44]

Interfaith activism also remained minimal. Canon law forbade priests to debate Catholic doctrine in public; in 1948 the Vatican renewed its earlier warning against religious indifferentism, and the Newman Federation promulgated such bans widely.[45] In 1954 the federation's executive secretary proudly announced that "most Newman chaplains" kept "joint activities to the lowest possible minimum," and were participating in the popular Religious Emphasis Weeks and other interreligious discussion groups "rather reluctantly."[46] Although some students and chaplains did participate out of narrow traditionalism, many others scanted the weeks as tokenism while conducting quite active dialogues and joint religious ventures "underground" the year around.

Meanwhile, the episcopal moderator for the Newman Club Federation carried out his routine duties, such as issuing calls to observe "Cardinal Newman Day" and choosing the national chaplain. He also performed well his most significant charge, that of reporting each year to the rest of the hierarchy on the needs and growth of the movement. Between 1941 and 1952 Bishop Kearney steadily educated the bishops on the magnitude of the problems facing their Church on the public campuses. On the basis of such information, Archbishop Richard Cushing of Boston declared in 1948 that it would "never be physically possible for our Catholic colleges to accommodate the thousands of Catholic students in higher education."[47] Already stretched tightly, the line securing religious education as the Catholic Action prerogative of the colleges appeared to be fraying.

CHALLENGE AT MID-CENTURY

By 1950 the Newman Movement had survived over sixty years of struggle and rejection, both on campus and in the Church, and in June of that year nearly 1,000 delegates, eight chaplains, and three bishops gathered in Cleveland for a gala celebration, not of longevity, but of possibility. They listened to a "National Alma Mater of the Newman Club" that D'Artega composed; heard a message from President Harry S. Truman that praised "the moral force of the Newman clubs in American college life"; and bestowed the Cardinal Newman Honor Award on the Ambassador to the Vatican, Myron C. Taylor.[48]

Two appraisals of the Newman Movement appearing in *America* that summer highlighted its growth. The editors lauded the work of "Father John Keough [sic]" and presented a somewhat ambiguous review of the antagonistic position their predecessors had taken twenty-five years earlier before launching into extended praise of the federation's efforts "to promote an adult knowledge of the faith and a frank recognition of Catholic social principles."[49] Jerome Kerwin, professor of political science at the University of Chicago, outlined some of the challenges facing the movement. He praised Catholic students in non-Catholic universities who "in ever greater numbers" were showing maturity and "seriousness of purpose" in demanding the study of "liturgy, apologetics, philosophy, social problems, and theology." He urged chaplains to be more sensitive to intellectual issues, asked Catholic colleges to drop vocational and pre-professional courses and concentrate on the liberal arts that they were "so eminently fitted" to treat, and recommended "the establishment of houses of study at the great secular universities" where chaplains and students could hold "seminars for interested groups on the campus and invite eminent Catholic scholars from time to time to meet local scholars in the fields of specialized knowledge."[50]

Kerwin's appraisal of the Newman Movement once again brought to the surface those contradictory assumptions encountered thirty years earlier when it was officially regarded as a "part of the Catholic educational system."[51] Granted the majority of Catholic young men and women who attended college were, and would continue to be, enrolled on non-Catholic campuses, were Catholic colleges prepared to relinquish their protected status as the "heart of Catholic Action" in the intellectual sphere and to view themselves as partners in a dual project of educational responsibilities shared with Newman clubs? Were state universities ready to reverse policies promoting their own academic imperialism and cooperate with private and denominational colleges, even with centers that campus ministers erected, in programs of religious study? Indeed, were the leaders of the Newman Movement capable of accepting the kind of intellectual challenge that Kerwin said they must?

These leaders examined the last question with considerable perplexity. Their busy clubs and centers could scarcely meet existing social and pastoral needs. The chaplains realized that their efforts to promote theological literacy and clear understanding of the relationships between religious and profane learning depended largely upon the enlistment of Catholic philosophers and theologians, as well as upon the assistance they could get from Catholic members of secular university facilities. But how could campus priests win the serious consideration of professors and other academic professionals as long as the bishops regarded the Newman Movement, not as a fully authorized agency for advanced religious education, but as part of a youth program? How could professors and students develop into a significant lay apostolate as long as the restrictive philosophy of Catholic Action bound them close to the clerical enterprise?

Such questions cut to the bone of how the Church would eventually come to terms with modern society, especially as represented by its centers for higher learning. In 1950 the outlook was brighter than ever, but not dazzling.

NINE

Working on the System

*Newman Club as a movement is ... the best way to
describe the national educational work of the Church
on the non-Catholic campus.*

Father Paul Hallinan
"Progress Report," 1953

In 1906, two years before it became necessary to form the Catholic
Student Association of America, the first chaplains' organization, the
American Federation of Spiritual Directors of College Catholic Clubs,
came into existence; its founder, Father John J. Farrell of Harvard,
claimed members in New England, Georgia, Canada, the Midwest,
and California.[1] The absence of any records for this organization
suggests that its tenuous beginnings did not survive the reversal the
Newman Movement suffered in connection with the Catholic Educational Association convention the next year.[2] During the decades that
followed, priests assigned to serve Newman clubs operated as rugged
individualists, something Father John W. Keogh often lamented as he
attempted to fashion a national effort.[3] In almost every case, these men
wielded considerable influence among Catholics on their campuses
and even left lasting impressions on the universities they attended.[4]
But, apart from Keogh himself, they had little impact on the developing national student movement.

The post-war years, with their burgeoning Catholic enrollments, demanded that the singular pioneers give way to corporate
strategists. As the cold war spread, leaders of the Newman Movement
believed that "The Battle of the Twentieth Century Will Be Fought
for the Minds of Youth!"[5] They questioned the wisdom of a Church
policy that limited their ministry to social and pastoral matters. The
campuses were the nation's centers for intellectual development. By
1950 non-Catholic institutions were again enrolling the majority of
Catholics going on to college, and the more intellectually inclined of
these young people seemed to be furthest from the Church.[6] The

Newman Movement must be allowed to take up once again what had been part of its original commitment: instruction in the truths of faith and in principles of Christian life for students who attended public universities. The good of souls demanded this; the good of the Church could not ignore it; the very survival of western civilization might well depend upon it.[7]

After three years of preliminary soundings, the priests attending the Mid-century Convention at Cleveland announced on June 15 the organization of the National Newman Chaplains' Association "to offer mutual aid and to unify the work of Catholic Chaplains working on non-Catholic College and University campuses"; the group proposed as its specific aim the setting and achieving of "goals and standards for pastoral and educational programs."[8] Led by Father Edward Duncan, chaplain of the symbolically important Newman Foundation at the University of Illinois, the chaplains were confident they could help to build the Newman Club Federation into a powerful agency for an intellectual as well as a spiritual mission, and in so doing provide the American Church with a system of chaplaincies which its leaders would one day have to endorse wholeheartedly and support generously.

DOLLARS FOR BOOKS

The Newman Movement entered the 1950s struggling toward development as an educational enterprise against a financial situation that made such an ambition seem hopeless. Although in 1949 the federation had operated on its largest budget in history, nearly $15,000 spent on overambitious programs plunged it almost $5,000 into the red. The chaplains were able to set things right by sending in eleventh-hour donations.[9] Soon thereafter they started a four-year campaign to raise the per capita dues from twenty to twenty-five cents. Totally dependent upon its own resources, the movement, in the colorful phrase of Father Paul Hallinan, had to stop trying to nourish itself on "one lonely, unvarnished hamburger."[10] After what he termed an extensive "educational campaign," the officers were able, in 1954, to achieve this objective; within two years their coffers once again bulged, this time with $28,000, one-third of which went to the national office for its work of coordination and publication.[11]

Father Hallinan, who served as national chaplain from 1952 to 1954, characteristically called budget boosting an "educational" task, for concern about education guided his chaplaincy. A doctoral candidate at Western Reserve University as well as a loyal disciple of John W. Keogh and an ardent reader of John Henry Newman, he insisted that the Newman Movement was "*primarily intellectual* in the very real sense of supplying Catholic principles of apologetics, theology, philosophy, history, and social education." He demanded that "every other project . . . be judged relentlessly in the light of that principle."[12] By mid-decade the federation was doing just that.

"Aware that a good Catholic is an informed Catholic," delegates at the 1955 convention set out to "promote an increased interest and inculcate a feeling of pride in our rich cultural heritage"; they further resolved "to contribute to the development of Catholic intellectual traditions in the United States."[13] The federation set up a Religious Education Committee, adopted criteria governing the development of club libraries and the organization of courses, and urged students at every campus to form local boards of education so they could design and implement programs that would win their clubs certification as "superior Catholic centers."[14] In 1958 the national chaplain reported that in nearly every college and university, Newman leaders had "stopped wringing their hands" and were working ardently "on the teaching assignment."[15]

During the second half of the 1950s, two lines of educational endeavor proved to be especially heartening. Panel-commission sessions, introduced at the Detroit convention of 1954, resurrected the discussion group techniques Keogh had inaugurated in 1928. Chaplains and students, prepared to discuss selected theological topics, led several sessions of the convention in a free give-and-take of information. The scheme helped to establish a new tradition of intellectual inquiry alongside the internal political and social activities of the national meeting that often threatened to smother its apostolic effectiveness.[16] Federation leaders also succeeded in launching a program of summer seminars, and only prohibitive costs kept them from returning to Cliff Haven, which during the movement's first ten years had been the site of similar gatherings. The first in the new series convened in 1952 under the sponsorship of the University of Notre Dame and the Ohio Valley Province and offered the twenty-six attending students a week-long series of lectures and workshops on such topics as the theology of the Incarnation, Church history, family life, social principles, liturgy; the layman and the Church, and ecumenical relations. An overwhelming majority of those enrolled indicated they would come again, and by 1958 five Newman Schools of Catholic Thought were instructing 500 club members.[17] In two years these numbers doubled; chaplains and students hailed the seminars as "the most valuable" educational experience the federation provided. Meanwhile twenty-six provinces set up weekend "capsule" schools.[18]

These educational programs benefited from a host of publications that the national office could now afford to issue. These included: *The Newman Club in American Education*, a statement of philosophy for campus work and a survey of fourteen religious courses underway at Newman centers;[19] *Tools and Techniques*, a comprehensive, scholarly manual on the teaching of apologetics;[20] *Outlines for a Reading Program*, a coordinated sequence to guide the inquisitive student;[21] *Chaplains' Source Book*, a selection of lectures and articles to help the newly appointed campus priest;[22] *Focus*, a thick, densely annotated listing of pertinent books and periodicals especially prepared for Catholics in secular colleges by the Jesuits at Woodstock College;[23] *Spot Educational Outlines*, lecture plans arranged by chaplains and Catholic specialists on theological and philosophical subjects;[24] *Handbook of Educational Programming*, a description of the successful instructional systems of forty clubs;[25] and *The Idea of a Univesrity*, a discussion outline offering "an antidote to the educational philosophy of John Dewey."[26] Nearly half of the fifty federation publications during these years were educational, and the chairman responsible for their distribution reported that students and chaplains received them enthusiastically.[27]

Chaplains devised a number of ways to tailor courses to the needs and resources of their campuses. Those at downtown professional schools read up on medical ethics and law and invited Catholic practitioners in these fields to staff regularly scheduled seminars. Others developed prototypes of the "free university" of the 1960s. Full-time chaplains with centers were able to present more standard fare. They provided regular weekly or biweekly inquiry classes, pre-marriage courses, and sequences in Church history, current problems in philosophy, "theology for the layman," and liturgy. Most centers also provided art-film series, featuring discussions in which priests or graduate students highlighted theological themes, and a few others annually mounted liturgical arts shows. Chaplains at the University of Minnesota set up the Newman Forum, which enrolled subscribing townsmen to finance public lectures by prominent Catholic thinkers from every continent. Similar programs elsewhere generally also assigned the speaker to lecture in several university classes during his two- or three-day stay on campus. The wealthier Newman centers regularly engaged such speakers for a quarter or a semester as "theologian in residence." Campus priests were also joining forces with ministers of other denominations in joint sponsorship of addresses and seminars.[28]

But these vigorous efforts to reconsecrate the youth movement to intellectual purposes did not go unwatched, nor, in some circles, unfeared. Nor did the students always welcome priestly leadership that seemed, at times, to control rather than to encourage their programs. About 1955 the Newman Movement was making waves that sometimes broke upon hostile shores.

TROUBLE IN WASHINGTON

Almost from the day in 1940 that the National Newman Club Federation became part of the National Catholic Welfare Conference, chaplains repeatedly asked for "a priest director . . . devoting all of his time" to student affairs.[29] Eight lay executive secretaries came and went within ten years, and the national office was in chaos. By 1952, 75 percent of the addresses on the chaplains' mailing list were incorrect, two-fifths of the listed clubs either did not belong to the federation or had gone out of existence, and the true number of Newman clubs was one tenth of those reported.[30] Letters from priests and students criticizing operations in Washington evidenced widespread disaffection and threatened the continuation of the long-sought-for central bureau. Furthermore, the absence of stable adult guidance at the national level permitted student turnover and, at times, whimsy to obstruct or divert critically important federation programs. The chaplains by no means wanted student leaders to be "puppets or rubber stamps," but they also dreaded the "unknown but personable young man or woman" graced with superficial piety, innocent of theological reading, and untutored in the major goals of the movement, who could "sweep into a convention and walk out the representative leader of some 40,000 Catholic students."[31]

For their part, the students did not agree that a priest should hold the most influential position in their federation. The executive secretary interpreted their affairs to the bishops and communicated the bishops' wishes to them. He coordinated leaders and activities on provincial and local levels, worked with the national officers, supervised mailings, monitored programs, and contributed advice. He also cooperated closely with the chaplains' association, whose president traveled about the country to dedications and provincial conventions where he delivered addresses that sometimes challenged club members' traditions and understanding of the movement. Some students suspected that Youth Department policy, chaplains' association philosophy, and the growing influence of the national chaplain (who after 1950 was their federation chaplain as well), tended to knit the affairs of the federation more tightly into the clerical bureaucracy and would eventually wrest it from the layman's grasp.[32]

When Father Thomas A. Carlin, O.S.F.S., accepted the post of first full-time executive secretary of the Newman Club Federation in July 1952, he came as the answer to the prayers of many chaplains and as the fulfillment of the fears of many students. Some quite innocent developments soon confirmed the latter. For example, Carlin incurred student ire when he agreed to help the chaplains redraw province boundaries to match those of the dioceses. Unable to convince the young leaders of the federation that he was not the agent of a chaplains' master plan, Carlin complained to a friend of the "deviousness of student thinking," which, he said, was "inconceivable" to an outside observer.[33]

Meeting at the University of Colorado in June 1953, the chaplains responded to such misunderstandings in a statement which its author, Monsignor Robert Tracy of Louisiana State University, called "The Boulder Memo." "The local chaplain," wrote Monsignor Tracy, should "moderate, not run" the Newman Club. As the official representative of the bishop, he was responsible for supervising all matters concerning faith, morals, and official policy. But he should breathe a spirit of "tact and charity" into his work with students, and he should approach them as "a wise, respected, fatherly moderator" summoning "a vigorous group of leaders" to an "apostolic adventure." Tracy insisted that local projects could "best come from student thinking no matter how good the chaplain's ideas may be or seem to him to be."[34]

Concerning the issue of clerical *versus* student leadership at the national level, Tracy's memo warned that "to camouflage authority too much is to court trouble," and suggested clear, agreed-upon lines of authority that left great room for student initiative. Father Hallinan pointed out that students brought innovation to the Newman Movement, while the chaplains contributed stability, and he called the harmonious fusion of the two a philosophy of "creative continuity."[35] In the years that followed chaplains took special pains to single out promising students, and spent extra hours with them in discussion and prayer. They soon concluded that "efforts ... to groom student candidates for province and national offices" were bearing good results.[36]

While such efforts helped to smooth over disruptions between students and chaplains, however, the bonds that held the chaplains' association to the executive secretary and the Youth Department began to snap. Many part-time campus priests lacked the time and money to attend national meetings and to consult with the Washington leadership, and they often failed to see what benefits membership in the Youth Department afforded. On the other hand, those deeply involved at the national or provincial levels could see snags, as well as advantages, in this relationship; some believed that the Newman Movement could not fulfill its potential until the national chaplain himself took over the executive secretaryship of the federation. By 1955 Father Carlin, the federation's executive secretary, had heard enough remarks at meetings and read enough between the lines of letters to feel that he had lost the confidence of the chaplains as well as much of the cooperation of students. He concluded that he had neither the appetite nor the personality to "stay on as an office boy," and in April he accepted a new position as assistant director in the NCWC Youth Department.[37]

The confusion following this move plunged the chaplains' association and the department into a bitter controversy. Monsignor Tracy, who had become national chaplain the previous year, scoured the country for Carlin's successor, and in June received permission from the Paulists to ask for the services of Father Charles Albright, then serving at Wayne State University.[38] Meanwhile, the NCWC Executive Secretary was under the impression that Carlin's work with the Newman federation would continue, and he had not made any provisions for hiring another full-time staff member.[39] Tracy complained that the Youth Department had gained an assistant director at the expense of the Newman Movement "through a queer misunderstanding," and he cited the ambiguous wording of some of the memorandums concerning Carlin's transfer.[40] Other chaplains viewed the affair as the "latest episode" in a long series of attempts to swallow the Newman Movement "in the anonymity of the Youth Department to the detriment of its progress" and insisted that Tracy fight back.[41]

Resolution of the difficulty finally came after Bishop Maurice Schexnayder, a former chaplain who had become episcopal moderator of the Newman Club Federation in 1952, and Monsignor Howard Carroll, the NCWC executive secretary, intervened. By the first week of July, Tracy was able to announce that the appointment of Albright was certain.[42] The outcome boosted the sagging morale of the chaplains' association, kept the central office intact, put one of their own members in charge of it, and served notice on those in the NCWC who did not take the Newman Movement seriously that its leaders were fully determined to meet any resistance to their cause with decisive measures.

RERUNS FROM THE TWENTIES

Struggling fitfully against the unbalanced competition of tax-supported schools, Catholic colleges were also feeling a financial pinch. Furthermore, their administrators were now called upon to defend the academic excellence of these institutions,[43] an issue that might not only depress current enrollments, but in the long run could complicate plans to expand for the student boom looked for in the 1960s and 1970s.[44] The college leaders were not flattered by Newman spokesmen who would not rest until every secular campus had a "religious educational program comparable to that available in Catholic colleges."[45] In answer, they launched a campaign to preserve their favored status as centers for religious schooling.

In 1954 they found an ally in a former Newman chaplain writing under the pen name "Ralph Strode," who published an article in *America* purporting to expose the subversion of faith by intellectuals on the secular campus. His analysis of professorial slur techniques, campus moral dangers, and the ineffectiveness of Newman clubs presented a dark picture.[46] Father James J. Maguire, C.S.P., of the Newman Foundation at Wayne State University, countered in a subsequent issue of the journal. While admitting the accuracy of most of Strode's assertions, including those about Newman *clubs,* the chaplain insisted that those Newman *Centers* or *Foundations* offering a full round of liturgical and educational programs met quite well the religious needs of Catholics at secular schools. Maguire also cautioned schoolmen against exaggerated indictments of secular culture that alienated "men of goodwill" who were beginning "to look to the Church for wisdom and enlightenment." Such counterattacks, he said, "create ... a new and most disastrous type of ghetto mentality."[47] While several thousand reprints of the Strode article were making the rounds of Catholic college and alumni circles, some from these ranks joined the debate by charging that mediocre religious teaching in Catholic schools also subverted faith, thus lending new credence to an opinion Newman chaplains had long expressed.[48]

Meanwhile, the *Catholic Digest,* publicizing the newly completed Newman Hall at the University of Minnesota, made some assertions that further threatened Catholic institutions. The author claimed that over 60 percent of all Catholics in higher education were in secular

colleges and concluded that "within twenty years Newman Foundations ... could be the major instruments of Catholic higher education." In his opinion, it was apparent that "our only hope" lay in a
"greatly expanded Newman Apostolate."[49] Father Leonard Cowley,
chaplain at the University of Minnesota, had no desire to kick up the
ashes of old controversies. He pointed out that the *Digest* piece had
placed his customarily good-humored banter into a context of mili-
tancy, and called upon Catholic journalists, professors, and chaplains
to respect their colleagues and to "try to help each other in a time when
unified thinking and action is demanded by the press of secularism."[50]

Newman chaplains expressed fears that, for the third time in
their history, concern for the preservation of the colleges would injure
the movement, and determined to state their position collectively and
clearly.[51] Accordingly, in May 1955 the chaplains' association issued a
statement of reassurance, largely the work of Father Tracy, entitled,
"Principles and Policies of the Newman Club Movement." It set forth
ten affirmations dealing with the higher education of Catholics.
"There can be no ideally perfect education which is not *Christian
education,*" the statement began, and "this is best achieved by the
Catholic college and university where God is *centrally* studied and
daily worshipped. . . . The best place for the Catholic student ordinar-
ily is the Catholic college." Other points noted that the Newman
Apostolate was the response to "the presence of more than 300,000
Catholic young men and women" on secular campuses; urged action
on their behalf; and suggested that Newman programs could bridge
"the chasm that separates Catholic and non-Catholic centers of culture" if they were supplied with more and specially trained priests,
"more attractive and effective centers," and more cooperation from
"the entire Catholic intellectual effort at the college and university
level." The statement concluded with Bishop Schexnayder's words:
"We must not do as little as we can for the Catholic student in the
secular college and university, *but as much as we can.*"[52]

"Principles and Policies" artfully served the purposes the chaplains' association intended. Some of its members did sincerely believe
that all Catholic students should be in Catholic colleges; others
strongly held that they were better off in secular schools. The studied
ambiguities and generalizations the document used in describing
Catholic institutions contrasted with factual assertions about the status
of the Newman Movement. Nearly all the chaplains could accept a
rationale so diplomatically worked out.[53] At the same time, the policy
statement appealed to most Catholic college leaders, some of whom
even quoted portions favorable to their institutions in occasional

debates with federation officials.[54] Furthermore, its temperate appeal for unified action on behalf of Catholics on the secular campus helped win the chaplains a place within the College and University Section of the National Catholic Educational Association that year.[55] It seemed that the iceberg blocking the chaplains since 1907 was beginning to crack.[56]

END-OF-DECADE BALANCE

In 1950 Professor Jerome Kerwin had summoned Catholic educational leaders to collaborate with Newman chaplains and, where possible, secular universities in setting up houses at the latter for the study of Catholic theology and philosophy.[57] A fair appraisal of the response to his challenge indicates that ten years later only the Newman chaplains had taken him seriously.

By 1960 the National Newman Chaplains' Association, which had begun the 1950s with eight charter members, listed on its rolls over half of the estimated 500 priests assigned to work with Newman clubs. Dividing the roles that Father John W. Keogh earlier had tried to perform single-handedly, thirty-one priests headed up committees on such things as building and planning, education, international students. liturgy and music, new chaplain's training, policy and agenda, and publicity. Working closely with students and bishops, the association had led the way in dramatically redirecting the Newman Movement back to the task of providing religious education for the non-Catholic campus. Vigorous as these efforts had been, however, its own estimates claimed that only about one in ten of the 500,000 Catholic students on these campuses joined Newman clubs, and that only about one in 100 enrolled in programs of religious study. The swiftly growing population of Catholic graduate students had virtually no contact at all with the movement.[58]

The fault, if there was one, did not lie entirely within the Newman Movement. Its leaders returned from a 1956 conference with representatives of Catholic colleges to announce that "Newman educational programs are not regarded officially as Catholic education."[59] A similar series of meetings with spokesmen for secular institutions on the accreditation of religious studies led the national chaplain to comment that it was not clear whether such conferences were "designed to promote or to curb the dissemination of religious knowledge."[60] Leaders of the Newman Movement knew they could do little to speed up the academic gates that were slowly opening to receive theology as an authentic intellectual pursuit. Faculties would accept this area of study on their own scholarly terms according to a deliberated schedule, and pressure from religious professionals might actually retard progress.[61]

Newman leaders were on surer ground when they insisted that the hierarchy had to take a stronger stand regarding their role in religious education. And here they enjoyed some little encouragement. During the 1950s eleven priests who had been Newman chaplains became bishops; three of them—Leonard Cowley, Auxiliary of St. Paul; Paul J. Hallinan, Bishop of Charleston, South Carolina; and Robert Tracy, Auxiliary of Lafayette, Louisiana—had been national chaplains. These new bishops made sure that the problems of the Church on campus were kept before the rest of the hierarchy. They promoted the appointment of more chaplains, encouraged the erection of more centers, and forged closer links between the bishops and the Newman Club Federation. Another former chaplain, Auxiliary Bishop Maurice Schexnayder of New Orleans, served as episcopal moderator of the Newman Club Federation from 1952 to 1960. His diplomatic but determined advocacy did not accomplish all that he desired in his frequent behind-the-scenes skirmishes with college and church officials; but his sincere interest and encouragement raised the morale and fulfilled many hopes of Newman leaders. For example, in 1956, when the hierarchy refused to finance Newman Federation educational publications, "Bishop Schex" won a yearly $5,000 subsidy from the Our Sunday Visitor Press in Huntington, Indiana;[62] and two years later he got the hierarchy to agree that the Newman Federation was its "official" agency in secular higher education.[63]

The constraint imposed on the federation by its relegation to NCWC's Youth Department in the interest of protecting the role of Catholic colleges as designated centers of higher religious education loomed for most Newman leaders as their most formidable obstacle. The federation was still dependent for financing upon student dues and chaplain assessments, and Father Albright found at times he could not draw his own salary and was in danger of not being able to meet the modest payrolls of the staff assisting him in the executive office.[64] The bishops did not feel free to finance the movement on a national level since this would constitute "assisting Catholics not to attend Catholic schools," something which canon law forbade and which thus would make them "vulnerable . . . to attack from Catholic colleges and universities."[65] It was true that on the diocesan level during the academic year 1958–59, bishops individually had authorized the construction of fifty new Catholic student centers, that the movement had sponsored four schools of Catholic thought, eight area seminars, twenty-one leadership weekends, and a club president's conference in the interest of developing Catholic cultural and theological leadership. But Bishop Schexnayder concluded at the decade's end that "a realistic appraisal of the situation" required him to tell the bishops that the movement had developed only to the stage it actually should have reached "twenty-five years ago."[66]

The 1959 Report of the National Chaplain agreed with Schexnayder's evaluation. "Any priest who is not somewhat discouraged," wrote Father George Garrelts of Minnesota, "is not a bona fide Newman Chaplain." Garrelts claimed that the typical priest on campus was still single-handedly trying to muddle through overwhelming problems. He had to serve students individually while attempting to influence the course of academic life that moved in broad and vigorous currents on all sides. He still awaited a helping corps of Catholic professors. Impulses toward more interfaith activities continued to jostle him against Church regulations and policies. Aloofness on the part of Catholic college educators continued to frustrate him. Yet Garrelts had also traveled far and wide over the country consulting with chaplains and students about past crises and hopes for the future, and he noted how, during the decade, the chaplains' association had gained strength, confidence, vision, and influence within the movement and the hierarchy. He added: "Any Newman Chaplain who is not overall optimistic does not see the full picture."[67]

TEN

Out from the Shadows

We have a mandate!!

Monsignor Alexander Sigur,
address to newly appointed
Newman chaplains, 1962

During the years following World War I, American Catholics claimed more and more of their country for themselves; at times they even felt they were actually more American than their non-Catholic fellow citizens. The cohesiveness of the various forms of their Catholic ghetto culture fortified them for accomplishing the former and insisting upon the latter. Their sons and daughters who graduated from parish schools into colleges operated by the religious orders of the Church continued to enjoy the support of a Catholic environment. Students matriculating to the secularistic campuses, however, found themselves in a strained situation. They entered a region of American life dominated by a worldly ideology which their Church judged to be hostile to the Christian teachings and natural law underpinnings of the nation, a condition which these young Catholics fully recognized and lamented. But, because their Church termed their chosen schools "occasions of sin,"[1] because Catholic colleges enjoyed a "prior right" in canon law to receive the attention and benefits of the Catholic body,[2] and because this population imposed a huge task upon leaders seeking to organize and staff parishes, parochial schools, hospitals, orphanages, and other agencies for the ministries of the Church, little of an "official" nature could be done to help these students in their plight.

As early as 1907 leaders of the movement to provide pastoral care and religious education for these growing thousands of young Catholics started to work their way toward acceptance into the official philosophy and administrative mechanisms of the American Church. They achieved this minimally in 1940, when the National Newman Club Federation became part of the College and University Section of the Youth Department in the National Catholic Welfare Conference.

For the next twenty years advocates of the Newman Movement worked on the system. Students, chaplains, and an increasing number of bishops collaborated to circumvent policies hindering, and to fashion ones furthering, their Newman mission. Vindication very much like that experienced by their patron was at hand for those who had never given up hope that one day the American Catholic bishops, as a national body, would see things their way.

BALANCING ACTS

By 1960 Newman chaplains began to ease off from the promotion of schemes for formal religious instruction that had dominated their activity for a decade and began to rethink the pastoral implications of their situation. Though they agreed among themselves that their work was educational "in the very real sense of supplying Catholic principles of apologetics, theology, philosophy, history, and social education" where university policy withheld such options from students,[3] some of them insisted that "the spiritual and religious development of the student in liturgical practices" was an "important part of the educational process."[4] Bishop Paul J. Hallinan of Charleston, South Carolina, who had led the crusade for Newman educational programs as national chaplain early in the 1950s, summed up the dilemma. "The Apostolate called the Newman Movement," he said, "is an exercise in poise" between the Catholic college and the Newman center, between the secular teacher and the religious educator. Until priests and lay scholars joined its ranks in enough numbers "to permit the luxury of specialization," he thought, "the *pastoral-educational* conflict" would find only unsatisfactory solution in "compromise."[5]

When the Advisory Board of the National Newman Chaplains' Association met at St. John's Seminary, Plymouth, Michigan, in July 1961 to review reports from campuses around the country, the members agreed that as long as the scales tipped in favor of pastoral care, they would compromise. Though there is no Newman Movement "without an educational program," they said, "the essential priestly and pastoral role is the root of our mission to the secular campus." Their discussions supported this view by an appeal to accepted theology on the nature of the priesthood and statements by recent popes describing the liturgy as the "primary and indispensable source of the true Christian spirit." They also pointed to the many young Catholics who were leaving home to attend college or were enrolling in commuter schools; both groups tended to ignore services in local parishes.[6] Furthermore, as Father John Bradley of Ann Arbor had already argued, the appearance of an unprecedented number of full-time chaplains and student centers had carried the movement "beyond the framework of the Newman Club" into the "broader and deeper . . . work of the student parish."[7] Finally, the vast majority of chaplains were also ready to admit their need for additional preparation and qualification before they could hold forth on their campuses as theologians or philosophers.

With their own policy somewhat clarified, the chaplains at Plymouth turned to the role they wanted the bishops to play. They cited the small number of chaplains and the meagerness of their resources. Whereas the ratio between priests and students on Catholic campuses was one to thirty, they said, a priest on a large secular campus might have to look after as many as 2,000 young coreligionists and also several hundred other students seeking advice or religious instruction. What, then, in the chaplain's estimation, should the bishops do? First, they should assign one priest full-time for every 300 Catholics at residential campuses and for every 500 at commuter campuses, with another full-time priest for each additional 500 students in the first situation and 1,000 in the second. Most critical of all, bishops could also clearly and emphatically notify pastors that curates assigned part-time to the campus ministry were to devote a specific number of hours each week to this apostolate. Finally, the bishops could also upgrade the entire Newman Movement if they would find some way to give priests entering it special preparation and training.[8]

While the last two recommendations had considerable merit, the chaplains overlooked several factors complicating their assessment of ratios and priorities. Not all priests on Catholic campuses were chaplains; rather, the overwhelming majority were full-time teachers, and most of them had neither the time nor the inclination to be chaplains in the usual sense. Furthermore, chaplains in these schools were themselves often part-time teachers or curates, and they were actually less organized as a group and more burdened with institutional responsibilities than many Newman chaplains.[9] Again, problems facing Newman chaplains at commuter schools, where students often held jobs and attended classes at a wide range of day and night hours, indicated more clergy might well be needed there than in residential situations, as the chaplains proposed. Nevertheless, their review of the situation supplied the hierarchy with a helpful guideline.

Although changing conditions on the campus justified the new emphasis on pastoral involvement there, the shift was also part of a grand strategy. The chaplains knew that bishops, as chief pastors, would respond to meet spiritual needs with more readiness than they would to advance instructional programs. Furthermore, at a time, as Hallinan noted, when the rapidly expanding Newman Movement had to move with more caution than before, chaplains would do well not to threaten the Catholic colleges by direct assertions of their own mission as educators. The long-range view suggested that when the hierarchy had invested considerable sums in the erection of facilities near secular campuses and had transferred a larger proportion of their personal to man them, they might very well come to the point where they would themselves begin to pressure religious orders, not only to staff chapels, but also to supply teachers from their colleges — a development some members of the orders were also hoping would soon take place.[10]

Meanwhile, concentration on the pastoral function of the chaplaincy accompanied two other developments in the movement. At the forty-sixth annual conference of the federation, held in Cleveland during the closing days of August and the first days of September 1960, the National Newman Association of Faculty and Staff came into being to promote "spiritual welfare, ... research and scholarship among Catholic faculty and staff, [and] to assist Newman Chaplains, students, and alumni on national, province, and local levels."[11] That same year the executive secretary of the federation, Father Charles W. Albright, C.S.P., announced the incorporation of the National Newman Foundation, an agency to attract the support of Newman alumni around the country and to approach the growing number of funds and foundations, Catholic and non-Catholic, which were then concerning themselves with religion in higher education.[12]

In autumn 1961 Bishop Hallinan, newly appointed moderator of the Newman Club Federation, approached the episcopal moderator of the NCWC Youth Department, Archbishop John Dearden of Detroit, to present a summary of the Plymouth meeting and to sketch the history of the student federation and its auxiliary branches: the Alumni Association, which began in 1924, the Honor Society that originated in 1938, the eleven-year-old Chaplains' Association, and the new faculty-staff group and foundation. He found Dearden "very sympathetic" and ready to use his position to give "prestige and real stature" to the movement. Their four-hour conference produced, said Hallinan, "a real step forward." He assured Monsignor Alex Sigur of Southwestern Louisiana State University, national chaplain from 1960 to 1962, that the other components of the movement were prepared to accept the chaplains' understanding of pastoral-educational relationships and that officials within the Youth Department stood ready to grant it a more appropriate status. Hallinan rejoiced especially because "for the first time, a new total concept of the Newman Movement" was emerging, with everyone playing "a well-defined role" in the process. Most important, these developments had "the agreement of the bishops."[13]

The moderator was not alone in his evaluation of the situation. In February 1962 the newly elected president of the National Newman Club Federation, Edward Orlett, at the General Motors Institute of Dayton, Ohio, sat down to write his monthly column for *Newman News* and decided to express himself forthrightly on a sensitive issue. "Is the Newman Club, a student organization of part-time apostles, capable of meeting the spiritual, intellectual, and social needs of half a million Catholic students on the secular campus?" he asked. He thought not. The Newman mission required "a great many more lay people" who had "authority and responsibility." Even at the risk of playing down the role of students, Orlett thought the time had come to admit that the Newman club was only a part of a broader endeavor on the campuses.[14] Simultaneously, he set forth in a letter to Monsignor Sigur, the national chaplain, his ideas on "the possibility of a meeting ... to create a better understanding among all elements" and how best to meet them.[15]

The national chaplain and the executive secretary of the federation, Father Albright, had hardly congratulated Orlett on his vision and intentions when the young president moved into action. On March 17 he mailed to the officers of the several sections of the movement a summary of problems and a proposal to remedy them. His list mentioned "rapid expansion" that endangered relationships between chaplains and student leaders, generated confusion within student ranks, and sapped time and energy needed for "long-range thinking or planning." He proposed what he termed a "summit" to impress "clergy, students, faculty, and alumni" with the conviction that each group must "share equally in responsibility and authority" for the work of the Church in nondenominational colleges and universities.[16] Though Fathers Sigur and Albright, and Hallinan, who was now Archbishop of Atlanta, had already decided such a meeting should take place some time in the summer of 1962,[17] Orlett's impetuous intrusion seemed to them to jeopardize efforts they were making to paper over some recent misunderstandings between students and chaplains.

Here was the situation. For several months preceding Orlett's announcement, a student committee had been raising money to produce a film describing the nature and needs of Newman work. At a recent meeting they had agreed to transfer their collections to the National Newman Foundation. However, a press release issued by the treasurer of the foundation indicating that $15,000 had been earmarked for a documentary motion picture did not acknowledge the students' contribution.[18] Furthermore, invitations to view the rough footage and determine the final content of the film excluded students. Predictable tremors of mistrust ran through federation ranks and joined rumors suggesting that Orlett was about to be disciplined by ecclesiastical authority for his forwardness in speaking up.[19] How could the clergy point out to Orlett that he was moving a bit too fast without seeming either to discount the importance of the meeting he suggested or to discourage full and open student participation in it?[20]

Fathers Albright and Sigur mixed reassurance with admonition. They explained to Orlett that the Newman Foundation had not "stolen" the money, but that a regrettable error in reporting its origin had distorted the whole matter; nor were the chaplains really stepping into student territory. They went on to say that the president had made a tactical blunder. He should have issued his proposal jointly with the national chaplain, if not with the episcopal moderator himself. Furthermore, they said, while Orlett assumed "each element" of the operation could enjoy "equal responsibility and authority," this was incorrect and even appeared to dictate the outcome of a meeting called precisely to discuss such important matters.[21]

Archbishop Hallinan, who did not want the conference to become a "confrontation" between vying chaplains and students, as the term "summit" suggested to him, feared Orlett had "prejudiced the whole thing" and wrote him a stern dressing down—one of the severest he ever penned during his years of association with students. But the moderator concluded on a note of "high hope." He was confident the national chaplain and the federation president could lead the movement into greater unity and purpose and agreed "to proceed with the course of action" Orlett had outlined.[22] In publicly announcing what all finally agreed would be called the "Ann Arbor Summit," Hallinan said the idea for the conference "originated with Mr. Edward Orlett,"[23] a typical flourish.

Word about the summit soon came from the authorities. On April 24 Archbishop John Krol of Philadelphia, the new moderator of the Youth Department, issued an announcement "formally" recognizing the various Newman organizations as "official members of the 'Newman Family'" and raising the movement, which previously had been a part of the College and University Section of the Youth

Department, into the status of a section in its own right. "This new structure for the first time," commented Hallinan, "officially and formally" recognized the Newman Movement as "a vigorous arm of the Church in Catholic higher education, and a vital apostolate for the Christian formation of students . . . tomorrow's leaders in the nation and in the Church."[24] Meanwhile, invitations went out and responses were encouraging.[25] Representatives of the federation, the chaplains, alumni, honor, and faculty associations; and the National Foundation prepared for their important meeting, set for the Gabriel Richard Catholic Student Center at the University of Michigan from June 22 to 24.

AT THE SUMMIT

Though Monsignor Sigur told the opening session that the Ann Arbor Summit was "a grass roots operation" and no one had made "notes ahead of time,"[26] Archbishop Hallinan had already listed what he thought were the "primary tasks" of the movement. These numbered five: "To reach every Catholic student on the non-Catholic campus; to identify him with the Church on campus; to enroll him in a sound program of religious education; to provide pastoral care and spiritual formation; to encourage and form a vigorous leadership for the Catholic lay apostolate."[27] When the seven lengthy sessions had ended, one of the students remarked that for the first time in his life he had not only met an archbishop, but had been "able to talk back" to one,[28] and the final form of a definition and goals for what was now officially to be called The "National Newman Apostolate" only approximated Hallinan's ideas. The Newman Apostolate, concluded the delegates, was "the work of the Catholic Church in the secular campus community." Their list of goals placed "the intellectual and moral development of the Catholic on the secular campus" in first place, followed by his "religious education," "apostolic formation," then "the responsible participation of the Catholic in the Academic and Civic Community."[29]

In remarks closing the meeting Sigur said that "the strongest and most experienced elements in Newmanism" had met face to face, debated, concurred, and fulfilled the dreams of Timothy Harrington and John W. Keogh. At last, he went on, alumni, fund raisers, Catholic faculty and staff, and chaplains were coordinated to assist students, whose federated clubs directly touched the lives of their peers on campuses across the nation. Enlightened by an episcopally sanctioned concept of their mission and guided by a national office with greater autonomy, jubilant priests, professors, laymen, and students now went forth under "a mandate" to "bring the Church to Catholic students and Christ to their campuses."[30]

Hard evidence of the new status of the Newman Apostolate came almost immediately. Catholic architectural magazines "discovered" Newman centers as a potentially important object of artistic and financial interest.[31] Nevertheless, as a survey of 600 prominent Newman alumni, chaplains, and students indicated in July 1962, other Catholic Americans had less specific ideas about the apostolate. It indicated that the support and approval of the bishops was unknown or "traditionally minimized" among Catholics, the "majority" of parish priests and laity "neither understood nor appreciated . . . the work and problems of the Newman Apostolate"; its role in formal religious education was virtually unknown; and most students in secular schools showed "little interest" in other Newman activities.[32] The Chaplains' Association and the Newman Foundation agreed to launch immediately a "program of public relations" to alert Catholics to financial needs pressing upon the apostolate so its ultimate goals of religious formation and education could achieve their "full potential."[33]

Half a decade of promotional activity followed. Chaplains and others who joined their cause submitted articles to Catholic magazines and diocesan papers, wrote letters to editors of almost any journal mentioning the work of the apostolate, prepared brochures for university administrators and entering students, and did their best to promote invitations to tell their story to professional and business groups. From 1963 to 1966 the *Catholic Periodical Index* listed seventy-seven articles dealing with the responsibilities of the Church toward non-Catholic campuses, a number nearly equalling the total published during the previous three decades. Many of these presentations dwelt on the transformation of the old, apologetically and socially oriented Newman club into the new, pastoral and educational "mission on campus." Some claimed that the new directions and emphases called for "a crash program" to enlist personnel and funds in a massive kind of Marshall Plan for Catholics in secular colleges. Though a few articles recognized the complications involved in any program of national engineering for the apostolate or pointed to existing flaws, all had the cumulative effect of alerting Catholics to the new field that had been opened to their energies and generosity.[34]

Statistics measuring growth showed significant increases. In 1962, 169 full-time and about 600 part-time chaplains were operating in 79 centers and 65 "houses."[35] Five years later, the number of priests full-time in the apostolate had grown to 423, a third of the total, with 109 of these also serving as "diocesan directors" specially commissioned to promote and organize in their immediate areas. In addition, 71 sisters had joined Newman staffs around the country. The number of well-equipped centers rose to about 300, and at another 54 campuses, priests and Newman students were sharing facilities on an "ecumenical basis."[36] Yet this burst of expansion was already stretching diocesan resources to the limit. Between 1955 and 1960 the number of Catholics in nondenominational schools had risen approximately 43 percent, while bishops had been able to boost the total of chaplains and centers by nearly 70 percent.[37] In the five years following Ann Arbor, Catholic attendance increased to 920,000, a rise of about 50 percent, while the number of chaplains serving them rose by 31 percent, that of centers by 139 percent.[38]

Other apostolate projects also moved forward, though sometimes haltingly. Guidance of the Newman Foundation passed through the hands of two directors between the appointment of the first in May 1962 and the arrival of Mr. Jerry Burns in June 1963.[39] The original goal of $5 million for capitalization receded further from possibility as Burns found bishops often hesitant to divulge the names of generous donors, chaplains jealous of their alumni lists and the addresses of many benefactors they had already reached, and board members slow to beat the bushes after donors said to be "just waiting" for the foundation to come along. By 1965 gifts from bishops comprised 50 percent of its income; sums from Catholic-related foundations and other sources the rest.[40] In 1966 the foundation allocated between $40,000 and $50,000 to national and regional Newman projects, and in 1967 more than doubled the allocation. Some of this money went into study grants for doctoral students in theology, research projects on the Newman Apostolate, and libraries for individual centers. The bulk, however, supported eight Newman institutes of Catholic thought, student leadership training schools, the Newman chaplains' training schools, and the international desk of the apostolate.[41]

All observers agreed that the series of Newman chaplain's training schools the foundation first financed in 1962 were a long-needed and important benefit. After the inaugural four weeks of classes at Ann Arbor, the sessions moved to Minneapolis for two years; to Boulder, Colorado, for three more years; and in 1967 had an additional year at Harvard. Further plans called for four schools in four regions of the country, each one accommodating about fifty priests and sisters.[42]

In format, these training institutes brought prominent chaplains and guest lecturers from the fields of psychology, history, philosophy, theology, and university administration to present theoretical and practical aspects of campus religious work. The participants studied Newman's writings, experienced varying forms of liturgical celebration, visited model centers where they examined successful programs and projects, read recommended books, and shared ideas and experiences in formal and informal seminars. While the "curriculum" changed from summer to summer as the chaplains tested what courses were most practical for their purposes, the schools continued to instill in beginners a common perspective on campus life, foster a spirit of unity, and supply them with a handful of how-to's that gave the corps a semi-professional status. Eventually a few chaplains from both Catholic and Protestant colleges began to enroll. Promoters of the schools were somewhat dismayed, however, at the proportion of priests— about 40 percent—graduating into the apostolate and then being reassigned to other work three or four years later. To find a remedy, they began asking for research into the problems and opportunities in campus ministry, criteria for those entering it, and ways to strengthen the chaplains' association.[43]

The international desk, which opened in 1965 with a foundation grant, considerably broadened the vision and the work 6f the apostolate. Its director, Laurence T. Murphy, a Maryknoll priest who had served missions in Bolivia, Peru, and the Philippines before teaching at the University of Notre Dame, believed that American higher education was, in fact, involved in international education and furthermore, that this would be true if not even a single foreign student were in the United States. He argued that the curriculum of the American university influenced the way Americans thought about other peoples and cultures, that its task forces and "think tanks" served overseas American military, economic, and diplomatic aims, and that its programs in technology and political science carried forward the westernization of the entire globe.

Father Murphy committed his office to furthering among non-denominational colleges and universities an appreciation of the worldwide problems of disease and poverty as well as the principles of justice and peace that would harness the American educational enterprise for the achievement of human dignity everywhere. With such a view, Murphy did not think his primary task was "to help foreign students." Rather, it would be to promote the traditional commitment of the Newman Apostolate to the examination and inculcation of values in academia by providing a program of lectures featuring scholars from the developing nations.[44]

VIEW AT THE TOP

"You cannot stay in isolation in your club," Monsignor Paul Tanner, assistant general secretary of the NCWC, had told Newman leaders in 1948; "you must be part of the campus, or you are seriously deficient in social responsibilities."[45] During the years that followed, as the number of Catholics in nondenominational colleges and universities zoomed to new all-time highs and bishops responded by doubling the number of priests serving them, the students followed Tanner's advice. They transformed the federation from an often faltering collection of clubs into a more tightly organized and expanded mechanism for linking Newman activity with that of other student organizations at home and overseas, and they strengthened the club instructional programs by a massive flow of program aids and textbooks. Meanwhile, the chaplains organized their own quasi-professional association and concentrated on developing theologically informed and liturgically inspired leaders to shape activities in their growing number of centers.

In one sense, the Ann Arbor Summit of 1962 put an end to the Newman Movement. From the beginning of the Federation of College Catholic Clubs in 1915, students and priests had struggled to bring the leaders of the Church in America to accept several facts of higher educational life: that there were good reasons for many Catholic young people to attend non-Catholic colleges; that it was useful to organize them into Newman clubs; that it was even more sensible for these clubs to have adequate facilities for worship and religious education; that this necessary response to a condition required full-time, specially prepared priests, sisters, brothers, and lay leaders; that the end result of such developments would usually assume the form of a worshipping university community of Catholic students, professors, and staff members.

In 1940 the hierarchy admitted the Newman Movement into the Youth Department of the National Catholic Welfare Conference under the rubric of "Catholic Action," but this move did not substantially alter the movement's "underground" character. Even though after 1940 it gained in official prestige and received a better hearing among the bishops, the movement nevertheless remained a part of a large bureau that also monitored the activities of clubs in Catholic colleges, high schools, and parishes. Frustrating encounters with various segments of the ecclesiastical establishment demonstrated to Newman leaders how lightly the "official Church" regarded their mission to make the heritage of Catholicism an integral part of the lives of students outside the sponsored schools of that faith. In 1962 the bishops put an end to all that. They transformed the "movement" of Catholics on secular campuses to win sanction from ecclesiastical authority for their societies and programs into an "apostolate" mandated to win loyalty from academicians and students to the person and wisdom of Christ.

Flushed with the victory of Ann Arbor, the fashioners of the Newman Apostolate could be forgiven for thinking that they had hastened the dawn of a new era and had only to carry out their recently approved plans. They had been so preoccupied with working on the system that they had failed to notice that, although the sky was indeed brightening, its color was red. A decade of student religious revival along more or less conventional lines was giving way to a period of upheaval and apparent rejection of institutional forms. The Church itself was in the first stages of a penetrating self-scrutiny that would lead to a raveling of the close-knit American Catholic culture. Secular campuses were beginning to discover the sacred, while Catholic institutions were courting the secular. It would soon become apparent that the brief history of the Newman Apostolate exemplified Cornford's Law: "Nothing is ever done until everyone is convinced that it ought to be done, and has been convinced for so long that it is now time to do something else."[46]

PART THREE

PRESENT POSITION

In a higher world it is otherwise, but here below to live is to change, and to be perfect is to have changed often.

John Henry Newman
An Essay on the Development of Christian Doctrine

ELEVEN

Religion Succeeded in College

A University by its very name professes to teach universal knowledge. Theology is surely a branch of knowledge.

John Henry Newman
The Idea of a University

Shortly after the start of World War II Jesuit theologian John Courtney Murray declared that "humanism closed in itself and consciously divorced from all religious . . . inspiration" had reached its moment of truth.[1] At public and independent universities, where irreligion had often been fashionable during the years between the wars, presidents and professors once again mooted the possibility that perhaps higher education should reexamine the neglected theological dimensions of learning and take responsibilities for character formation more seriously. Observers of student affairs discovered a religious revival during the 1950s that continued past the middle of the next decade when one of the most astute of them wrote that young people were not only continuing their search for "resacralization" of life, but were pressing the quest more vigorously than ever before.[2]

RUMORS ABOUT ANGELS

Editorial revisions in the drafts of letters and speeches that university presidents prepared after 1940 indicate a new appreciation for religion in college life. Though he was unsure of what title to assign to the proposed office, Lotus Delta Coffman of Minnesota that year "was on the point of naming a university chaplain because he felt that the time was at hand when some religious services on campus should be arranged."[3] When Edmund Broun Fred of Wisconsin prepared a talk for the Milwaukee branch of the American Association of University Women, he opened one paragraph with the formula,

137

"The university has no commitment for or against any church or even religion itself"; he struck the last four words from the final draft.[4] Officials at Ohio canvassed seventeen other public colleges and discovered "rapidly changing . . . attitudes toward religion, both on campus and in the curriculum."[5]

University leaders were once again "proposing and carrying out policies and programs on all levels for the spiritual development of their students."[6] In 1942 the dean of students at Yale University reported "a widespread awareness among deans of women and men and other college personnel officers of the important contributions that religion and religious groups can make to the adjustment problems of students." The "student personnel point of view . . . imposed upon educational institutions the obligation to consider the student as a whole," and, the dean continued, this included "his moral and religious values."[7]

In line with this philosophy, deans and counselors began to draw existing religious programs and services into their structures. Minnesota's Henry E. Allen, the first coordinator of students' religious activities employed by a state institution, wrote in 1952 that thirty-one public colleges had officially commissioned fifty-four staff members to look after the religious welfare of students, and thirty-nine were paying full or part salary for nearly as many religious workers from churches. At over sixty public universities freshmen were able to record their religious preference as they filled in registration forms.[8] Eight years later the supervision of student religious organizations was the responsibility of personnel officers in 40 percent of tax supported institutions and the majority of these also provided rooms where these groups met. [9] Administrators believed chaplains should serve faculty and staff as well as students, thought they should receive "faculty privileges . . . almost automatically," and lamented the "lack of competent, professional campus ministers who . . . remain long enough to become effective, trusted, and respected."[10]

Presidents advanced a number of reasons for their renewed interest in campus religious life. Some viewed separation of church and state in a new perspective. "By interpreting the sensible theory of separation to mean the divorcement of religion from education," said Walter C. Langsam to his faculty at the University of Cincinnati in 1957, American higher education had "actually . . . been favoring the anti-religious and even atheistical elements of the population."[11] Other presidents were concerned for the role of religion in the formation of faith and character. Robert Hutchins astonished a 1962 convocation audience at the University of Chicago when he said, "We are agreed that it is more important to be good than to be intellectual, and that it is hard, if not impossible, to be good without being religious." He advocated the appointment of "moral and religious men" to professorships, or men who "at least take religion seriously."[12] Other administrators awoke to a special duty to provide for the religious living and enlightenment of students simply in terms of preparation for responsible citizenship.[13]

Professors generally were not so enthusiastic in expressing a readiness to welcome religious influences back into college life, but during the 1940s some of them began to prepare the way for the later revival. Faculty members at the University of Toledo set up a religious council that sponsored chapel services widely attended by teachers and students and sparked the founding of a Newman club.[14] Professors investigating the feasibility of setting up a department of religious education at Louisiana State declared that the study of religion was "not only a part of a liberal education" but contributed "more directly than most other studies to the development of character."[15] Faculty members also began to manifest increasing interest in their own religious lives. In 1939 those of Protestant Episcopal persuasion held the first national meeting of their newly formed Guild of Scholars. The next year other teachers interested in relating religion more directly with their lecturing helped the Student Christian Movement launch an interdenominational fellowship of faculty personnel.[16]

While administrators justified the renewed emphasis upon religion on grounds of fair play, personality development, and good citizenship, professors preferred to talk about the role of the campus in preserving civilization. One group acknowledged in 1941 that they felt "under a special constraint to realize a unity of thought and effort" because of the "growing threat to the democratic way of life."[17] Others were taking to heart criticisms that a specialist in the history of science, Arnold Nash, leveled at them in 1943. In his treatise, *The University in the Modern World,* Nash argued that science is neither "neutral" in its pursuit of truth nor free of value judgments in its application of learning. Rather, it proceeds from both the "moral assumption" that man has intrinsic dignity and the "metaphysical assumption" that he is perfectable. What was most alarming of all, claimed Nash, was that although science pretended to champion mankind against ignorance and folly, it was unable either to demonstrate the validity of or to act effectively in defense of these assumptions.[18] Professors who engaged in such reflections also realized that the future of university education rested largely in the hands of tax-supported schools, which, as Walter

Lippmann wrote, had for half a century "progressively removed from the curriculum . . . the Western Culture which produced the modern democratic state" and were graduating men and women who no longer understood "the creative principle of the society in which they will live."[19]

For some intellectuals, however, claims about the value of religious beliefs amounted to academic heresy. Such professors viewed the rise of the American university as the fulfillment of an Enlightenment dream and recoiled in horror at the thought of turning back history. The conflict latent between the radical secularists and professors more open to previous intellectual traditions erupted during the conference on Science, Religion, and Philosophy in Their Relation to the Democratic Way of Life that met at Columbia University in 1940 and again in 1942.

Mortimer Adler jolted the first meeting with a widely reported address which he titled, "God and the Professors." The Chicago Thomist said he did not "expect professors to understand what was wrong with modern culture and modern education" because this would exact from them an admission of what was "wrong with their own mentality." Behind the "multiplicity of technical jargon," he insisted, lay "a single doctrine . . . the affirmation of science and the denial of philosophy and religion." For Adler, any colleague who claimed "to respect the distinct place of religion in modern culture," but refused to admit that it was "superior to both philosophy and science" either did not know what he said or was "guilty of profound hypocrisy." Since science contributed "nothing whatsoever" to the understanding of the democratic way of life, Adler concluded that America had "more to fear" from professors than from Hitler.[20]

The conference of 1942 dealt an even more severe blow to the scientific humanists. The participants termed "the malady" undermining western civilization "intellectual and spiritual" and claimed that if civilization were "to endure," all men of intelligence had to join in thwarting present attempts "to fasten paganism on the world." They accepted the "pluralistic" concept of learning that the Thomist Jacques Maritain advocated as the most realistic way to ensure the survival of intellectual endeavor and the ultimate synthesis of knowledge. They also asserted the "need . . . for men to attain that increased measure of knowledge, which according to Francis Bacon, brings men back to God."[21]

Professor Sidney Hook of New York University led the counterattack against Adler and Maritain. The "progress of scientific knowledge," Hook argued, flew full in the face of every one of these "assumptions about the nature of knowledge." He thought that America must still rest its hope "in building the values and attitudes of scientific methodology more firmly into the living tissues of the democratic way of life." Hook deplored what he called the "new failure of nerve" among academicians and the "intellectual panic" beneath the "frenzied search for a center of value that transcends human interests." Such opinions, "bluntly put," said Hook, "are gateways to intellectual and moral irresponsibility." He warned professors not to surrender to "obscurantism" by appealing to "a superior insight not responsible to the checks of intelligence." To do so, Hook concluded, "was nothing else but to spread the 'blight of Hitlerism'," a dogmatic attitude that could remain to rot democracy "even though the tyrant be annihilated."[22]

The atrocities of the next several years profoundly shook the faith of the secular humanists. "The freedom of science to pursue the open search for knowledge" may not have fostered Fascism or Nazism, as some traditionalists implied, but that was not the issue; the issue was simply "rampant nationalism" anywhere on the spectrum of political ideology that enslaved science and crushed all freedom.[23] "It is one of the paradoxes of our time," wrote Supreme Court Justice Robert Jackson at midcentury, "that modern society needs to fear little except men, and what is worse it needs to fear only the educated men."[24]

THE CAMPUS GETS RELIGION

Observers commonly describe the 1950s as a decade in which all America underwent a religious revival, one that was especially visible on college and university campuses. Those who wish to discount the importance of such phenomena as religious revivals argue that ebbs and flows of religious fervor seem to follow regular cycles; thus the 1950s are impressive not so much for the fact of a return to religion as for the quality of that return. To these critics, the decade was especially conducive to a rebirth of traditional commitments and mores. Neo-orthodoxy had finally taken hold among intellectuals in the United States; Bishop Angus Dun was their national chaplain, Reinhold Niebuhr their house theologian. On the campuses, professorial timidity and student apathy generously gave ground before a number of reactionary forces. Everything seemed to favor an era of conformity, and "everyone" knew that caution and religion mixed well.[25]

The argument we shall explore differs from this explanation. An examination of attitudes and actions of students and professors during these years bares a much deeper involvement in religion than such an interpretation honors. The ostensibly uninvolved professors came quietly to a new realization and appreciation of religious values. This methodical discovery produced a major shift in their own professional self-understanding and opened American higher learning to a refreshingly new course. Rather than in any return to church membership or pious manifestations, here lay the fundamental revolution in the campuses of the 1950s.

A large number of professors in the 1950s continued to harbor "a vague, uncomfortable suspicion" that American civilization was infected "with a sickness unto death."[26] Their therapy took several forms. At an increasing number of campuses they joined with students in reinstating chapel meetings and setting up programs within denominational centers.[27] Others attempted to develop an "intellectual gospel" by forming, in 1953, the Faculty Christian Fellowship, a league of Disciples, Lutherans, Presbyterians, Methodists, Evangelical, Reformed and American Baptists, and Episcopalians, who carried on somewhat in the tradition of the earlier Guild of Scholars.[28]

Through its annual meetings and papers appearing in *The Christian Scholar,* the forum served as a questioning remnant among colleagues who had prepared for their life work when "immunity to religion" was "symptomatic."[29] In fifteen years "informed concern about the relation of faith and learning ... spread from a minute coterie to a large body," numbering an estimated 15,000 professors; the journal of the fellowship, *Faculty Forum,* had a subscription list of over 37,000 names.[30] All this gave evidence of a substantial interest in campus religion among teachers who were willing to organize their concern. What is more, though the group of Christian faculty seemed unable to come up with all the answers it sought,[31] it nonetheless framed urgent questions with rigor and promulgated them to a wide audience.

A new sophistication also began to take hold within academic departments and committees. Natural scientists withdrew from old battles over evolution and immortality of the soul to huddle over the adequacy of their own contemporary interpretations of human existence. Social scientists applied their methods to conclude that traditional academic scanting of religion seemed to be "an historical accident arising from the peculiar circumstances of the period when the social sciences developed."[32] A few philosophers were ready to admit that religion was a fact because religious men existed; even theology seemed "possible," argued one as he debated whether "The Rugged Cross" or "The Open Tomb" were the best symbol Christianity could

hold before a stricken world.[33] Developments in two critical areas of
university life, the inculcation of values and the teaching of religion,
signaled most dramatically the new self-awareness and religious appreciation within the professoriate.

Scholarly studies of value changes among students during the
1950s supported the notion that colleges were doing little more than
reinforcing conventional, even nonreligious, outlooks and commitments. In 1950 Professor Harold Tuttle of the University of Oregon
discovered that only 20 percent of administrators in 300 institutions
offering courses in religion thought the courses had any "ethical
implications."[34] Later in the decade, Philip Jacob of the University of
Pennsylvania and Edward D. Eddy of the American Council on
Education separately came to a similar conclusion for all of American
higher education. Jacob reported in 1957 that 75 percent of undergraduates were "gloriously contented with their present day-to-day
activities and their outlook for the future." Their aspirations for
material gratification were "unabashedly self-centered," and students
"cheerfully" expected to "conform to the economic *status quo*." While
they subscribed to "traditional moral virtues" like sincerity, honesty,
and loyalty, they did not feel "personally bound to unbending consistency" to these ideals.[35] A year later Eddy's more sophisticated study
produced substantially the same conclusions,[36] and both men agreed
with Tuttle that nearly all courses were "nerveless and flaccid" in the
matter of changing student values because they were poorly taught.[37]

Such findings might seem to argue against our thesis; professors
during the 1950s apparently were little concerned about morals nor
were they helping their students to develop any new ethical apprecia-
tions; later research substantially confirmed these pessimistic findings.[38] But the fact remains: During the religious revival on campus,
which began in the 1950s and continued into the 1960s, professors
began to come to a new comprehension of their power to mold
students for good or evil.

Other evidence supports this contention. About 1960 Professor
Robert Pace of UCLA decided that instead of lumping findings from
different campuses together and then drawing conclusions about
American higher education in general, he would examine campuses
separately to see if specific educational programs and environments
were changing the values of students in different places in different
ways. Pace also concentrated on longitudinal investigations of student
populations; that is, he examined the results of tests for values which
freshmen took when they entered a specific college and again when
they were seniors. Reviewing forty-seven such studies, Pace found

that in 75 percent of them, "significant" changes in students' values took place, and in a number of instances appeared to last after graduation.[39] He and Lawrence Thomas of Stanford warned scholars that "teachers in colleges and universities have many influences, whether intended or not, on the moral and spiritual values of their students"; they should "examine the nature and effects of these influences in order to be morally responsible."[40] While professorial concern for the formation of appropriate values still awaited considerable development, such concern had returned to the campus because professors themselves had elected to push back the night.

A QUIET REVOLUTION

This same pattern of internal renewal was also present, and much more dramatically so, in the matter of academic religious teaching in secular institutions. To improve this situation, professors had to solve three problems that previously had restricted the formal investigation of religion: constitutional prohibitions of a religious establishment, fear of indoctrinating students, and the cult of objectivity in teaching.

The wall between religious study and the college classroom began to crack in 1953. That year Leo Pfeffer, the noted constitutional lawyer who had led the fight to oust released-time catechetical instruction from Illinois public schools, professed to find "no objection to having three chairs of theology, Protestant, Catholic, and Jewish, in the university of any state."[41] Lawyers, though aware that church-state legislation never in fact exercised a great influence on the place of religion in higher education, were nonetheless encouraged that so formidable a champion of strict separatism concurred with their views.[42] Professional theologians, however, were not sure whether the fissure would admit religion on an academically sound basis. Professor Clyde Holbrook of Princeton argued that if public universities had to hew in their religious investigations to "the three faiths approach," they might well encounter some of the old sectarian rivalries. In any case, he asked, if competent faculties wanted freedom to range beyond these three American manifestations of religion or to develop entirely new systems of religious thought and principle, should they be limited by what amounted to public opinion?[43] Within a decade the United States Supreme Court handed down a decision that all but leveled the wall. In the Schempp case of 1963 the justices ruled that "study of the Bible or of religion, when presented objectively as part of a secular program of education, may be . . . effected consistent with the First Amendment."[44]

The other two issues, indoctrination and objectivity, lay closer to specific professorial concerns. An English teacher at the University of Minnesota raised the issue of indoctrination in classical fashion early in the 1950s. He termed theology courses "indoctrination rather than education" because whatever students and professors regarded as "purposeful and idealistic" depended entirely upon their private religious and ethical persuasions, and "to pump for one religion or ethical" system over another was "no business of the university."[45] Yet during these years faculty discussions exposed the assumptions and consequences of this supposedly protective position.

First of all, to insist that religious and ethical beliefs were inherently individualistic and subjective virtually amounted to a quasi-establishment in state universities of the essentially Protestant notion that religion was "a matter of faith, not knowledge."[46] Furthermore, to withhold from students the opportunity for religious study already constituted a type of indoctrination. "The college must give some respectful attention to the study of religion," concluded a faculty committee at the University of Michigan in 1953, "if its neutrality is not to be a malevolent neutrality."[47] A professor of engineering could see no problem of indoctrination arising as long as teachers of religion observed the same limits his colleagues did. Both subjects, he said, contained material for application and had to be taught precisely for their usefulness. Yet he did not think it was the role of the teacher in either discipline to impel the student to apply or use what he learned; "the knowledge itself" provided the appropriate motivation.[48]

But to say that professors could teach about religion without directly promoting sectarian commitment was not the same as saying that they could remain personally impartial and objective, as the conventional canons of academic respectability presumably required. Let the students take from the classroom what they wanted; did not the professor have to remain uninvolved in what he taught precisely to serve them best? As the discussions of the 1950s proceeded, instructors discovered their exaggerated notion of "objectivity" had led them in many cases "to dissemble and put aside . . . or even to atrophy their own convictions."[49] Some did so out of "duty," others because they were timid and conservative.[50] Many concluded that a "heartless neutrality"[51] eviscerated good scholarship. Since the mission of the university called for the communication to students of an understanding the teacher possessed, it was not at all clear that the professor could claim greater competency in proportion to the degree that the inner consistency of his discipline eluded him.[52] If religion "is taught for purposes of general education ... descriptively, at any level of scholarly thoroughness," wrote a philosopher at Ohio State University, "the problem of commitment is no more serious than it is in any other subject matter area."[53]

The rapid development of academic religious study in nonsectarian colleges and universities during the 1950s and early 1960s evidenced how thoroughly professors were solving these long-standing problems and how much more freedom they had to expand university commitment to scholarship. Taking the 1920s as a base line, and remembering that state universities increased in number from 109 in 1920 to 671 about 1960, the figures appeared quite impressive.[54] In 1922, 91 percent of state universities provided courses dealing with various aspects of religious study—chiefly philosophy, history, sociology, and psychology of religion. The low point came in the mid-1930s, when about 76 percent of public campuses reported such courses. By 1960 the proportion again exceeded 90 percent. The number of courses available to students within these universities also rose sharply: from 2.5 religion courses per campus during the 1920s, it reached 5.0 in the 1930s and stood at 8.7 in 1958.[55]

The way these programs converged in new departments of religion provided an even more significant index of academic commitment. One investigator of the early 1920s found only two "distinct departments of religion" on state university campuses.[56] Between 1946 and 1955, however, thirty new departments appeared and by the mid-1960s about 20 percent of public universities had either autonomous departments or formal interdepartmental programs.[57] While these new divisions of academic study often lacked criteria either for what constituted a "religion course" or for the selection, tenure, and degree qualifications of their instructors,[58] they nevertheless confronted Catholic, Protestant, and Jewish religious traditions of learning directly, and exposed students to such thinkers as Aquinas, Barth, Tillich, and Bultmann.[59] Between 1940 and 1952 these departments prepared an average of forty-seven students each year for the doctorate; by 1969 the annual figure for doctorates in religious study was but four short of 300.[60] A "quiet revolution" on campus was well under way.[61]

When investigators tested student response to this restoration, they found the professorial new assertion of nerve was helping higher education to serve learning and life in appropriate ways. The majority of students taking religion regarded themselves as only "moderately or casually" religious. They entered the study out of "intellectual curiosity," though some admitted to a "search for religious meaning." The courses had only a minimal correlation with students' religious affiliation, practice, or acceptance of traditional teachings. On the other hand, they stimulated graduate and undergraduate students to attempt their own syntheses of knowledge.[62] Acceptance of such academic religious study suggested that, whether they were themselves believers or not, the professors of the post–World War II era were not retrograde when they dared to help the university save its soul by recommitting it to the study of all learning, both human and divine.

TWELVE

Crises of Faith in College

*In Catholic Education the course of Philosophy takes
first rank. (Religion is not a course in the ordinary
sense of the term. It is a life. As such, it should control
and guide all the activity, academic and otherwise, of
the Catholic student.)*

Gerald B. Phelan
addressing Catholic educators in 1932

In 1946 Father Charles A. Hart, professor of philosophy at The
Catholic University of America, virtually gave the game away. That
year he wrote: "It may be taken for granted that the day of mere
catechism in religion in our Catholic colleges is now definitely
passed."[1] Did this assumption indicate that during the 1920s and 1930s
these protected institutions had been offering religion courses below
that "university grade" demanded of those taught in accredited
Newman centers such as that in his home state of Illinois?[2] More
importantly, did his good-hearted premise accurately describe the
situation in the 1940s? The irony that the favored status of Catholic
colleges vis-à-vis the Newman Movement during these years may
have contributed to the spread of many academically mediocre institutions[3] now leads to another. This policy apparently allowed the
study of philosophy, and especially of religion, to rank among the
most intellectually impoverished of Catholic college offerings. A
British observer summed it all up in 1963 when he concluded that
American Catholic universities did not exist "to provide great schools
of theology . . . but to prepare Catholics for careers."[4] Other scholars
added that the careers Catholics found most congenial during these
years favored "security-seeking, authoritarian, uncreative, and anti-
intellectual thinking."[5]

More recent investigation calls this latter conclusion into question,[6] and this in turn points to the phases of growth through which
Catholic higher education in the United States had to pass as it

accepted and trained the children of immigrants. While challenges to secularistic faith were taking place in public universities after World War II, Catholic colleges were also passing through a time of severe testing. As the secular campuses had done, Catholic higher education turned inward to reappraise fundamental assumptions governing relationships between religion and academic enterprises. But where some elements in public education had opened toward the sacred, Catholic educators showed a definite trend toward secular principles of organization and styles of operation. By the end of the 1960s, it was becoming clear that such efforts were secularizing Catholic schools in a way that upset many of their students who expected a strong religious life as well as competent education in the arts and sciences, including religion.

THE LIVING NON-CENTER

Although apologists for the Catholic college claimed in the 1920s that its commitment to religious study served as the "interpretation of all else" in the curriculum,[7] this was hardly the case. Prior to World War II neither Catholic graduate schools, teachers' colleges, nor seminaries offered a "thoroughgoing scientific course in moral education." Only three colleges offered an undergraduate major in religion; when professors tried to develop a religion department at Notre Dame, the rest of the faculty resisted the move on the grounds that it would probably fragment the curriculum![8] A graduate student at Marquette claimed in 1938 that "nothing in the present framework of the Catholic college program" distinguished it "from secular schools." If a teacher of religion fell sick for a day or two, he said, "the students' actual program would rather parallel that of the neighboring state university."[9] Not until the mid-1930s did religion teachers begin to call professional meetings to analyze their "failure to present . . . the Catholic ethos."[10] Among other things, they discovered that chaplaincies and spiritual guidance were "not clearly conceived as part of the religious education" in Catholic colleges.[11]

Instead of providing competent chaplaincies to head up the religious life of the extracurriculum, college administrators depended upon the entire institutional setup to accomplish this. Professors of "religion" debated the relative effectiveness of Bible study, theology, philosophy, liturgy, athletics, and good conduct codes, as if each of these were equally potent for developing mature Christians. Schools where girls never had the opportunity to read Aquinas on the virtues of prudence and temperance published codes regulating the use of tobacco and the width of straps on evening gowns. Most colleges publicized the fact that they adhered to obedience to the Church laws of Friday abstinence from meat and observance of Catholic opinion about movies rated "B" by the Legion of Decency, while they simultaneously made acceptance of Pius XI's condemnation of artificial contraception and divorce the heart of their apostolate. Enforced attendance at weekly services, periodic lectures on piety, and yearly retreats rounded out the moralistic system in the typical institution.[12]

But important as the protection and building of character might have seemed, should it have detracted from the academic programs of these institutions? We have seen how religious study in state universities during this period failed to achieve scholarly prominence partly because administrators expected it to perform as a moralizing influence.[13] Catholic colleges also tended to bend as many secular subjects as possible toward guaranteeing the preservation of morals. In 1925 their leaders admitted the lower academic standing of their schools, but they expressed belief that it was "better far" to go through life without what seemed "a liberal education" than to gain one at the "broken cisterns and poisoned wells" of public universities.[14] Nor could all Catholic administrators concur with Father George D. Bull, President of Georgetown, a decade later when he castigated "present tendencies in our educational system" for teaching philosophy "to show boys how they can give an answer to the atheist . . . the Communist or birth controllers," and not for "its liberalizing power over the human mind."[15]

Not until the 1950s did the faculties and administrators of Catholic colleges begin to view "theology" as an authentic academic discipline in its own right. This term started replacing "religion" in papers that professors delivered at annual meetings. The word "integration" came to denote the role of theology in the intellectual synthesis of learning instead of the achievement of psychological balance in the senior in accounting who earned "B's," dated only Catholic girls, and made the sign of the cross before a basketball free throw.[16] Teachers of sacred doctrine in Catholic colleges formed their own association. Increasing numbers of them returned from catechetical and theological centers in Europe determined to reform the content and methods of courses in the colleges their orders operated. Meanwhile, liturgical and biblical movements began to sensitize students of the late 1950s to social action as well as personalist dimensions in the study of their religious heritage and in their struggle for holiness. Within a few years professors of philosophy, theology, and the scriptures were asserting their right to lay aside their customary responsibility for an elaborate catechetical system and to speculate and write on doctrinal and moral matters free of restraint from chancery officials.[17]

MASTERPLANNING

By the early 1960s, however, Catholic college leaders were discovering two significant realities of great importance for the development of the Newman Movement. The first was the harsh fact that in a nation committed to the total education of all young men and women who wanted to get a college degree and could manage it, the Church grew increasingly unable to provide programs "from nursery through graduate and professional schools."[18] The second realization came from the Vatican Council. Months of research and review that preceded that assembly, as well as interventions on the floor of St. Peter's and the final drafts of the documents, opened the institutions of the Church not only to the world, but to each other.

In 1964 Father Paul C. Reinert, President of St. Louis University, had these new perspectives in mind when he called for a "masterplan" to deal rationally with the list of "mandates" he thought the times had presented Catholic colleges. The colleges must restrict their growth, he warned, "lest it reach a point of proliferation where quality is seriously impaired" and where sky-rocketing costs would threaten their very existence. Administrators, he said, had to replace unplanned expansion with the methodical development of first-rate programs and faculties in theology and philosophy while reshaping other aspects of their institutional programs to complement rather than compete with those in neighboring Catholic colleges. Finally, officials in each school should launch a thorough review of financial practices toward assuring a broad and stable plateau for support and growth. All these requirements converged, Reinert concluded, on the need for "an objective, carefully prepared, flexible blueprint for the general development of Catholic higher education in this country."[19]

Although some Catholic educators had been brooding about these points for years, Reinert's address "brought the entire problem out into the open" and won almost "unanimous support for its position on the 'needless proliferation' of smaller colleges."[20] Nevertheless, the idea of a "blueprint" was especially threatening. Who was to tell a religious congregation that it should not build a new college or expand an old one? College officials resented suggestions that some schools might do better as junior colleges or academies, even when such demands came gently from within their own ranks. Should lack of regional accreditation, uneconomically low student-teacher ratios, duplication, proximity, or poverty make the closing of a Christian institution reasonable? Nostalgia recalled how Notre Dame and Fordham had once been struggling little schools. Hope remained a virtue if only because it outshone bleak reality.[21] "Professional educators," said one archbishop, referring to Reinert's conclusions, "are going down the wrong path when they attempt to restrict the freedom of development in the light of urgent need and the problem of supply and demand."[22]

While they did not entirely reject the masterplan idea, Catholic college leaders preferred to soften its implications by espousing less drastic proposals. In the late spring of 1964 they formed an advisory committee headed by Auxiliary Bishop James P. Shannon, President of the College of St. Thomas in St. Paul, Minnesota, to study the situation and draw up guidelines for future action. Two years later responses to the committee's *Working Paper* acknowledged its accuracy in describing the "weaknesses and problems" of the Church's institutions, but some officials expressed a fear that the catalogue of inadequacies "could be misunderstood and thus bring more harm than good to Catholic higher education." When published in 1968, the final document placed special emphasis on two proposals designed to strengthen the over-all system: interinstitutional cooperation; and the sharing of administrative authority with lay persons.[23]

Both of these moves had long-standing precedents in American higher education. Non-Catholic colleges had begun to share facilities, faculties, specialized curricula, and administrative responsibilities during the Depression years when 230 institutions entered into 115 "compacts." A host of regional federations after World War II confirmed this trend.[24] However, Catholic colleges tended to shun such ventures, even among themselves. Between 1904 and 1950 only six cooperative plans came into existence. In the following decade, twenty-six new ones got under way.[25] By 1959 a majority of Catholic college presidents were pleading for "the sharing and pooling of resources, plants, curricula, and faculty," and a third were ready to limit course offerings in their schools "to areas in which the colleges can offer strong programs."[26] Some even toyed with the idea of setting up campuses adjacent to state universities. By the mid-1960s, seventy-two more programs of regional, state, national, and international scope were in operation, and some Catholic schools were also linking themselves with their Protestant and independent counterparts. "A small college cannot stand alone any longer," said the Sister-President of Immaculate Heart College, Los Angeles, which joined the pioneering Claremont College Group in 1965; she added that interinstitutional cooperation "might help" to end the insularity experienced at so many Catholic institutions.[27]

The declericalization of administrative boards seemed to offer a way out of financial difficulty as well as a means of liberalizing faculty policy. In January 1967 administrators of Webster College and St. Louis University, both in Missouri, initiated such steps and several other Catholic institutions signalled their readiness to follow suit.[28] Proponents of declericalization explained to disturbed constituents that the religious orders were not "giving up" ownership of the schools, because legally they had always merely been "acting as trustees of funds devoted to the cause of Catholic education." Moreover, the aim was only to eliminate direct church control, not to lessen church-relatedness, a step that would perhaps facilitate fund raising and create eligibility for federal money.[29] Protestants commented, however, that sixty years of experience in "secularization" had taught them some lessons Catholic religious orders might perhaps review, lest they make a virtue of necessity.[30] If, as a number of observers claimed, the American university was beginning to replace the Church as the center of highest spiritual effort and aspiration and as the primary shaper and transmitter of values, perhaps Catholics could best serve the nation by remaining more closely bound to the traditional structure of the Church. Furthermore, it was not at all clear how increased lay governance would ensure either "Catholic identity" or liberal academic policies.[31]

Even while leaders of Catholic higher education searched for ways to maintain their institutions through more efficient organization, members of the religious congregations began in rising numbers to challenge the very idea that their communities ought any longer concern themselves with operating schools. The Jesuits provided a significant focus of these debates. Simply to meet 1955 rates of expansion, said one, would require a doubling of the size of Jesuit schools by 1970.[32] Some members believed their predecessors had developed universities beyond the limits imposed by "the principles and policies" of the order's constitution and "the letters of our recent Generals."[33] Even more alarming were the strident voices of other members questioning the entire Jesuit apostolate in higher education. While older Jesuits described many of these doubters as "anti-intellectual," others acknowledged the validity of sweeping indictments of a deep commitment to immobile structures and conventional practices.[34]

FACING THE FACTS AGAIN

While administrators and faculty in Catholic colleges agonized during the 1960s over ways to increase confidence in their mission, students in these institutions were growing restive about the quality of spiritual care and religious education they were receiving. A walk across campus now brought preceptors into the midst of students more involved in analyzing institutional shortcomings than in wrestling with personal problems of career choice or morality. Priests, the students said, were "dogmatic" inside class and reluctant conversationalists outside.[35] A "pastoral vacuum" on campus deadened the transforming word of the Gospel.[36] One out of every three students harbored a "certain feeling of alienation"[37] from the Church, and an equal number graduated as "atheists."[38] At some prominent campuses, only half of the students attended Sunday Mass and as many as 30 percent denied that Jesus Christ was "really and truly present" in the eucharist bread and wine. Nearly half of the students in one survey indicated that they preferred to think of themselves as "Christian" instead of "Roman Catholic."[39] Many young Catholics were gleaning greater religious satisfaction in small groups that practiced spontaneous prayer or developed "underground liturgies," while others seemed to find the intense personalism of social action groups a more compelling substitute for traditional pious exercises such as novenas or First Friday observances.[40] Catholics on the Catholic campus showed "a radical impatience with many of the structures and procedures of the institutional church," wrote the head of a Christian Life Council in one school; though these students were not yet showing signs of mass defection from Rome, the possibility that they might "must haunt and trouble the American hierarchy."[41]

Scholarly investigations confirmed these trends. A study of personnel services in Catholic colleges in 1955 found no formalized connection between courses in religion, many of which were still designed primarily to strengthen the personal quest for Christian perfection, and the counseling program.[42] The author of a survey of pastoral care at Catholic colleges warned early in the 1960s that administrative and canonical impediments rendered these chaplaincies "inimical" to the fundamental religious mission of Catholic colleges; that is, to help students arrive at a mature appreciation and practice of the faith.[43] An investigation of worship on campuses in 1966 led to the conclusion that even where an "advanced" liturgical program was in operation, the majority of students who continued to attend Mass had only "mild or moderate" involvement in the services and did not grasp the essential meaning of worship or comprehend the significance of important sections of the Eucharistic liturgy.[44] Studies of the religious outcomes of Catholic higher education did little to brighten the outlook. The colleges served a clientele largely disposed by financial resources and home conditioning to profit from their programs of religious study and formation. Yet the measurable impact of these programs was quite slight and seemed to be more dependent upon pre-college influences than the four years of collegiate life.[45]

Challenged by the calls to internal renewal issuing from Vatican Council II, and especially concerned about the absence of strong chaplaincies to serve the needs of questioning, even alienated, student populations, officials of the College and University Section of the National Catholic Educational Association began to regard the Newman Movement as a potential helper rather than as a historic threat. At the NCEA meeting in 1962 a spokesman for the movement urged the college leaders to realize that Newman clubs and centers did not compete with Catholic collegiate education.[46] Twelve months later a former Newman chaplain, quite familiar with the methods necessary to work on the system, Archbishop Paul J. Hallinan of Atlanta, told them that the time had come to "broaden the whole definition of Catholic higher education" so as to include "every Catholic student" no matter what kind of school he attended.[47]

Ironically, the Jesuit weekly, *America,* perhaps did more than any single agency to influence the popularization of the notion that the secular campus was a promising field for Catholic educational effort. In May 1960 the editors published an article on Catholics in public and independent colleges that attempted to demolish the long-standing myth that defection from the faith prevailed at them.[48] An accompanying editorial commented that "while the perennial arguments for and against Catholic undergraduates attending non-Catholic universities and colleges" had been bandied back and forth, a new factor recently had entered the debate: "simple necessity." Since the Church could not educate all college-bound Catholics in its own schools, what was it to do? The editors proposed a "new kind of Newman Club, more on the scale of a 'Catholic Institute' . . . complete with library, lounge, study facilities, lecture halls, seminar rooms and, above all, a faculty competent to create the scholarly climate of Christian culture" that would attract, challenge, and form students in the "distinctive values, attitudes and instincts arising from the great philosophical synthesis of Christian humanism." Noting how some bishops had already "provided men and money to start such centers," the editors concluded that Catholic colleges and universities would "have to be even more generous than heretofore in sharing facilities, making credit courses available, and even loaning faculty members."[49]

In effect, these Jesuit editors were realizing the truth of what proponents of the Newman Movement had declared more than fifty years earlier: on the secular campuses of the nation the Church faced "not a theory but a condition."[50] What is more, their response to the condition was a proposal very similar to the Catholic Foundation Plan their predecessors had so harshly condemned in the 1920s. A month later the editors welcomed to their pages the pioneer of that much-attacked scheme, Father John A. O'Brien, whom they now termed "an outstanding authority on the Newman Club apostolate."[51]

Writing from his research office at Notre Dame in the serenity that vindication supplies, Father O'Brien termed the editorial "far visioned and carefully reasoned," and said it heralded "the dawn of a new day in the discussion of one of the most important and delicate problems of Catholic higher education: making adequate provision not only for the spiritual care but also for the religious instruction of the Catholic students attending secular colleges." He noted that "the sons of Loyola had probably taken less part in any effort to minister to or instruct the Catholic students at secular institutions than any of the other religious communities" and had "generally opposed, covertly or overtly, any effort to establish an adequate Catholic student center on a secular campus." The former chaplain continued by citing statistics showing the large number of Catholics in non-Catholic colleges, discussed what he called the "pathetic inadequacy of priestly personnel and of physical facilities" supplied for them, recounted the history of the Newman Foundation at the University of Illinois and its accredited courses in religion, and asserted that "the entrance of Jesuits into this important field would meet the widely felt need of properly trained priests to provide scholarly guidance and instruction on a par with that of the university faculty."[52]

In the fall of 1964 *America* carried the discussion further with the publication of a "study of the next twenty years" that also supported the idea that Newman chaplaincies and centers at secular colleges were "part of the total Catholic higher educational system in the United States."[53] The authors, two young Jesuits holding degrees from Harvard and Johns Hopkins, declared that in the school year 1963–64, Catholics comprised 23.5 percent, or slightly over one million, of the 4.5 million students enrolled in American colleges and universities. Since the number registered in colleges operated by the Church was only 366,000, about 2 of every 3 Catholics attended public, independent, or Protestant institutions. The writers then cited projections drawn by the Fund for the Advancement of Education predicting that college enrollments would reach 12.6 million in 1984. Assuming that the Catholic proportion of this population would remain at least at 1964 levels, the authors concluded that 2.4 million Catholics, over 80 percent of the Catholic total, would be receiving their education at non-Catholic colleges, and Catholic institutions would enroll only about one of every 25 students in all colleges and universities.[54]

The authors believed, however, that the Church had the "resources . . . to meet this challenge and to . . . bring higher education and intellectual endeavor into close contact with Christian life and thought." Comparing figures representing the number of full-time priests engaged in Catholic higher education, and assuming that religious would not resign from the orders in large numbers, the Jesuits concluded that the orders could supply two-thirds of the priests needed for the Newman Apostolate without tapping more than 4 percent of their manpower. Similar calculations suggested that two members of religious congregations of women could take up residence at each secular campus and drain national reserves of the sisterhoods by less than 2 percent.[55] The writers added that religious superiors could promote such an apostolate among students and faculty at non-Catholic universities at moderate financial expense and perhaps reap in return a harvest of religious vocations.[56] Thus the secular campus took on the aspect of a missionary challenge, a place where the hardier members of religious orders might contribute to the religious renewal in American culture, something founders of the Newman Movement had urged six decades earlier.[57]

It seemed that another turn-of-the century prophecy was also coming true. In 1908 John Talbot Smith had noted "the rise of the diocesan priest in the American democracy to the important place which the religious priest occupied in the Old World."[58] Newman chaplains acknowledged that members of religious orders, not diocesan priests, traditionally pioneered new ventures for the Church, but the emergence of the chaplain's pastoral and educational ministry within nondenominational institutions for higher education in the United States offered a dramatic reversal of this tradition.[59] Although the American-founded Paulist Fathers had significantly helped in this ministry, the Newman Movement had been predominantly the enterprise of diocesan priests, often in battle with religious orders in secondary and higher education. The resultant Newman Apostolate remained almost exclusively the province of diocesan priests. Around mid-decade 206 priests and 86 sisters representing about three dozen religious congregations had taken up work in the secular campuses; but the largest portion of the burden was still being borne by 272 full-time and 876 part-time diocesan clergy.[60]

Was it possible for communities of religious to enter this ministry without proliferating its clerical leadership among hundreds of overlapping jurisdictions and provinces and without interpreting its loosely formed ideology according to principles of spirituality that often differed widely among orders? Or could the architects of the Newman Apostolate restructure it to make the great potential represented in these thousands of men and women religious, many of them highly educated in academic and personnel specialties, available to the work of the Church in the secular campus community?

THIRTEEN

To Live Is to Change

The reform at which the Council aims ... is ... an honoring of tradition by stripping it of what is unworthy or defective so that it may be rendered firm and fruitful.

Pope Paul VI, 1963

For many persons in the United States, the 1960s were a "time of lost hopes." During these years they discovered that widespread poverty, racism, rebellious youthful countercultures, assassination and other forms of violence, urban ugliness, and environment degradation were as much a part of national life as the Fourth of July; and also that government could cope with these domestic diseases no better than it could heal the running sore its military involvement had widened in Southeast Asia. The new attitude toward religious influence in higher education, which we have reviewed in the previous two chapters, appears to have been the leisurely beginning of what now became an urgent review of national values and priorities. In plain terms, the upheavals and the reversals of the 1960s made Americans face up to the limits of their way of life.[1]

Such traumatic awakenings plunged American Catholics into a doubly perilous disillusionment. Gradually moving from their ghetto cultures into the mainstream, they found that instead of serving as the embattled guardians of the American dream, they were themselves part of its problems. And there could be no retreat, for the Second Vatican Council, which adjourned in December 1965 after four years of intense review of the place of the Catholic Church in the modern world, initiated the dismantling of the doctrinal and disciplinary structures that had made ghettoism, and its security, possible.[2]

Involved with one of the nation's most vulnerable institutions, the university, and infused with the reformist spirit of the council, the Newman Apostolate could not escape this turmoil, and by the end of the decade it no longer existed. Its demise, however, did not also signal the end of the Newman Movement that had given birth to the national apostolate. The movement itself was able to survive because it returned to those forms of diocesan-based campus ministry that had first appeared before 1910. It could, moreover, look to its future with some degree of confidence because, in a nation whose institutions presupposed a Supreme Being, the chaplaincy now appeared to be the most feasible agency, in both secular and Catholic higher education, for encouraging forthcoming leaders to develop the kind of religious faith that both nation and church required.

WHATEVER BECAME OF NEWMAN?

By the mid-1960s the student section of the National Newman Apostolate was, according to its president, "on the verge of eventual death."[3] Federation membership plummeted from over 47,000 in 1963 to about 18,000 a year later. Though its proposed budget stood at $41,000, its treasurer announced that incoming dues came to less than 10 percent of this amount.[4] Some of this decline may have reflected dissatisfaction with the emergence of a full-time, full-salaried national president who was not a student,[5] but this one reason could hardly account for reports coming from everywhere that Newman clubs were declining in membership even though Catholic enrollment on the secular campuses continued to soar.[6] Another reason was that these associations bore traces of ghettoism, which still seemed to be in control. For example, at the Golden Jubilee Congress held in New York City in 1965 delegates tabled even a mild resolution on peace, virtually boycotted an address on the challenges of ecumenism delivered by the noted church historian, Jaroslav Pelikan, and ignored the various student activist movements then in prominence. For many potential Newmanites, "the tremendous amounts of love and scholarship" generated over social issues by "secular student groups such as the Students for a Democratic Society"[7] seemed much more in tune with Pope Paul's invitation to "build a bridge to the contemporary world"[8] than did clubbish standpatism.

As a matter of fact, although the pronouncements of Vatican II confirmed the spirit and mission of the Newman Movement, they nevertheless subverted many of the assumptions that had underpinned the development of the Newman Apostolate. How could the movement any longer be thought of as "bringing the Church to Catholic students on the secular campuses"[9] when the *Dogmatic Constitution on the Church* described the laity as already a constitutive part of it?[10] How could the work of the Church in the secular campus community ever again be dominated by the old Catholic Action notion that such work was a participation in the mission of the hierarchy, when the *Decree on the Apostolate of the Laity* taught that Catholics were directly called to the prophetic ministry of Christ by the fact of their baptism[11] and the *Declaration on Religious Freedom* implied that they now enjoyed a new liberty of conscience?[12]

Again, could Newman clubs remain officially aloof from interfaith activities, including worship, when the *Decree on Ecumenism* for the first time in history called Protestant communities "churches" in which the Holy Spirit was authentically at work?[13] Indeed, the *Declaration on Non-Christian Religions* urged Catholics to seek out the helpful wisdom of pagan systems.[14] In view of these edicts, then, would not excessively critical and cautious attitudes toward secular higher education have to change? The *Pastoral Constitution on the Church in the Modern World* termed the triumphs of human culture "a sign of God's greatness and the flowering of His mysterious design," and credited everyone dedicated to "the earthly service of men," whether a believer or not, with responding to the Spirit of Christ.[15]

Even more yeasty than these changes in understanding were those in attitude promoted by the council's liturgical reforms. "Ritual is religion in action; the cutting edge of the tool ... which accomplishes what religion sets out to do," wrote an anthropologist in the mid-1960s. Giving students increased participation in and power to shape the forms of the Mass carried far more import for the future of Catholicism than what went on in schoolrooms or in bishop's offices.[16] For the Catholic laity Mass had always been a "hands off" matter, the preserve of the priest, his mysteriously wonderful and quiet service to his flock. Vatican II restored to worshippers the vernacular Mass and functions of the Mass they had lost four centuries earlier, responsibilities in the preparation and celebration of the Eucharistic Memorial which not even the Holy Father himself could usurp.[17] Presumably, an adult attitude toward the most sacred experience within Catholicism would nourish a similar response toward the Church and life itself.

Also contributing to the ferment within the Newman Apostolate was a central concept that emerged from the council: that of "collegiality." This concept expressed the way in which the bishops exercised "supreme authority" over the entire church in union with the pope and over their local jurisdictions in union with their own priests and lay leaders.[18] Newman chaplains found that this emerging sense of partnership complemented many of the ways in which they had tried to work with students and faculty. In a more far-reaching sense, it also rendered older canonical lines of authority obsolete, and accordingly, it put a great strain on the concept that the Newman Apostolate required a national headquarters operating under a legally sanctioned mandate.

By the middle of an already paranoid decade, Newman activists, at times more informed by media interpretations of these developments than by theological commentary on them, began to question the control exercised by the NCWC Youth Department, in which the Newman Apostolate resided as a full member, and to challenge policies that seemed to be subverting the student federation. The conflict broke into the open in June of 1965 as students planned their annual conference around the theme "The Emerging Layman." They complained that in some places chaplains had actually fired Newman club officers and perpetrated other indelicacies, thus giving a lie to the notion that Vatican II liberated lay people from arbitrary clerical supervision.[19] Reacting against these abuses as well as against the Youth Department's justification that Vatican II had made the chaplain an "official representative" of the bishop, federation president Julius Gilbertson of Wisconsin State University, Eau Claire, issued a proclamation of emancipation. He proposed a "pro-student" movement: graduates and undergraduates would operate "outside the ecclesiastical framework of the Church but within the spirit of it" and exercise freedom of self-determination "in accordance with the special nature and relative autonomy of the temporal order." In this way young lay persons would "emerge," learn responsibility as well as respect for authority, and develop a mature comprehension of their mission in the world. If such a view did not capture a central place within the Newman Apostolate, Gilbertson warned, the clerics would succeed in "submerging ... the laity."[20]

Federation leaders were not fully convinced when the chaplains' advisory board met shortly thereafter in "crisis session" and passed a resolution favoring more student autonomy, at least in relation to the Youth Department.[21] Later, when students heard rumors that the bishops were ready to relieve the federation's financial anemia with a kind of matching grant, some feared a scheme designed to transmute concern into control; the bishops "are going to have a real fight on their hands," vowed one Washington-based federation officer.[22] After some meetings with representatives of Protestant and Orthodox student groups, the Newman Student Federation joined in to form the University Christian Movement in September 1966.[23] The secretary of the federation explained that the move was "probably the beginning" of a dynamic and relevant campus educational and ecumenical regeneration, one which certainly assured desired lay autonomy at a time when Christian influence was essential within campus uprisings.[24] Unfortunately, the leadership had consulted neither its own constituency nor its NCWC proctors and "caught a little hell"[25] for its efforts.

Meanwhile, chaplains were also growing increasingly frustrated with NCWC oversight. Since its establishment in 1962, the Newman Apostolate had maintained two offices in Washington, one for the president and executive secretary of the student federation, the other for the coordinating secretary of the apostolate. The chaplains argued that because bishops had created the latter and made it directly accountable to them, they should also finance it. But NCWC officials insisted that "Newmanism" was a student affair to be funded by student dues. This meant that the apostolate coordinator, Father Charles Albright, C.S.P., seldom had enough money to assist its chaplain, alumni, honorary, faculty-staff, and fund-raising divisions. Indeed, between September 1963 and March 1964 the students gave him less than $800 for his offices, expenses, and salary, and that of his lay administrative assistant.[26]

The irony was exquisitely painful. Albright was authorized to promote, especially in poorer dioceses, chaplaincies, Newman centers, and diocesan directorates. Such developments supplanted federation provincial organizations and resulted in quasi-campus parishes that replaced Newman clubs. This meant, in fact, that he was undermining the national student federation which was expected to fund his activities! Yet it was difficult to win enthusiastic support from bishops when some chaplains, such as those involved in the interdenominational "Atlanta Statement" that appeared in 1965, called for "freedom to discover forms of the Church which best serve the campus community," including intercommunion.[27] Although the statement's Catholic signers represented only themselves, they were symptomatic of a considerable disaffection among Newman chaplains with traditional church ways.[28]

Leaders of the Newman Movement, clerical or lay, national or local, looked to the second half of the 1960s only to see their long-awaited, carefully designed apostolate unravelling. It seemed they had gotten into the system just in time to attend its collapse.

Interpreting these signs of the times during the federation congress which met at Dallas in August 1966, Episcopal Moderator James W. Malone of the diocese of Youngstown began to promote the restructuring of the apostolate. In plain talk that reviewed with devastating accuracy the shortcomings of each of its six sections, he called for innovation and decentralization, especially in light of the need to adapt the work of the Church to differing conditions among colleges and universities. Bishop Malone insisted that the Newman Apostolate existed primarily for students; but he noted with equal conviction that any section not fulfilling its mission, even the Newman Student Federation, should be ready to change, even cease to exist.[29] After considerable thought in private, prayer in community, and debate on the floor, the delegates voted by acclamation to create the Catholic Commission on the Church in the American University comprised of ten chaplains and twenty students authorized to "re-evaluate the structures and organization of the Newman Apostolate in the light of Vatican II and the changes in the university world."[30]

The work of the commission, coordinated by Father John T. McDonough, who replaced Albright in the Washington office in 1965, went on throughout the next year. Its first phase produced surveys revealing how students were shifting their concern for organizational interests to those revolving about identity, community, ecumenism, and direct service on and off campus. Chaplains' responses indicated a similar shift from national structures to local involvement and also reflected a desire for more professionalism in their own preparation and work.[31]

Meeting at the Maryknoll Seminary in Glen Ellyn, Illinois, during March 1967, the commission redefined the Newman Apostolate from "the work of the Church in the secular campus community" into "a searching, believing, loving, worshipping . . . presence of the Catholic Church in the campus community." Sensitivity to "oneness with other Christian communities" and dedication "to the service of human needs" were to inform this presence. With an outlook that harked back to the 1920s rationale of the Federation of College Catholic Clubs, the Glen Ellyn statement termed each campus assembly of Catholic students, faculty, staff, and priests the "basic functional unit" of the apostolate. Now, however, instead of interposing a provincial structure between the clubs and the national headquarters, the commission favored the establishment of diocesan boards to foster development. To finance the national office, each "Newman entity" was asked to tithe 1 percent of its annual budget.[32] Although some leaders of the federation mounted a last-ditch counterconference that July in Hyattsville, Maryland, claiming that the Glen Ellyn proposals would "destroy the movement as a lay student organization" and reduce the federation to a "mere managerial" agency,[33] the congress of the Newman Apostolate, held the next month at Northern Illinois University, overwhelmingly adopted the commission's recommendations.[34]

With this vote, the Newman Apostolate virtually passed out of existence. Its national coordinating board was dissolved. Its alumni, honorary, and faculty-staff associations were reduced to the status of local branches attached to campus units that wanted them. In 1969, with the collapse of the University Christian Movement, membership in which had been supposed to guarantee "continuance" no matter what the priests did, the Newman Student Federation fell apart. In April of that same year, the Newman Chaplains' Association reorganized itself into the Catholic Campus Ministry Association (CCMA), an autonomous, professional group which also enrolled sisters and lay personnel.

The 1960s, then, had been a decade that saw the National Newman Apostolate develop from six organizations that had laboriously emerged over half a century. At the decade's close only one of the constitutent sections, the National Newman Foundation, existed according to its original charter, and its director was planning to change it from a "foundation" granting funds, something it had never done prominently, into a "development office" to solicit financial aid in behalf of specific programs drawn up by local leaders or the CCMA.[35]

For over sixty years one aspect of the idea of the Newman Movement, the student federation, had preserved the dream and the momentum, and had become, by that curious law according to which "the Church follows its students," the exuberant parent of helping adult associations. Resentful of what they regarded as clerical machinations, some embittered student leaders were ready to argue that the spawn had devoured the sire. But the truth lay much deeper. The national federation had been a necessary, in a way unfortunate, alternative. It served as a kind of lobby working toward return to the original inspiration, that "new link in Catholic evolution" comprised of chaplaincies and Catholic halls that bishops pioneered at the turn of the century. These predated the federation in time and could, by the very nature of things, provide superior pastoral care and religious education. It was to this original diocesan-centered conception that the Newman Movement had returned. In a sense, after a long migration imposed by the timidity of the hierarchy and the obstinacy of Catholic college proponents, the movement had returned to its origins.

SECOND SPRINGTIME

What advantages did the Newman Movement enjoy as its leaders, in anticipation of the closing decades of the century, reorganized

it as a diocesan oriented and directed ministry within higher education? Considering the turbulence that continued to batter American
society, it seemed to occupy a relatively strong position, if only
because it had never been better off.

In the first place, the highest authority in the Catholic Church
had accepted the Newman concept of religious education. Although
the Vatican II *Declaration on Christian Education* fell far short of giving
the support for their movement that Newman chaplains had hoped
for,[36] it nevertheless did support their view that Catholic *schooling* and
Catholic *education* were not synonymous. Instead of insisting, as the
1931 encyclical of Pius XI had done, upon the right of the Church to
provide general education that included catechetical elements, the
new declaration asserted, rather, that the Church bore special responsibility to serve society through various kinds of educational agencies.
Preempting the traditional argument for Church colleges, Bishop
Hugh A. Donohue of Stockton, California, urged his fellow bishops to
promote Newman chaplaincies and centers as generously and as
zealously as they did parish schools.[37] Such advocacy represented a
belated but normative reply to the appeal Fathers John W. Keogh and
James Ryan Hughes had issued forty years earlier when they argued
on behalf of the educational mission of Newman clubs.[38] Furthermore,
Newman chaplains received assurance that their views would be
adequately represented in the forthcoming national pastoral on
Christian education that the bishops were drafting to apply the
conciliar principles in the United States.[39]

In 1969 the post–Vatican II reorganization of the Catholic
Church in the United States led to two other significant advances
which leaders of the Newman Movement had sought, especially since
the Glen Ellyn meeting. First, the United States Catholic Conference
(USCC), as the NCWC was now named, set up a Department of
Christian Education housing the former national office of the Newman Apostolate; this department now included the new Division of
Campus Ministry, with a sister as full-time assistant to its priest-
director. This meant that the movement no longer received direction
from the Youth Department but, at last, was accorded both recognition and inclusion in the bishops' national budget as an educational
agency with a direct means of communicating upwards from the local
level. That same year the Knights of Columbus, supplying a $50,000
annual budget, opened in Washington's Center for Applied Research
in the Apostolate (CARA) a Department of Campus Ministries to
assist in the training and performance of Newman chaplains.[40]

Reports coming from both of these newly established sources

soon indicated how healthy the Newman Movement was. It was entering the 1970s with 1,450 chaplains, eighty of whom were sisters, at work on about 1,200 campuses. Of the priests, 500 were appointed full-time to campus ministry, a third had canonical status as pastors or associate pastors, over one-fifth of the total served on ecumenical teams, and about 80 percent of them regarded campus ministry as a career in itself. They operated out of 327 Newman centers, over half of which were adapted older buildings, about one-third especially designed; two-thirds of the priests described their facilities as "adequate." In sixty other places the chaplains shared buildings on an interfaith basis. In addition to whatever facilities they had, over three-fourths of the priests could use campus rooms for social affairs, two-thirds could use them for religious services, and more than half had access to rooms provided by neighboring parishes. Over three-fourths of the priests provided religious services on weekends, about two-thirds on a daily basis; two-thirds also regularly organized social activities and gave religious instructions. Although less than 40 percent of the chaplains found the quarterly or semesterly retreat a viable institution, over half reported that some form of intensive "Christian weekend" experience proved to be quite successful. Slightly fewer than half of the priests indicated they participated in social action movements on their campuses. Figures also suggested a turnover in personnel of about one-third of the total each year, chiefly among part-time chaplains.[41]

Also indicative of the new strength and collaboration among elements in the Newman Movement was a related study of sisters in campus ministry; this survey was organized with CARA by Sister Sheila Doherty, S.N.D., assistant director of the USCC office charged with the development of the sisters' role. This review of the background, self-perception, acceptance among students and priests, and performance of 62 full-time and 14 part-time sister-chaplains led to some quite optimistic conclusions. These women regarded themselves, not as "sisters on campus," but as professional ministers who performed many of the roles "scripturally and historically ascribed to deacons"; i.e., they taught classes and led discussion groups, counselled, organized student religious and welfare programs, visited the sick, planned and conducted rehearsals for liturgical celebrations, and in some instances helped to prepare couples for marriage and preached. The majority of the sisters felt "highly accepted, even esteemed" by students. Most of them also were regarded as "professional members of the ministry team" on the campus they served. Although only about one-third wore contemporary dress in contrast to the traditional or modified habit, over half recommended that sisters in campus ministry do so. The study found turnover higher than among priests, and it suggested that sisters and laywomen serving as campus ministers receive greater support from their sponsoring communities and even be ordained as deaconesses.[42]

When compared with figures for 1962, the year in which the Newman Apostolate was mandated, these surveys indicated that the movement was not expanding as rapidly as the size of the Catholic population enrolled in secular higher education. Enrollments slightly more than doubled between 1962 and 1969, rising from about 700,000 to 1,471,000, while the number of chaplains increased only by about one-half, from 969 to 1,450. Furthermore, because the vast majority of the students commuted, problems of communication and organization seemed at times to be insurmountable. The greatest turnover of personnel took place precisely among chaplains assigned part-time to nonresidential campuses. In addition, well over half of the chaplains reported that funding for their operational expenses and staff salaries came from other than direct diocesan subsidy. On the brighter side, however, 400 chaplains did receive diocesan support. And the ratio of *full-time* chaplains and Newman centers to the student expansion was quite favorable—up from 169 to about 500, full-time chaplains had nearly trebled in number, while facilities, moving from 144 to 387, showed a similar growth.

The conclusion that approximately 300 campuses out of over 1,200 had full-time chaplains with adequate centers and financial support offered some encouragement. At least it could be said that American Catholics had never before provided so well for those of their ranks who wanted the care, or just the companionship, of priests and sisters as they prepared for their adult roles by attending secular colleges and universities. Furthermore, the Catholic Campus Ministry Association, now numbering about 350 chaplains and utilizing a yearly budget approaching $15,000, was developing national workshops and other training programs aimed at helping experienced chaplains with the specialized problems posed by community colleges, minority groups, campus activists, and the training of peer ministers. Also, Father Laurence Murphy, M.M., Director of the Division of Campus Ministry, continued to assist the CCMA in offering two annual training schools for newly appointed priests and sisters. These two agencies also jointly arranged for a month-long ecumenical institute in July 1970 at Cuernavaca, Mexico, where several dozen chaplains probed deeply into the questions surrounding the role and relevance of the campus minister in an age of revolution.[43]

Always hopeful and "cautiously optimistic," Father Murphy viewed himself as the facilitator of decentralization and cooperation within the movement, and he expressed the opinion of most chaplains when he proposed that they undertake two new developments: first, the enabling of chaplains on Catholic and secular campuses to work together more closely through membership in the CCMA and under the guidance of local diocesan directors; second, the organization of the latter into a supportive and professionally prepared leadership corps.

The first objective appeared to be as needed as it was formidable of accomplishment. Academic trends on public and independent as well as on church-related campuses during the previous two decades had left chaplaincies as one of the more important structural means for linking studies with life; perhaps as the only means for permeating both with religious faith. As we have seen, secular colleges and universities had for years shied away from teaching religion, while Catholic institutions had claimed such studies to be a chief reason for their existence. Then state universities discovered that religion could be treated speculatively, not necessarily involving the imposition of value judgements, and Catholic faculties transformed their religious offerings in much the same way. The very fact that during the 1960s religion gained a widely recognized academic respectability posed a new problem. Even when well-taught, "religious studies" or "theology" still remained abstract. Though speculation about religious thought was part of the young person's quest for identity and involvement with life, it could not ultimately accomplish either one. The academic teaching of religion on any campus should produce theological literacy; alone, it could not form the religious man or woman.

In the developing division of labor on campus, eyes increasingly turned to the chaplain to assist students to convert religious knowledge into faithful and operative conviction. For one thing, he was "marginal": in the university, but not of it. He represented the older generation, and yet most often enjoyed the confidence of students. He stood between the town and the gown, the pulpit and the lectern, the sacred and the profane. He was free to legitimate or to criticize, to force divisions or to heal. The theologian was not by that fact a liturgist, but the campus minister was. The professor of ethics was not a moralist, the campus minister had to be. The instructor in social doctrine or sociology need not be an activist, but the campus minister could scarcely ignore the idealism of students or the needs of the times. The idea that the "campus pastor" operated a "laboratory of religious life" was not new among university officials;[44] but in an era of heightening academic specialization and dissatisfaction, the campus minister was emerging as a principal catalyst for testing the assumptions and values of higher learning and fusing knowledge with life.[45]

Important as the chaplaincy seemed to be, could the institutional chaplain in the Catholic college and his diocesan counterpart on the secular campus mutually benefit by getting together? Nearly two-thirds of Newman chaplains had no connection with their counterparts in Catholic colleges, and research indicated that most Catholic college chaplains suffered by being isolated from each other. Of over 400 of the latter listed in 1969, the overwhelming majority — including the 150 diocesan priests providing weekend religious services, usually in small women's colleges — worked in complete separation from their colleagues. Many held administrative or counseling posts; nearly half also taught. Meetings, class preparation and schedules, time spent in offices instead of in lounges or dormitories, the stigma of holding an official disciplinary or academic position, all conspired to separate them from the deep involvement with the students they wanted to serve. Predictably, many of them complained simply of "fatigue," while a number who got too thick with activists suffered the chagrin of being discharged as "embarrassments" to their institutions. As for regional or national unity, while such congregations as the Jesuits, Dominicans, Benedictines, Franciscans, and Holy Cross Fathers had a dozen or more of their members serving in chaplaincies, few of these priests had a forum where they could pool their experiences or have a voice in determining the religious policy within the institutions operated by their orders. Although the suggestion had often been made, Catholic college chaplains did not have a coordinating or training agency such as did Newman chaplains, nor did they have even a separate address listed in the NCEA's College and University Department.[46] Murphy believed that "Newman has much to offer in term of models for campus ministry," and noted that CARA was compiling a directory of chaplains in Catholic institutions to serve as a companion to that for Newman chaplains.[47] The formation in 1970 of the NCEA Commission on Campus Ministry carried the possibility of mutual cooperation a step further.[48]

Central to this unification, as well as to the new conception of Catholic campus ministry, was the second development Newman leaders eyed for the 1970s. This was the project of professionalizing the office of diocesan director. From the appointment of the first director, Father John Bradley of the University of Michigan, in 1961, their numbers had grown in nine years to 114. Although they maintained status as chaplains at their own campuses, these priests were expected to recruit personnel, prepare job descriptions and contracts, preside over regular meetings of all the campus ministers in their dioceses, promote continuing education for them as well as leadership workshops and religious retreats for students, prepare and defend an annual budget, and be directly accountable to their bishops through yearly reports. They now had enough experience to start preparing their own handbooks and other aids, and steps were under way to organize a national board to facilitate communication, develop policy, and speed up the needed expansion, both locally and nationally.[49] Furthermore, CARA was conducting a survey of diocesan directors to determine their status and functions as part of the effort to establish norms for what Bishop William D. Borders, Chairman of the USCC Committee on Education, termed "an encompassing mission of vital importance to Church and campus."[50]

By April 1971 it seemed that the Newman agenda was off the memo pads and becoming fact. That month in Minneapolis the National Catholic Educational Association held its sixty-eighth annual convention, and its College and University Department hosted a special session on campus ministry. Sixty-four years earlier, a similar get-together had ended in a frustrated stalemate when college leaders conspired to turn bishops against the Newman Movement. At that time, Father Peter Edward Dietz, the indomitable chaplain at Oberlin, had predicted that some day the "lay of the land" would erase the rivalry between the two camps and unite college and Newman chaplaincies "in one mighty stream."[51] Now it appeared to be happening. Fathers Ray Sullivan, President of the Catholic Campus Ministry Association, and Jim Blumeyer, S.J., Coordinator of Religious Activities at Rockhurst College in Kansas City, shared their experiences and problems before an appreciative audience of bishops, administrators, professors, priests, and sisters dedicated to putting aside former differences and uniting in common effort. What is more, that same convention became the occasion on which Father Murphy announced plans for a venture which college administrators and chaplains had come to regard as essential. This was the establishment, in the neighborhood of the ecumenical Boston Theological Institute, of a national center for the preparation of campus ministers.[52]

For the American Catholic hierarchy to endorse this project suggested how different was the situation at the start of the 1970s from that shortly after the turn of the century when aspects of the idea of a

Newman Movement first appeared.[53] Then, the university, though generally friendly to religion, was about to enter a period of heightening indifference, even hostility, to its presence and influences; now, it had passed through secularism into open-mindedness, and religious concerns were once again finding institutional welcome on campus. Then, the hierarchy had turned from a moment of progressive engagement with American institutions toward increasing control, even restriction, of such initiatives; now, the bishops had voted in the post–Vatican II era of reform, and by national policy they were beginning again to provide lay persons with the freedom and assistance they needed. Indeed, the bishops were themselves taking the lead in mobilizing Church power to remedy critical social ills.[54]

Without doubt, hard times still lay ahead for the Newman Movement. Within the Church lurked such spectres as budgetary cutbacks, the continuing shortage of religious vocations, the failure of some dioceses to permit the pastoral innovations which chaplains deemed necessary for ministering to their communities, and the occasional practice of assigning priests and sisters insecure in their vocations to Newman centers, where they could "work out their problems" (the fact that a few of these individuals chose to re-enter the lay state suggested to casual observers that something might still be wrong in the Newman Movement). On campus, other familiar demons were to be found, along with some new ones. Chaplains continued to confront the seemingly omnipresent busyness and facelessness of most institutions of higher learning, the inadequacy of the term "campus" to suggest either the locale or the process that today educates most people after high school, the tolerance among most of the college-age group for permissive ethics governing alchohol, drugs, and sex, and the plethora of nonconventional forms of religiosity among young people existing simultaneously with unprecedented numbers of students claiming "no religious preference."[55] All these conditions suggested new challenges.

Still, friends and advocates of the movement could temper their anxieties by recalling that years of desperation had not thwarted their cause. They could reflect that in contrast to most American institutions, theirs emerged from the 1960s in better condition than it had entered them. And they could anticipate the continued benevolence of the Master whose mission they carried on. Their patron had invoked Providence at the start of an earlier second spring. "One thing I know," John Henry Newman then proclaimed, "that according to our need, so will be our strength." He could have been speaking of the Harringtons, the Keoghs, and the Hallinans who would inspire the American movement one day to bear his name, when, addressing English Catholics celebrating the reestablishment of the hierarchy on their soil in 1852, he voiced this challenge:

> Who is to stop you, whether you are to suffer or to do, whether to lay the foundations of the Church in tears, or to put the crown upon the work in jubilation?[56]

APPENDICES

Rejection of Secularization Theory

Apart from "secularism" and "secularistic," which I employ to identify a world view that eliminates a transcendent God and His revelation, "secular" and other forms of the term work in a purely descriptive sense. That is, their presence does not indicate agreement with the theory of secularization made popular by Harvey Cox in the mid-1960s through the publication of his very readable and witty *The Secular City*. He viewed the process of secularization as being "historical" and "almost certainly irreversible," and yet not resulting in "a new closed world view that functioned very much like a new religion." To him the true outcome of gradual liberation from religious dominance was "secularity." This new word named a new era: nonreligious social institutions, such as universities, operated on their own autonomous principles and according to their own inherent values. Unlike the distant past, the sacred realm no longer tampered with the profane; unlike the more recent past, the worldly did not necessarily exclude the religious. Rather, both orders now coexisted in the creative tension set up by gentlemanly dialogue between secular (not secularistic) and sacred institutions.[1]

This explanation of what secularization is all about seems to be naive on three counts.

First, as a theory of what has been happening in American life and education throughout the past nine or ten decades, secularization stands vulnerable to exploitation by intellectuals with an axe to grind. Cox and like-minded colleagues claim that non-believers must never interpret the gradual removal of religious tutelage over human affairs as ushering in the age of triumphant secularism. That is, atheists and friends are told it is not proper to interpret data pointing to secularization according to their anti-religious assumptions. But this sort of admonition is really very confusing: the only way to comprehend the Coxian view is precisely to read into the historical record the unfolding of Divine Providence. Believers are told that secularity is the inevitable outcome of a desacralizing process the Bible itself initiated. In other words, as a theory, secularization is so unfounded that both believers and nonbelievers can use it to justify their pet world views.

Since such confusion really does not advance knowledge or dialogue, David Martin has suggested that the term "be erased from the sociological dictionary."[2] And if from there, why not from the theological lexicon and the pastoral seminar as well?

Second, Cox argues that since modern folk are "no longer interested in the ultimate mystery of life," the process of secularization seems to be "almost certainly irreversible."[3] Yet modern folk seem to feel otherwise. How else explain the recent growth of fundamentalistic churches for adults? Beyond church walls, the organization of fundamentalistic sects (be they derived from Christian or oriental inspirations) among youth? Or how else explain the reemergence of religious issues among professors and other intellectuals? Robert Bellah offers an answer people in all walks of U.S. life would probably accept: "For practical historical reasons having to do with the increasing disillusionment with a world built on utilitarianism and science alone ... religion, instead of becoming increasingly peripheral and vestigial, is again moving to the center of our cultural preoccupation."[4]

Finally, the theory of secularization fails to take into account what Langdon Gilkey terms the all-pervading "worldly mood" in which secularity subsists, much as a spider's web hangs in fog. This secularistic spirit, he says, is "not a philosophy so much as ... the background, the foundation for all the philosophies." Indeed, whatever biblical interpretation as a mental exercise might conclude, the fact is that it was this-worldliness, not other-worldliness, that gave birth to secularization; and though it need not foreclose openness to God and religion, it has, as a matter of record, tried to do so.[5]

Available to illuminate contradictory world views, incorrect regarding the persistence of religion and concern for the ultimate among people, and inconclusive about the pressures of a dominant this-worldliness, secularization theory appears to be deceptive as a way to understand what has been happening during the course of American higher education in the twentieth century.

Presidents of the Student Federation, 1915–68

1915–18: James M. Kieran, Hunter College (Professor)
1918–21: Alexis I. duPont Coleman, City College New York (Professor)
1921–23: David A. Gibson, M.D.
1923–24: David A. Jordan, New York University
1924–25: Frank J. Murphy, University of Pittsburgh
1925–28: Thomas R. Swain, New York University
1928–29: Joseph B. Hearn, University of Pennsylvania
1930–32: John Paul Smith, City College New York
1932–34: Joseph F. Van Horn, University of Pennsylvania
1934–35: Thomas J. Pinkman, New York University
1935–36: Newman F. Mallon, University of Toronto
1936–38: John V. Kingston, Brooklyn Polytechnic
1938–40: John L. Ricketts, University of Pennsylvania
1940–42: William J. Hurley, New York University
*1942–43: Virginia Morrissey, Boston University
1943–44: Francis Gaddis, University of Alabama
1944–45: Lucille Becker, University of Colorado
1945–47: Elvira Caggiano, Hunter College
1947–48: Edward Stuart, University of Texas
1948–49: Richard Oliver, University of Alabama
1949–50: Dennis Duffy, University of Minnesota
1950–51: Gerald B. Nolan, University of New Hampshire
1951–53: Andrew C. Putka, Western Reserve
1953–54: Quinlan Halbeisen, Iowa State College
1954–56: Ronald Bedard, University of Rhode Island
1956–57: Joseph Cronin, Harvard University
1957–58: Walter J. Markel, Long Beach State College
1958–59: James J. Berdou, Louisiana State University
1959–60: William Hansell, University of Pennsylvania
1960–61: Edward Pronchinsko, University of Wisconsin

*The new constitution of 1942 permitted a student, "not necessarily an alumnus, as previously required," to serve as president.

1961–62: Edward J. Orlett, General Motors Institute, Dayton, Ohio
1962–63: Tim Dyer, Eastern Michigan University
1963–64: Julius Gilbertson, Wisconsin State University, Eau Claire
1964–65: Donn N. Kurtz, II, University of Southwestern Louisiana
1965–67: Charles T. Badrick, Kansas State University
1967–68: Michael V. Barry, New York City

National Chaplains to the Student Federation, 1917–66

1917–35: Rev. John W. Keogh, University of Pennsylvania
1935–38: Rev. Paul A. Deery, University of Indiana
1938–40: Rev. John J. Collins, New York State Teachers College
*1940–44: Rev. Donald M. Cleary, Cornell University
1944–45: Rev. Michael Mulvoy, C.S.Sp., University of Alabama
1945–47: Rev. John J. Dempsey, University of Buffalo
1947–48: Rev. Frank McPhillips, University of Michigan
1948–49: Rev. Leonard P. Cowley, University of Minnesota
1949–50: Rev. Joseph Connerton, University of Chicago
1950–51: Rev. Edward J. Duncan, University of Illinois
1951–52: Rev. J. Desmond O'Connor, University of New Hampshire
1952–54: Rev. Paul J. Hallinan, Cleveland Intercollegiate Newman Club
1954–56: Rt. Rev. Robert E. Tracy, Louisiana State University, Baton Rouge
1956–58: Rev. James J. O'Brien, University of Connecticut
1958–60: Rev. George Carrelts, University of Minnesota
1960–62: Rt. Rev. Alexander O. Sigur, University of Southwestern Louisiana
1962–64: Rev. Richard Butler, O.P. (served full-time)
1964–65: Rev. Paul F. Halloran, Mankato State University
1965–66: Rev. Raymond Kriege, University of Wisconsin, Milwaukee

*In 1942 the Episcopal Moderator of the Newman Club Federation began to appoint the national chaplain, who until then had been elected by the annual convention of the student federation. After 1950, when the Chaplains' Association came into existence, the moderator appointed the priest proposed to him by the association.

Executive Secretaries* of the Student Federation, 1941–62

1941:   Albert W. Rinehart
1941–44:   Tess Marie Gorka
1944–45:   Veronica VanderHeyden
1945–47:   Louise McNerney
1947–49:   Philip DesMarais
1949–50:   William Pinkel
1950–51:   Marion Andert
1951–52:   Joan Ellen Hickey
1952–55:   Rev. Thomas A. Carlin, O.S.F.S.
1955–62:   Rev. Charles W. Albright, C.S.P.

*Upon becoming a part of the Youth Department, NCWC, the executive secretary, appointed by the department and located in Washington, became also an officer of the student federation. The post was held by laymen until 1952 when the first priest–secretary was appointed. In 1955 the title was changed to "Coordinating Secretary of the National Newman Club Federation," in 1962 to "Coordinating Secretary of the National Newman Apostolate," and in 1966 to "Director of the National Newman Apostolate." For names during the years 1962–69 see Appendix VII.

The National Newman Club Chaplains' Association, 1950–68

Chaplains first tried to organize in 1906. Their next attempt of record took place in June 1950, during the Chaplains' Institute which met in conjunction with the Mid–Century Convention of the National Newman Club Federation. The association intended "to further the work of the chaplains on a local and on a national level, to pool their spiritual, intellectual and organizational resources, and to use the zeal and talents of all the chaplains in perfecting the Newman Apostolate." The president of the association was aided by an Advisory Board consisting of Past National Chaplains, the current National Chaplain, the province chaplains, and those chaplains serving as chairmen of the several committees of the association. To ensure contact with the daily work of the Newman Movement, the National Chaplain continued to serve in his local campus assignment during his tenure. In 1969 the association withdrew from the Newman Apostolate to become the Catholic Campus Ministry Association.

PRESIDENTS OF THE CHAPLAINS' ASSOCIATION

1950–51:   Rev. Edward J. Duncan, University of Illinois

1951–52:   Rev. J. Desmond O'Connor, University of New Hampshire

1952–54:   Rev. Paul J. Hallinan, Cleveland Intercollegiate Newman Club

1954–56:   Rt. Rev. Robert E. Tracy, Louisiana State University, Baton Rouge

1956–58:   Rev. James J. O'Brien, University of Connecticut

1958–60:   Rev. George Garrelts, University of Minnesota

1960–62:   Rt. Rev. Alexander O. Sigur, University of Southwestern Louisiana

1962–65:   Rev. Richard Butler, O.P. (served full-time)

1965–66:   Rev. John Bradley, University of Michigan

1966–67:   Rev. Philip J. Brannon, University of Vermont

1968–69:   Rev. Charles Forsyth, O.S.B., University of Colorado

APPENDIX VI

The National Newman
Foundation, 1960–69

In 1957 the Chaplains' Association resolved that since the future of the Newman Movement depended largely upon the establishment of a stable financial basis they should explore the idea of establishing a national incorporated and tax-exempt foundation. Monsignor James E. Rea, Chaplain at Columbia University, served as president of the temporary board that set up the foundation. On June 3, 1960, the National Newman Foundation was incorporated in the District of Columbia to "assist the Bishops of the United States in a most practical way to provide for the members of their flocks attending non–Catholic colleges." Specifically, the Foundation set out to attract "the support of the alumni of secular colleges, who have profited from the Newman program in their undergraduate days" and to appeal "to the growing number of funds and foundations, Catholic and non–Catholic, which are concerning themselves with religion in higher education."

OFFICERS OF THE FOUNDATION

Presidents of the Board of Trustees

1961–67: Andrew P. Maloney, Bankers Trust Company of New York City
1967–69: John J. Meng, Fordham University
1969– Vincent Burke, Riggs National Bank, Washington, D.C.

Directors

1962: John J. Burns
1962–63: Joseph S. McGrath, Jr.
1963–69: Jerry Burns
1969– William F. Tonne, Jr.

Executives in the Newman Apostolate, 1962-69*

Apostolate Office

1962–64: Charles W. Albright, C.S.P. (Coordinating Secretary)
1964–65: Joan Orlosky
1965–69: John T. McDonough (Director)

Student Federation

1962–65: Gail Benkert (Executive Secretary)
1965–69: Michele Fearing (Administrative Director)

*In 1969 the "Director of the National Newman Apostolate" in the Youth Department of the NCWC became the "Director of the Campus Ministry Division" in the Department of Education, United States Catholic Conference.

Notes

ABBREVIATIONS

AAB	Archives, Archdiocese of Baltimore
AACHSP	Archives, American Catholic Historical Society of Philadelphia
AANY	Archives, Archdiocese of New York
AAP	Archives, Archdiocese of Philadelphia
AASF	Archives, Archdiocese of San Francisco
AASL	Archives, Archdiocese of St. Louis
ACSP	Archives, Congregation of St. Paul, New York
ACUA	Archives, The Catholic University of America
ADSYU	Archives, Divinity School, Yale University
ANCCU	Archives, Newman Club, Columbia University
ANCEA	Archives, National Catholic Educational Association
ANCUMich	Archives, Newman Center, University of Michigan
ANHUI	Archives, Newman Hall, University of Illinois
ANNA	Archives, National Newman Apostolate
ASRUOre	Archives, School of Religion, University of Oregon
AUCB	Archives, University of California, Berkeley
AUI	Archives, University of Illinois
AUMich	Archives, University of Michigan
AUMinn	Archives, University of Minnesota
AUMo	Archives, University of Missouri
AUND	Archives, University of Notre Dame
AUOre	Archives, University of Oregon
AUP	Archives, University of Pennsylvania
AUT	Archives, University of Texas
AUW-M	Archives, University of Wisconsin, Madison
AYU	Archives, Yale University
CARA	Center for Applied Research in the Apostolate, Washington, D.C.
CAT	Catholic Archives of Texas, Austin
CCD	Confraternity of Christian Doctrine
CCMA	Catholic Campus Ministry Association
CEA	Catholic Educational Association (1904–1926; see NCEA)

CSAA	Catholic Student Association of America
FCCC	Federation of College Catholic Clubs (1915–1938; see NNCF)
JCUM	Joint Collection, University of Missouri Western Historical Manuscript Collection–Columbia and State Historical Society of Missouri Manuscripts
NCAPU	Newman Center Archives, Purdue University
NCEA	National Catholic Educational Association (1927–)
NCWC	National Catholic Welfare Council (1919–1922) National Catholic Welfare Conference (1922–1967; see USCC)
NFCCS	National Federation of Catholic College Students
NNCF	National Newman Club Federation (1938–1965; see NSF)
NSA	National Student Association
NSF	Newman Student Federation (1965–1968)
SCPC	Special Collections, Pomona College
SCUI	Special Collections, University of Iowa
SPC	Files of St. Paul's Chapel, Madison, Wisconsin
USCC	United States Catholic Conference (1967–)

FOREWORD

1. Quoted from Michel Tronchai, *Vie de Lenain de Tillemont, avec des relfexions sur divers sujets de morale, et quelques lettres de piété* (Cologne, 1711), p. 114, in David P. Jordan, "LeNain de Tillemont: Gibbon's 'Sure-Footed Mule,'" *Church History* 39 (December 1970), 489.

2. *The Future of Man,* trans. Norman Denny (New York: Harper & Row, 1964), p. 12.

3. Martin W. Davis, S.D.S., *The Sister as Campus Minister* (Washington, D.C.: Center for Applied Research in the Apostolate, 1970), p. 8.

1. RELIGION STAYED IN COLLEGE

1. Wallace N. Stearns, "Moral and Religious Training in Universities and Colleges in the United States," *Religious Education* 2 (February 1908), 203.

2. Commissioner of Education, *Reports,* 1901, 2:16–19, and 1910, 2:850–51; U.S. Department of the Interior, Bureau of Education, *Bulletin,* 1922, no. 28, p. 3; *Biennial Survey of Education,* 1928–30, 1:458; U.S. Office of Education, Federal Security Agency, *Biennial Surveys of Education in the United States,* 1938–40, 1940–42, pt. 2, ch. 4, p. 12.

3. Harold Bolce, "Blasting at the Rock of Ages," *Cosmopolitan* 16 (May 1909), 665–80.

4. "F.L.," "Dangers of Secular Universities," *The Catholic Mind* 14 (August 22, 1916), 432.

5. Compare the *Bulletin of the University of Missouri* 6 (February 1905), 64, with that of 16 (March 1915), 97–98.

6. "College Aims, Past and Present," *School and Society* 14 (December 3, 1921), 499–509.

7. Quoted in "Educational Notes," *The Catholic Educational Review* 21 (February 1923), 116.

8. "Oration," *University Record* (Chicago) 9 (May 1904), 13–17.

9. "Religious Life at the University of Texas," brochure c. 1959, folder, Religious Life, Main Library, University of Texas, Austin.

10. R. A. Seligman, ed., *Encyclopedia of the Social Sciences* (New York: Macmillan, 1934), p. 631.

11. For example, see discussions by Huston Smith and Guy E. Swanson in *The Religious Situation: 1968* (Boston: Beacon Press, 1968), pp. 583–600 and 801–34.

12. Harvey Cox, *The Secular City* (New York: Macmillan, 1965), pp. 20–21, 61.

13. For further discussion see Appendix I.

14. Charles S. Braden, "Enrollment Trends in Religious Courses," *Christian Education* 31 (December 1938), 306–17.

15. See Ch. 11, pp. 137ff.

16. Lois Kimball Rosenberry Matthews, *The Dean of Women* (New York: Houghton Mifflin, 1915), p. 186.

17. See *Literary Digest* 20 (March 17, 1900), 338ff.; E. S. Boyer, *Religion in the American College* (New York: Abingdon Press, 1930), p. 74; Gould Wickey, "A National Survey of the Religious Preferences of Students in American Colleges and Universities," *Christian Education* 21 (October 1937), 49–55.

18. Michael Argyle, *Religious Behaviour* (London: Routledge and Keegan Paul, 1955), pp. 63–67; George H. Betts, "Religious Attitudes and Activities of 1,600 Northwestern University Students: A Report," *Religious Education* 23 (November 1928), 919.

19. V. P. Robinson, "The Conception of God of College Students," *American Journal of Religious Psychology and Education* 3 (November 1908), 247–57; Read Bain, "Religious Attitudes of College Students," *American Journal of Sociology* 32 (March 1927), 262–70; C. F. Thwing, "Significant Ignorance about the Bible," *The Century Magazine* 38 (May 1900), 123–28; R. H. Edwards, et al., *Undergraduates: A Study of Morale in Twenty-Three American Colleges and Universities* (Garden City, N.Y.: Doubleday, 1928), p. 243; Bernard E. Meland, "The Present Worth of Jesus," *International Journal of Ethics* 42 (April 1923), 324–33.

20. Herbert L. Searles, "An Empirical Inquiry into the God Experience of One Hundred and Forty College Students," *Religious Education* 21 (August 1926), 334–41.

21. "Student Religion," *The Outlook* 135 (September 19, 1923), 110.

22. Edwards, *Undergraduates,* p. 247.

23. James Leuba, *The Psychological Study of Religion* (New York: Macmillan, 1912), pp. 213–18.

24. Daniel Katz and Floyd H. Allport, *Student Attitudes* (Syracuse, N.Y.: Craftsman Press, 1931), p. 765.

25. H. W. Prentiss, Jr., "The Cult of Competence," Address, Midwinter

Commencement, Univ. of Pennsylvania, February 6, 1945, p. 7, ms., AUP, Archives General, Commencement Addresses.

26. "Educational Philosophy of College Undergraduates," *The School Review* 35 (April 9, 1927), 246–49.

27. Edward Aswell, "The Students Prescribe," *Forum* 76 (November 1926), 712–18.

28. Quoted in "Colleges Keeping the Faith," *Literary Digest* 82 (July 12, 1924), 31.

29. Quoted in the *Columbia Herald* (Columbia, Mo.), June 5, 1891.

30. "Student Union Committee, 1915," Wheeler Papers, 1915, Bancroft Library, Univ. of California, Berkeley.

31. Quoted in "Proceedings of the Conference on Religious Education," pt. 2, *Bulletin of the University of Illinois* (October 1906), p. 120; see also Henry D. Sheldon, *History of the University of Oregon* (Portland, Ore.: Binfors and Mort, 1940), pp. 63, 139; "Chapel Regulations, 1904," AUP, Archives General, contains a summary of practices at several campuses; Frank H. Strong, "Religious Education in the Universities," *NEA Proceedings* 52 (1914), 489–92, and Clyde K. Huder, "The Chancellors of K.U.," *The University of Kansas Alumni Magazine* 60 (January 1962), 4–5; John W. Keogh, "Report to Cardinal Dougherty, 1918," pp. 85–92, ms., AAP, Newman Club.

32. "The Supervision of the Religious Life in Educational Institutions," *REA Proceedings* 1 (1904), 127–29.

33. "President's Reports, 1901–1912" Report of June 13, 1904, n.p., typescript, SCUI, MacLean Papers. Jesse, however, preferred to establish a "Dean of Manners and Morals" in each university to function as a "sort of college pastor." See Shailor Matthews (Chicago) to Jesse (Columbia, Mo.), September 15, 1904, AUMo, microfilm, reel 69, "Minutes, Executive Board, June to September, 1906."

34. See Howard Hopkins, *History of the YMCA in North America* (New York: Association Press, 1951), pp. 289–90; Harry Melvin Philpott, "A History of the Student Young Men's Association" (Diss., Yale, 1947) and Clarence Prouty Shedd, *Two Centuries of the Student Christian Movement* (New York: Association Press, 1934).

35. In AUW-M, Van Hise Papers, 1913–14, series 4/10–1, box 42, YMCA.

36. "Amounts Appropriated to YMCA by School Administrators," AUT, President's Records, box UF-2D, Student Life, 1907–1929, folder YM and YWCA.

37. W. T. Moore (Columbia, Mo.) to Campbell Wells (St. Louis, Mo.), September 27, 1904, JCUM, box 3501, School of Religion; and Richard C. Hughes, "The Church and the Religious Problem in State Universities," *Religious Education* 10 (April 1915), 178–85.

38. *Bulletin of the University of Texas*, no. 129 (August 15, 1909), p. 5.

39. Daniel B. Purinton, "The State University and the Teaching of Religion," *Religious Education* 3 (June 1908), 54; Norman Wilde, "Religion: A Luxury or a Duty?" *International Journal of Ethics* 20 (July 1910), 470–81; Walter S. Athearn, *Religious Education and American Democracy* (Boston: Pilgrim, 1917), pp. 265–66; Shedd, *Two Centuries of the Student Christian Movement*, p. 392; and "Christian Student Awakening and Bible Study at Colleges and Universities," *Current Opinion* 68 (June 1915), 422–23.

40. Wallace N. Stearns, "Religious Education in the State Universities," *NEA Proceedings* 45 (1907), 731.

41. Quoted in minutes of the 1932 meeting of the National Association of State Universities, SCUI, O. D. Foster Papers, Notebook 25.

42. Daniel Callahan, *The Mind of the Catholic Layman* (New York: Charles Scribner's Sons, 1963), pp. 57–72.

43. Ibid., p. 61.

44. Ibid., pp. 59–64; also Thomas T. McAvoy, C.S.C., *A History of the Catholic Church in the United States* (Notre Dame, Ind.: University of Notre Dame Press, 1969), pp. 320–28.

45. William Michael Halsey, *The Survival of American Innocence: Catholicism in an Era of Disillusionment, 1920-1940* (Notre Dame, Ind.: University of Notre Dame Press, 1980), pp. 37–39.

46. See Robert D. Cross, *The Emergence of Liberal Catholicism in America* (Cambridge, Mass.: Harvard University Press, 1958), passim.

47. Quoted in Callahan, *The Mind of the Catholic Layman,* p. 69.

48. Ibid., pp. 77, 110.

49. McAvoy, *History of the Catholic Church in the United States,* pp. 332–38. For the text of the papal letter and a helpful commentary, see John Tracy Ellis, *Documents of American Catholic History* (Milwaukee: Bruce Publishing Co., 1956), pp. 553–62.

50. Michael V. Gannon, "Before and After Modernism: The Intellectual Isolation of the American Priest" in John Tracy Ellis, ed., *The Catholic Priest in the United States: Historical Investigations* (Collegeville, Minn.: St. John's University Press, 1971) pp. 293–383.

51. John Tracy Ellis, *American Catholicism* (Chicago: University of Chicago Press, 1969), pp. 124ff.

52. See Canon #682, *Codex Juris Canonici* (Westminster, Md.: The Newman Press, 1951), p. 227.

53. Between 1885 and 1916 22 percent of the 155 bishops appointed in the United States studied in Rome; between 1916 and 1966 40 percent of the 409 U.S. bishops studied in Rome. During the latter period so also did 70 percent of the U.S. cardinals. See John Tracy Ellis, "On Selecting Catholic Bishops for the United States," *The Critic* 27 (June–July, 1969), 47.

54. See McAvoy, *History of the Catholic Church in the United States,* pp. 371–78.

2. STRANGERS IN A STRANGE LAND

1. Quoted in "Wayside Notes," *The Catholic Citizen* (Milwaukee), October 27, 1906. See discussions of Catholics on secular campuses in *CEA Reports* 1 (1904), 79–81; 2 (1905), 125–33; 3 (1906), 119ff; and F. Hiermann (Buffalo, N.Y.) to Austin O'Malley (Notre Dame), October 25, 1897, AUND, O'Malley Papers.

2. Interview, Aurora, Ind., July 9, 1964.

3. Thomas Lantry O'Neill, C.S.P., "Newman Hall, 1912–13," p. 5, brochure, AUCB, "Student Life—Newman Club."

4. "Memorial to His Holiness, Pope Pius X," April 1906, ACUA, Papers of the Rector's Office, 1903–09, box L, folder C.

5. Interview, Clarence Luhn, Aurora, Ind., July 9, 1964. See also comments on priests criticizing Harvard's Catholics in John LaFarge, "Report on the Condition of Catholic Students at Harvard University," typescript, ribbon copy, dated Christmas Day, 1904, 13 pp. unnumbered, signed by the author. This typescript, hereafter identified as LaFarge "Report," was found in the papers of The Most Rev. Thomas H. McLaughlin, Bishop of Paterson, N.J., by Bishop Francis Rodimer; it is now in the possession of this writer.

6. Quoted in "Loyola School Letters," n.p., brochure, AUND, McDevitt Papers.

7. Edward Dennis Kelly (Ann Arbor, Mich.) to O'Malley, November 9, 1897, AUND, O'Malley Papers.

8. J. M. Naughton (Madison, Wis.) to O'Malley, November 9, 1897, in ibid.

9. Keogh, "Report to Cardinal Dougherty, 1930," pp. 2–3, AAP, Keogh Papers, Newman Clubs, 1923–30.

10. LaFarge, "Report."

11. Quoted in Oscar W. Firkins, *Cyrus Northrup: A Memoir* (Minneapolis: University of Minnesota Press, 1925), p. 502.

12. Harry James Towey, "A History of the Principal Catholic Student Groups on the Main Campus of the University of Minnesota" (Thesis, St. Paul Seminary, 1949), p. 51.

13. "The Old and the New Ideal of Scholars," Baccalaureate Address 1905 (Ann Arbor: University of Michigan Press, 1905), p. 11.

14. John W. Keogh, "Report to Cardinal Dougherty, 1918," pp. 71–80, AACHSP, Keogh Papers, box labeled "Notebook."

15. Helen Vogt, "Report from the University of Iowa," *The Catholic Student* 1 (November 15, 1910), 16–18.

16. The Paulist Fathers, "The Religious Situation at the University of Texas" (Austin, 1908), p. 7, brochure, CAT, Newman Club.

17. *The Undergraduate and His College* (New York: Houghton Mifflin, 1917), p. 190.

18. Keogh, "Report . . . 1930," pp. 2–3.

19. Thomas H. Dahm (Moscow, Idaho) to H. C. Hengell (Madison, Wis.), April 13, 1927, SPC, Hengell Papers. See similar reports in R. L. McWilliams, "The Presence of Catholic Students at Our State Universities," *American Ecclesiastical Review* 35 (Augist 1906), 197–200.

20. John J. Farrell (Cambridge, Mass.) to Denis O'Connell (Washington, D.C.), January 16, 1907, ACUA, Rector's Correspondence, 1903–04, box 2; and "Discussion," *CEA Reports* 3 (1906), 119ff.

21. E. M. Kerwin (River Forest, Ill.) to this writer, May 31, 1964.

22. H. P. Conway, quoted in "Discussion," *CEA Reports* 3 (1906), 122.

23. As remembered by R. A. Muttkowski (Columbia, Mo.) to H. C. Hengell, December 8, 1916, SPC, Hengell Papers.

24. "History of the Catholic Students' Association at the University of Wisconsin," typescript, ribbon copy, n.d. [c. 1910?], 4 pp. unnumbered, SPC, Hengell Papers.

25. Timothy Harrington, "Memoirs of the Earliest Days of the Oldest Newman Club," *Newman Quarterly* 5 (Summer 1921), 135–36.

26. See entries for December 7, 1888, March 14 and December 4, 1890, and February 8, 1891 in "Diary of a Student at the University of Wisconsin, 1886–1892," mimeograph, 1939, AUW–M, Record Group 20/0/1.

27. Quotations from letters of recommendation written by President Chamberlain and Professor D. A. Frankenburger, in possession of Harrington's son, Dr. Earl Harrington, Milwaukee, Wis.; cited with Dr. Harrington's permission.

28. Interview, Earl Harrington, Milwaukee, June 16, 1964.

29. Timothy Harrington, "Memoirs of the Earliest Days of the Oldest Newman Club," pp. 135–36.

30. Ibid.

31. For brief biographies of Harrington see Horton L. Roe, *The History of the Knights of Columbus in Wisconsin* (Milwaukee: Wisconsin State Council, 1952), pp. 164–65, and "Obituary," *Wisconsin Medical Journal* 47 (January 1948), 242–43.

32. See "History of the Catholic Students' Association at the University of Wisconsin"; *Public Ledger* (Philadelphia), February 26, 1897; *The Old Penn Weekly Review* (University of Pennsylvania) 2 (April 9, 1904); and *Catholic Standard and Times* (Philadelphia), February 14, 1903.

33. Quoted in *Catholic Standard and Times*, February 14, 1903.

34. The summary that follows is based upon a review of constitutions and other descriptive material found in "Minute Book, Spalding Guild, 1905–1910" in Newman Foundation, University of Illinois, the most complete record, and on reports from several dozen clubs found in files of *The Catholic Student*, 1909–1916, and *The Newman Quarterly*, 1917–1926. In addition to the Towey history already cited see: Peter Alegi, "A History of Catholicism at Yale to 1943," departmental essay in American Studies, Yale, 1956; Louis William Doll, "History of the Student Chapel," and Michael Burke, "History of St. Mary's Chapel for Catholic Students," ms., n.d., ACUMich; Robert Melvin, "History of St. Thomas Aquinas Parish at Purdue University," ms., n.d., NCAPU; Barry McDermott, "History of the Newman Foundation, Univesrity of Illinois" (Thesis, Univ. of Illinois, 1958); and Mary Ruth Torpey, "The Newman Club of the University of Iowa," Historical Paper, State Univ. of Iowa, 1945, SCUI.

35. Quoted in Torpey, "The Newman Club of the University of Iowa," p. 9.

36. See Clarence Prouty Shedd, *The Church Follows Its Students* (New Haven, Conn.: Yale University Press, 1938), passim.

37. In "Proceedings, Fifth Convention of Church Workers in Universities," Iowa City, February 12, 1912, p. 5, Pamphlet Collection, ADSYU.

38. Quoted in "Minute Book, Spalding Guild," entry February 21, 1905.

39. See McDermott, "History of the Newman Foundation," n.p.

40. "Minute Book, Spalding Guild," entry September 30, 1906.

41. *Daily Illini,* March 20, 24, 1906.

42. *The Catholic Universe* (Cleveland), July 5 and August 2, 1907.

43. As reported in "Church Workers in State Universities," *Religious Education* 6 (July 1911), 223.

44. Keogh, "Report . . . 1918," pp. 1–19.

45. Quoted in *The Monitor* (San Francisco), March 19, 1910.

46. Quoted in *Newman Quarterly* 8 (Fall 1923), 3; also "Notes and Remarks," *Ave Maria* 15 (March 4, 1922), 277.

47. Quoted in "Newman Club," brochure [c. 1911], n.p., CAT, Newman Club.

48. Melvin, "History of St. Thomas Aquinas Parish," n.p.

49. See William J. McHale, "Report from the University of Minnesota," *The Catholic Student* 1 (November 15, 1910), 14–15; and W. P. Nemmers, "Report from Iowa State College," ibid., pp. 13–14.

50. Riordan (San Francisco) to John J. Hughes, C.S.P. (New York), March 13, 1911, ACSP, Hughes Papers.

51. Archbishop Messmer's job description, in *The Catholic Citizen*, September 9, 1914.

52. See John Tracy Ellis, *Documents of American Catholic History*, pp. 416ff.

53. La Farge, "Report."

54. In *The Catholic Universe*, August 2, 1907.

55. Ibid., July 19, 1907, and August 2, 1907.

3. A NEW LINK?

1. *The Catholic Citizen* (Milwaukee), November 24, 1906; see also *The Transcript* (Boston), December 1, 1906, and John J. Farrell (Cambridge, Mass.) to Denis J. O'Connell (Washington, D.C.), January 8, 1907, ANCEA, Howard Papers.

2. Writer's translation; the original Latin text is in *Analecta Ecclesiastica* (1905), p. 143, and this, with an Italian parallel, is in *Civiltà Cattolicà* 2 (April 26, 1905), 275.

3. To Joseph W. Cochran [New York?], September 28, 1907, SCUI, MacLean Papers, Religious Education Association, 1905–09.

4. *The Catholic Universe* (Cleveland), July 5, 1907.

5. To Francis W. Howard (Cleveland), January 26, 1907, ANCEA, Howard Papers.

6. See *Civiltà Cattolicà*, Quaderno 1346 (July 1906), 131–32, quoted in *The Monitor* (San Francisco), August 24, 1907.

7. To O'Connell, January 19, 1907, ACUA, Rector's Correspondence, 1903–09, box 2.

8. Reported in *The Catholic Citizen*, October 13, 1906.

9. LaFarge, "Report."

10. Arthur N. Lambeck (Milwaukee) to Lawrence B. Murphy (Madison), September 13, 1904, SPC, Hengell Papers.

11. See "Students' Petition" reprinted in a brochure Hengell prepared for fund-raising purposes in 1907, in ibid.

12. The account of Messmer's visit appears in a form letter prepared by the Catholic Students' Association of the University of Wisconsin and circulated in 1907; now in ibid.

13. Messmer quoted in Hengell, "The Catholic Mission at the University of Wisconsin," *American Ecclesiastical Review* 47 (January 1912), 99.

14. See typescript, ribbon copy, of charter in SPC, Hengell Papers: quotations from it appear in *The Monitor*, August 24, 1907. This "copying" is one of several incidents suggesting how these founding bishops and chaplains provided each other with "ammunition" and how some diocesan newspapers tried to help their cause. Hengell's correspondence contains a considerable number of letters from these early chaplains asking advice and help in setting up clubs and fund-raising schemes.

15. See promotional statement and list of donors in "The T. L. Harrington Fund," SPC, Hengell Papers.

16. For a more detailed story of these events see John Whitney Evans, "The Newman Idea in Wisconsin, 1883–1920," *Wisconsin Magazine of History* 54 (Spring 1971), 204–19.

17. To Hengell, January 12, 1914, SPC, Hengell Papers.

18. To Daniel Hudson (Notre Dame), April 21, May 9 and 30, September 9, 1907, AUND, Hudson Papers; see also *The Daily Journal* (Ithaca, N.Y.), April 18, 1907.

19. John A. Miller (San Francisco) to Andrew D. White (Ithaca, N.Y.), April 27, 1907, quoted in Michael J. Murphy, "The Cornell Plan of Bishop Bernard J. McQuaid," *Essays in U.S. Church History* 12 (May 1959), 81ff.

20. Messmer to John Farley (New York), July 21, 1907, AANY, P–13, Varia: Education, 1907–20.

21. To Hudson, September 3, 1907.

22. To Richard E. Queen (San Francisco), April 21, 1908, AASF, Riordan Correspondence, Newman Club.

23. *The Monitor,* March 19, 1910.

24. Thomas L. O'Neill, C.S.P., "Newman Hall: Catholic Chapel and Library at the University of California, 1912–1913," pp. 7–17, brochure AUCB, "Student Life—Newman Club."

25. To George M. Searle, C.S.P. (New York), May 10, 1908, CAT, Newman Club.

26. See Carlos E. Castaneda, *Our Catholic Heritage in Texas, 1919–1936,* 7 vols. (Austin, Tex.: Von Boechmann-Jones, 1958), 7:338–39; also *Bulletin of the Association of Religion Teachers, 1916–17,* File, Religious Life, Main Library, University of Texas, Austin.

27. To Gallagher, January 3, 1916, copy in ACSP, Hughes Papers.

28. Quoted in Castaneda, *Our Catholic Heritage in Texas,* 7:338–39.

29. See the account in LaFarge, "Report," n.p.; and *The Pilot* (Boston), October 19, 1907.

30. To Alvin Kutchera (Madison, Wis.), December 22, 1938, SPC, Kutchera Papers.

31. Pius X, *Acerbo Nimis,* English language ed. (Paterson, N.J.: Confraternity Publications, 1946), p. 11.

32. Ibid., p. 12; see also similar translation in *The Catholic Mind* 3 (May 1905), 215.

33. For a translation respecting the pope's use of Latin see James Ryan Hughes, *Encyclical "Acerbo Nimis" of Pius X* (Philadelphia: Federation of College Catholic Clubs, 1929).

34. Letter to the editor, *The Catholic Universe,* May 24, 1907.

35. To Farrell, January 7, 1907, ACUA, Rector's Correspondence, 1903–09, box 2.

36. John J. Farrell, "The Catholic Chaplain at the Secular University," *CEA Reports* 4 (1907), 150ff.

37. To O'Connell, January 19, 1907.

38. To Howard, May 15, 1907.

39. To James A. Burns, C.S.C. (Notre Dame), April 27, 1907, ANCEA, Burns Papers.

40. Letter to the editor, *The Catholic Universe,* October 25, 1907; see also remarks of Professor James E. Haggerty of Ohio State University in "Discussion," *CEA Reports* 3 (1906), 120. For the general critique of Catholic collegiate education see the notes Archbishop Farley prepared as the basis for his address to the CEA in 1904, AANY, P–13, Varia: Education, 1907–20.

41. This description was commonly used; see, for example, Thomas J. Conaty, "The Catholic College of the Twentieth Century," *Catholic University of America Bulletin* 7 (July 1901), 304.

42. Quoted in O'Connell to Howard, April 7, 1905.

43. This alert from the Roman headquarters of the Jesuits is quoted in Joseph T. Durkin, S.J., *Georgetown University: The Middle Years, 1840-1900* (Washington, D.C.: Georgetown University Press, 1963), pp. 217–23.

44. See "Report of the Joint Committee on High Schools," *CEA Reports* 1 (1904), 41–59 and 3 (1905), 22–24, 28.

45. Ibid., 1 (1904), 54–56.

46. Minutes of the Annual Meeting, April 26, 1906, Roman Catholic Archbishops of the United States, Washington, D.C., n.p., at No. 13, AASL, John J. Glennon Papers.

47. Conway, "Letter to Members of the Conference of Catholic Colleges," *Catholic University of America Bulletin* 13 (July 1907), 507–08.

48. Ibid.

49. Burns to Howard, March 29, 1907.

50. Conway, "Letter to Members of the Conference of Catholic Colleges," p. 508.

51. To Howard, May 15, 1907.

52. Farrell, "The Catholic Chaplain at the Secular University," pp. 150–63.

53. Conway arranged for this "addition" in a letter to Howard, June 15, 1907.

54. See *CEA Reports* 4 (1907), 163–76.

55. Ibid., pp. 172–73.

56. Ibid., pp. 35, 123.

57. Conway, "Letter to Members of the Conference of Catholic Colleges," p. 507.

58. To Howard, December 16, 1907.

59. Ibid.

60. To Farley, July 2, 1907, AANY, Varia: Education, 1907–20.

61. See Minutes of the Annual Meeting, May 8, 1908, Roman Catholic Archbishops of the United States, Washington, D.C., n.p., at No. 2, AASL, John J. Glennon Papers.

62. "Introduction," *CEA Reports* 5 (1908), 1.

63. Lyman P. Powell, *The Religious Situation in Certain Colleges and Universities* (Northampton, 1912), p. 33.

64. Entry September 8, 1916, in John W. Keogh, "Diary," *AACHSP,* Keogh Papers, box II.

65. F. Lloyd (Columbia, Mo.) to Hengell, January 15, 1916; also J. P. Lynch (Columbia, Mo.) to Hengell, April 22, 1922. See also *Bulletin of the University of Missouri* 21 (April 1920), 57.

66. Writing in *The Catholic Universe,* July 5, August 2, 1907.

67. See above, ch. 2, pp. 23ff.

68. *The Church and Modern Society* (New York: D. H. McBride and Co., 1903), 1:92.

69. *The Church and the Age* (New York: The Catholic World, 1887), pp. 1, 106, 122.

70. McQuaid to Hudson, January 31, 1904, April 21, and May 30, 1907; see also Messmer's pastoral letter of 1909, "To Our Beloved Clergy and Laity," SPC, Hengell Papers.

71. Thomas T. McAvoy, C.S.C., *A History of the Catholic Church in the United States,* p. 349.

72. See Van Hise's appeal, "To the Public," March 18, 1907, copy in SPC, Hengell Papers; *The Catholic Citizen,* September 29, 1906.

73. *The Catholic Universe,* July 19, 1907.

74. "The State University of Iowa Plan for Religious Education," *Religious Education* 4 (April 1909), 160.

75. Ross to Gallagher, January 3, 1916; also "Newman Club," brochure, 1922, p. 20, CAT, Newman Club.

76. Quoted in Joseph Wilson Cochran, "The University Pastorate Movement," *Religious Education* 8 (April 1913), 78.

77. *Daily Journal,* April 22, 1907. *The Catholic Universe,* May 3, 1907, described McQuaid and White as "intimate friends."

78. See William Douglas Mackenzie, "The Standardization of Theological Education," *Religious Education* 6 (August 1911), 253.

79. See R. V. Achatz, "Notes on Catholic Student Organizations, Purdue University, 1906–1914," prepared for interview at Aurora, Ind., July 9, 1964; *The Catholic Student* 1 (April 1915), 55–57; "History of the Newman Club at U.C.," *The Monitor,* September 17, 1927. Also interviews, Alvin R. Kutchera, Madison, Wis., June 9, Peter Leo Johnson, Madison, Wis., June 15, 1964, and Edward Lange, Austin, Tex., July 21, 1965. See also lists of members published in year books, e.g., *The Cactus* (Austin), 1920, n.p. Hengell regarded national parishes as "a problem." *Capital Times* (Madison, Wis.), January 6, 1930.

80. Farrell (Cambridge, Mass.) to O'Connell (Washington, D.C.), January 16, 1907.

81. "A Student's Impression of Newman Hall at Berkeley," *The Monitor,* August 21, 1920.

82. Sister M. Andrew Jackson, O.P. (Austin) to the writer, August 7, 1965.

83. A number of such quotations appear in a manuscript prepared by Mrs. Thomas F. (Bride Neill) Taylor, CAT, Bride Neill Taylor Papers.

84. See Francis J. Cassilly, S.J., "Catholic Students at State Universities: a Growing Educational Problem," *CEA Reports* 3 (1906), 111–17.

85. James A. Burns, C.S.C., "Position and Prospects of the Catholic College," *Bulletin of the Educational Conference of the Priests of the Holy Cross* 2 (January, 1928), 46.

86. Cassilly, loc. cit.

87. See William J. Bergin, C.S.V., "The Conservation of Our Educational Resources," *CEA Reports* 14 (1917), 60–61, 64–66.

88. See ch. 12, pp. 151ff.

89. Thomas Shahan, Rector of The Catholic University of America, quoted in *CEA Reports* 14 (1917), 169.

90. See above, note 46.

91. See above, note 61.

92. E. W. Leach (Minneapolis) to Hengell, November 19, 1909; Louis William Doll, "History of the Student Chapel," ms., n.d., pp. 8ff., ANCU-Mich.

93. Reported in *The Catholic Citizen*, December 29, 1906.

94. Quoted in ibid., September 14, 1907.

95. Felix Thomas Seroczynski, "The Catholic Student," *The Catholic Student* 2 (November 15, 1910), 10.

4. THE ONLY ALTERNATIVE

1. Interview, Aurora, Ind., July 9, 1964.

2. Daniel Sheehan (Iowa City, Iowa) to H. C. Hengell (Madison, Wis.), December 22, 1907; same to same, March 13; and Achatz (Lafayette, Ind.), to Hengell, March 12, 1908, SPC, Hengell Papers.

3. *The Catholic Student* 2 (November 15, 1910), 7-8.

4. Ibid.

5. See entry, April 26, 1908, Minute Book, Spalding Guild, ANHUI.

6. Archbishop John J. Keane of Dubuque, Iowa, agreed to serve "until a more active prelate could be secured." *The Catholic Student* 1 (April 1, 1915), 4-5.

7. Interview with R. V. Achatz.

8. According to the draft of a letter in Hengell's handwriting, undated. In 1915 an officer of the CSAA urged the priest to attend a forthcoming meeting "in view of the sentiments expressed in his letter." The draft letter and a letter from Mary C. Kelly (Humboldt, Iowa) to Hengell, November 11, 1915, are both in SPC, Hengell Papers. About this time "Newman clubs all over the United States" were "planning to make a national organization" according to the *Southern Messenger* (San Antonio), February 5, 1914.

9. See *Newman Quarterly* 3 (November 1918), 19-20; and "The Federation of College Catholic Clubs," pamphlet, 1921, p. 10, AACHSP, Keogh Papers, box II.

10. *The Catholic Student* began publication in September 1909; after reorganization of the national association in 1914 a second series was begun. The four extant issues, upon which this section is based, are: 1 (September 1909); 2 (November 15, 1910); 1 (April 1, 1915); 2 (April 1916).

11. "Interview with James Kieran: The Federation of College Catholic Clubs, Its Rise and Early History," *Newman Quarterly* 5 (Summer 1921), 134; John W. Keogh, "A Jewish Convert Woman Lays Foundation of the Federation," typescript, ribbon copy, n.d., 2 pp., AACHSP, Keogh Papers, box II.

12. Frank W. Demuth, "Federation of College Catholic Clubs of New York," *The Catholic Student* 2 (April 1916), 8-9. See also Demuth (New York) to Keogh (Philadelphia), May 10, 1960, in which the former cites diary entries in recounting events between September 1915 and June 1917, AACHSP, Keogh Papers, box II.

13. Quoted in "Newmanites," *Newman Quarterly* 10 (Summer 1926), 17.

14. "Your Vacation and Ours," pamphlet, 1916, n.p., ANCCU, Demuth Papers; *Newman Quarterly* 2 (November 1917), 2.

15. Quoted in *Newman Quarterly* 1 (June 1917), 1.

16. "Purpose," ibid. (March 1917), 2–3. Some convention minutes are in ribbon copy in ANNA, but for the most part we must rely upon the files of the *Quarterly*.

17. *Newman Quarterly* 2 (November 1917), 3–5; Keogh, "Report to Cardinal Dougherty, 1918," "Preface" and p. 70, AACHSP, Keogh Papers, box labeled "Notebook."

18. "Albany Province Meeting," *Newman Quarterly* 5 (Summer 1921), 151.

19. Interview, Msgr. John J. Donnelly, Philadelphia, August 5, 1964.

20. See reports in *Newman Quarterly* 3 (November 1918), 21, 24–25, and (March 1919), 19.

21. Quoted in A. I. du Pont Coleman, "The Tenth Legion," *Newman Quarterly* 4 (March 1920), 55.

22. David Rosenstein, "Old Poetry for New," *City College Alumnus* 23 (June 1926), 269–70.

23. "Commemorative Brochure," June 4, 1949, n.p., ANCCU.

24. Interview, Joseph Van Horn, Philadelphia, August 3, 1964.

25. Biographical data on Keogh can be found in Chancery Files, Archdiocese of Philadelphia. See also obituary in *Evening Bulletin* (Philadelphia), October 15, 1960, and the short biography in *National Newman News* 1 (November 1960), 4.

26. "Address to Chaplains," typescript, ribbon copy, 1955, n.p., AACHSP, Keogh Papers, box labeled "Keogh."

27. Keogh, "Report to Cardinal Dougherty, 1930," typescript, ribbon copy, 27 pp., Part III, p. 3, AAP, Newman Club.

28. From Donnelly's eulogy, a copy of which is in ANNA, Chaplain's Correspondence, 1960–61.

29. Fathers James H. Ryan and John A. O'Brien were also mentioned. See Monahan (Washington, D.C.) to Austin Dowling (St. Paul), March 17, 1921, mimeograph, ACUA, Pace Correspondence, NCWC Department of Education, 1919–23. Coleman described these developments to Demuth (New York), April 10, 1921, ANCCU.

30. Coleman (New York) to Keogh (Philadephia), September 21, 1920, ANCCU.

31. *Newman Quarterly* 4 (December 1919), 29.

32. "Resumé of the Convention," ibid., 6 (Autumn 1921), 22. The field secretary was William F. Starsinic, who apparently served in this capacity from the opening of the school year in 1921 until the summer of 1924. Meanwhile, Monahan hired John A. Kennedy who served the NCWC in a similar capacity from April 1921 until sometime in 1923, when Charles N. Lischka replaced him. See Minutes of the Annual Convention, July 2–7, 1923, Federation of College Catholic Clubs, p. 12, ANNA, Convention Minutes, 1923. Available records do not make precise dating possible. What is important is the irony of *two* organizers suddenly coming on the scene and working quite independently of each other.

33. Coleman, "The Tenth Legion," p. 55.

34. "Progress," *Newman Quarterly* 4 (June 1920), 99.

35. Ibid. (March 1920), pp. 54–55, and 5 (Summer 1921), 148–49; also "Newsletter" [of the Tenth Legion], June and October, 1920, n.p., ANCCU.

36. See Williams, "The Catholic Program of Reconstruction," *Newman*

Quarterly 3 (June 1919), 4–8; Ryan, "The Colleges and Social Reconstruction," ibid., 4 (March 1920), 47–48, and "The Social Question," ibid., 5 (Summer 1921), 115; also Charles Briehl, "The Revolt Against Industrialism," ibid., 8 (Fall 1923), 10, 30; "Dr. Allison of Yale on the Middle Ages," ibid., 7 (Fall 1922), 6; Katherine Bregy, "Stray Thoughts on the Catholicity of Non-Catholic Art," ibid., 6 (Autumn 1921), 3–5; Hugh P. Smith, "The Catholic Church and Evolution," ibid., 7 (Fall 1922), 8–10; and Charles Briehl, "The Psychology of the Subconscious," ibid., 4 (March 1920), 83–85.

37. "The Aim of the Federation," ibid., 6 (Spring 1922), 86.

38. To Dennis Duffy (Minneapolis), February 21, 1950, AACHSP, Keogh Papers, box I. In addition to organizers working out of Monahan's bureau who assured the federation that it was part of the NCWC Education Department (Minutes of the Annual Convention, July 2–7, 1923, Federation of College Catholic Clubs, p. 12, ANNA, "Convention Minutes, 1923") representatives of the NCWC Councils of Men and Women were also inviting the federation to affiliate with them ("Resumé of Convention," *Newman Quarterly* 6 (Autumn 1921), 15). As late as 1936 federation officers claimed membership in the former (Minutes of the Quarterly Meeting, October 25, 1936, Executive Committee, Newman Club Federation, ANNA, Executive Committee); although the NCWC denied this (Vincent Mooney [Washington, D.C.] to Joseph Van Horn [Philadelphia], April 5, 1934, ANNA, Youth Department).

39. Coleman quoted Keogh to this effect to Demuth, September 13, October 12, 1920, and July 13, 1921, ANCCU.

40. Keogh to Demuth, October 8, 1920.

41. Coleman to Demuth, July 13, 1921; and "Resumé of the Convention," *Newman Quarterly* 6 (Autumn 1921), 22.

42. Keogh to Mrs. Charles O'Toole (Bronxville, N.Y.), February 13, 1957, AACHSP, Keogh Papers, box II, and to John Kieran (New York), November 9, 1955, ibid., box I.

43. To Demuth, July 13, 1921.

44. Ibid.

45. Coleman to Keogh, October 15, 1922.

46. "Password" [Bulletin of the Tenth Legion], mimeograph, August 1924, pp. 1–2, ANCCU.

47. To Duffy, February 21, 1950.

48. Minutes of the Quarterly Meeting, August 27, 1921, Executive Committee, Federation of College Catholic Clubs, in *Newman Quarterly* 6 (Autumn 1921), 15.

49. "Dear Newmanite," form letter, April 5, 1929, ANNA, Executive Committee.

50. "Resumé of the Convention," *Newman Quarterly* 6 (Autumn 1921), 22. See also above, n. 32.

51. Minutes of the Annual Convention, July 2–7, 1923, Federation of College Catholic Clubs, pp. 4, 8; and "Speech of Mr. O'Toole on Toronto's Withdrawal," *Newman Quarterly* 9 (Fall 1924), 13, 29.

52. "Annual Convention of the Federation," ibid., pp. 23–24.

53. Interview, Joseph B. Hearn, Philadelphia, August 4, 1964.

54. Quoted in Thomas Swain, "Plan of Organization," *Newman Quarterly* 10 (Winter 1926), 7.

55. Minutes of the Annual Convention, July 3–6, 1922, Federation of College Catholic Clubs, p. 2.

56. "Report . . . 1918," preface.

57. "Have We Made a Mistake?" *Newman News* 12 (November 1927), 3.

58. To Dougherty (Philadelphia), June, n.d., 1920, AACHSP, Keogh Papers, box II.

59. To Peter Dufee, O.F.M. (New York), March 10, 1938, ibid., box labeled "Letters."

60. Interview, Msgr. John J. Donnelly, Philadelphia, August 5, 1964.

61. Henry J. Browne, "A History of the Catholic Church in the United States," in Louis J. Putz, ed., *The Catholic Church U.S.A.* (Chicago: Fides Publishers, 1956), p. 36.

62. Keogh, "Report to Cardinal Dougherty, 1926," typescript, ribbon copy, 4 pp., pp. 2–4, AAP, Newman Club.

5. RELIGION SUFFERED IN COLLEGE

1. Joseph T. Karcher, *A Catholic Layman Speaks* (Sayreville, N.J.: Academy Press, 1955), p. 184.

2. William Michael Halsey, *The Survival of American Innocence: Catholicism in an Era of Disillusionment, 1920–1940,* pp. 4–36, 169–71.

3. Michael Joseph Curley (Baltimore) to John K. Cartwright (Washington, D.C.), April 26, 1927, AAB, Curley Papers, 1922–47, Car-Cass.

4. Henry S. Commager, *The American Mind* (New Haven, Conn.: Yale University Press, 1950), p. 193.

5. "Pastoral Letter of 1919" in Raphael M. Huber, ed., *Our Bishops Speak* (Milwaukee: Bruce Publishing Co., 1952), pp. 5, 10.

6. Archbishop Austin Dowling of St. Paul, quoted in *The Catholic Citizen* (Milwaukee), July 21, 1917.

7. Winfred Ernest Garrison, *Catholics and the American Mind* (Chicago: Willett, Clark, and Colby, 1928), p. 227; see also George N. Shuster, *The Catholic Spirit in America* (New York: Dial Press, 1927), p. 188.

8. Luigi Civardi, *A Manual of Catholic Action* (New York: Sheed and Ward, 1936), p. 105.

9. Callahan, *The Mind of the Catholic Layman,* pp. 83–90.

10. O. D. Foster, The American Association of Religion," typescript, ribbon copy, n.d., pp. 21–26, SCUI, Foster Papers, Notebook 13.

11. Ibid., pp. 87, 61–65.

12. Pius XI, "The Promotion of True Religious Unity," English language ed. of *Mortalium Animos,* January 6, 1928 (Washington, D.C.: National Catholic Welfare Conference, 1928).

13. Foster, "Genesis of the Iowa School of Religion," typescript, ribbon copy, n.d., pp. 5–8, SCUI, Foster Papers, Notebook 20; also, Seymour A. Smith, *Religious Cooperation in State Universities* (Ann Arbor: University of Michigan Press, 1957), pp. 27–30.

14. See correspondence between George Kay, M. Willard Lampe, and Bishop Henry P. Rohlman, SCUI, School of Religion, box 2, Catholic Participation.

15. John L. McKenzie, S.J., *The Roman Catholic Church* (New York: Holt, Rinehart and Winston, 1969), p. 22.

16. Letter, December 29, 1924, Protocol No. 301–9, and reply, February 15, 1925, AANY, Hayes Papers, V–9.

17. Interview, Joseph Hughes, Duluth, June 14, 1977; he added that Fumasoni-Biondi had lectured seminarians in St. Paul on the need of learning theology that was not only sound but was also taught in the Latin language.

18. We have only Hayes' reply of November 28, 1927, AANY.

19. To Joseph D. Connerton (Chicago), September 7, 1954, AACHSP, Keogh Papers, box I.

20. See "Resumé of the Minutes of the Tenth Annual Conference," *Newman Quarterly* 10 (Fall 1925), 9; "Constitution of the Federation of College Catholic Clubs," brochure, 1925, pp. 4–6, 10; "The Federation of College Catholic Clubs," brochure, 1921, p. 7.

21. See ch. 7, pp. 88ff.

22. "Pastoral Letter of 1919," p. 9.

23. Quoted in *Alumni Quarterly and Fortnightly Notes* (University of Illinois) 5 (November 1, 1919), 6.

24. "Report on Survey of Religious and Character Influences on State University and College Campuses in the Area West of the Rocky Mountains" (North American Board for the Study of Religion in Higher Education, 1933), mimeograph, pp. 5–8, SCUI, School of Religion Papers, box 5.

25. "Report of Senate Committee on Educational Policy, July 7, 1920," AUI, President's Papers, Kinley General Correspondence, box 20, University Senate.

26. See materials in folders labeled "Suggestions Regarding the Organization of Intercollegiate Schools of Religion" and "School of Religion Correspondence," SCUI, School of Religion Papers, box 1.

27. Interview, M. Willard Lampe, Iowa City, December 23, 1964.

28. O. D. Foster, "Developments at the University of California at Los Angeles," *Christian Education* 12 (November 1928), 105–09.

29. For Vincent see E. W. Blakeman, "The Church and State as Partners in Education," *Religious Education* 15 (April 1920), 115. For the faculty committee see "Minutes of the Meeting of Committee Considering a School of Religion at the University of Minnesota, February 17, 1926," AUMinn, Papers of the President's Office, Coffman Papers, 1927–28; italics in the original.

30. Quoted in C. F. Kent (New Haven, Conn.) to W. A. Jessup (Iowa City), April 5, 1922, SCUI, Jessup Papers, 1921–22, folder 59, School of Religion.

31. *Trends in American Sociology* (New York: Harper, 1929), pp. xi–xii.

32. Willard E. Hotchkiss, *Higher Education and Business Standards* (New York: Houghton Mifflin, 1918), p. 106.

33. Maurice Parmelee, "The Rise of Modern Humanitarianism," *American Journal of Sociology* 21 (November 1915), 34–59.

34. "General Declaration of Principles," *American Association of University Professors Bulletin* 1 (December 1915), 28.

35. O. D. Foster, "Critical View of the University Field," *Christian Education* 11 (March 1927), 362–63. See also David Cottrell, ed., *College Reading and Religion* (New Haven, Conn.: Yale University Press, 1948), pp. vii–ix, 116, 183, 229, 307, 324.

36. Quoted in Hugh Hawkins, *Pioneer: A History of the Johns Hopkins*

University, 1874-1889 (Ithaca, N.Y.: Cornell University Press, 1960), p. 309.

37. Burris A. Jenkins, quoted in *REA Proceedings* 1 (1904), 158–59.

38. *The Trend in Higher Education* (Chicago: University of Chicago Press, 1905), p. 56.

39. A. B. Hollingshead, "Climbing the Academic Ladder," *American Sociological Review* 5 (June 1940), 394; also, "Ingroup Membership and Academic Selection," ibid., 3 (December 1938), 836–42.

40. Quoted in Carl Murchison, ed., *A History of Psychology in Autobiography* (Worcester, Mass.: Clark University Press, 1930), pp. 194–95, 446–48.

41. William Houston, *The Church at the University: Her Opportunities, Obligations, and Methods* (Westminster Foundation of Ohio, 1926), p. 14; O. D. Foster, "Problems of Religious Cooperation," *Christian Education* 4 (June 1921), 42–43; James H. Leuba, *The Belief in God and Immortality* (Boston: Sherman, French and Co., 1916), pp. 221–81.

42. Charles I. Glicksburg, "The Religious Motif in Higher Education," *AAUP Bulletin* 43 (September 1937), 457.

43. Charles E. Raven, *Natural Religion and Christian Theology* (Cambridge: Cambridge University Press, 1953), pp. 193–94.

44. Hotchkiss, *Higher Education and Business,* p. 106.

45. *Religious Thought in the Last Quarter Century* (Chicago: University of Chicago Press, 1927), p. 111.

46. See Clark, "Paper before the Association of Deans of Men in the Middle West," *School and Society* 16 (July 15, 1922), 65.

47. See "Committee on Student Discipline" at November 16, 1923, Main Library, University of Texas, Files, Student Life.

48. To W. H. Twenhofel (Madison, Wis.), January 10, 1931, AUW-M, Series 5/87.

49. "Report of the Dean of Men," in *Report of the President* (University of Illinois, 1923–24), pp. 110–11, AUI.

50. See Edmund G. Williamson, *Student Personnel Services in Colleges and Universities* (New York: McGraw-Hill, 1961), p. 13.

51. "Prayer and Behavioral Adjustments," *International Journal of Ethics* 41 (October 1930), 75.

52. Ruth Barry and Beverly Wolf, *Modern Issues in Guidance-Personnel Work* (New York: Teachers' College, Columbia University, 1957), p. 78.

53. Quoted in AUW-M, Series 5/87.

54. Vera Somers Hopkins, "A Study of Some Opinions of Pomona College Students on Sex Relationships" (Bachelor's Thesis, Pomona College, Claremont, Calif., 1936), p. 15, SCPC.

55. "D. Clausen Survey," AUW-M, Series 5/87.

56. C. Gilbert Wrenn, "Philosophical and Psychological Bases of Personnel Services in Education" in Nelson B. Henry, ed., *Personnel Services in Education,* Fifty-eighth Yearbook of the National Society for the Study of Education, pt. 2 (Chicago: University of Chicago Press, 1959), p. 46. See also Joseph S. Zaccavia, "The Behavioral Sciences and the Identity Crisis of Student Personnel Work," *Journal of the National Association of Women's Deans and Counselors* 31 (Spring 1968), 103–05.

57. Nicholas Murray Butler, "Oration," *University Record* (Chicago) 9 (May 1904), 13–17.

58. *Report of the President* (Yale University, 1939–40), p. 8, AYU.

59. "Modernism versus Medievalism," *School and Society* 53 (January 4, 1941), 154.

60. See Oscar W. Firkins, *Cyrus Northrup: A Memoir* (Minneapolis: University of Minnesota Press, 1925), p. 502.

6. ALL THE WAY TO ROME

1. "Holy Father Commends Work of Newman Clubs," NCWC News Service (Washington, D.C.), May 15, 1922.

2. "Catholic Foundation Endorsed by Pope," *Daily American Tribune* (Dubuque, Iowa), November 14, 1922.

3. *NCWC Bulletin* 2 (February 1921), 9–10, 25.

4. James H. Ryan (Washington D.C.) to Edward A. Pace (Washington, D.C.), February 14, 1921, ACUA, Pace Correspondence, NCWC Department of Education, 1919–23.

5. Coleman (New York) to Frank Demuth (New York), April 10, 1921, ANCCU, Demuth Papers; see also Monahan's "Monthly Report" for November and December 1921, ACUA, Pace Correspondence.

6. "Newman Clubs' Aims Defined by Education Bureau," NCWC News Service, May 23, 1921.

7. Monahan, "Catholic Clubs in State Universities and Non-Catholic Colleges," *NCWC Bulletin* 4 (November 1922), 22; "The Newman Club Idea," *NCWC Editorial Sheet* 2 (February 1922), n.p., AANY, Hayes Correspondence.

8. "Resumé of the Conference," *Newman Quarterly* 6 (Autumn 1921), 22.

9. Monahan to Austin Dowling (St. Paul), March 17, 1921, mimeograph, ACUA, Pace Correspondence.

10. Pace to Ryan, February 12, 1921, in ibid.

11. Minutes of the Annual Convention, July 2–7, 1923, Federation of College Catholic Clubs, p. 12, ANNA, Convention Minutes, 1923.

12. Elizabeth B. Page, "Higher Education in Catholic Schools," *NCWC Bulletin* 5 (July 1923), 20; "Training for Lay Leadership," *Catholic School Interests* 1 (August 1922), 10.

13. Editorial, *America* 33 (October 3, 1925), 592.

14. Albert C. Fox, S.J. (Prairie du Chien, Wis.) to Francis W. Howard (Cleveland), November 29, 1919, ANCEA, Howard Papers.

15. Ryan, "Catholic College Week—April 30 to May 6," *NCWC Bulletin* 3 (April 1922), 2.

16. Ibid., p. 3.

17. Ibid., p. 4.

18. "Catholic College Week Widely Observed," *NCWC Bulletin* 4 (June 1922), 29.

19. See "Instructions for the Meeting of the Bishops, June 22, 1922" in Ellis, *Documents of American Catholic History,* 633–35.

20. "The Teaching of Christian Doctrine," *NCWC Bulletin* 4 (November 1922), 21.

21. Administrative Committee, "The Programme ... Proposed for the Coming Meeting of the Bishops," leaflet, August 12, 1922, n.p., AANY, P–13, Varia: Education, 1907–20.

22. Bureau of Education, *Education in a Democracy* (Washington, D.C.: NCWC Press, 1923), *Educational Bulletin* 5, p. 3.

23. Ryan, "Catholic College Week—April 30 to May 6," p. 2.

24. For a fuller discussion see David B. Tyack, "The Perils of Pluralism," *American Historical Review* 74 (October 1968), 74ff.

25. Charles Lischka summarized the survey in a final effort to keep Newman clubs before Catholic educators in his "The Attendance of Catholic Students at Non-Catholic Colleges and Universities," *CEA Reports* 22 (1925), 103. John Elliott Ross, the Paulist chaplain who conducted the study, published it as "Catholics in Non-Catholic Colleges" in *Religious Education* 21 (August 1926), 399–403; the ms. of the study is in ACSP, Ross Papers.

26. "Catholic Institutions for Higher Education," *NCWC Bulletin* 6 (February 1925), 18–20.

27. Notice in ibid., 7 (June 1926), p. 12.

28. James A. Burns, C.S.C., quoted in *The Catholic Citizen* (Milwaukee), May 23, 1925. See also his "The Position and Prospects of the Catholic College," *NCEA Reports* 24 (1927), 129, and *Directory of Catholic Colleges and Schools, 1932-33* (Washington, D.C.: NCWC Department of Education, 1933), p. 29.

29. Interviews, Fathers John A. O'Brien, Notre Dame University, May 21, 1965, and Edward V. Cardinal, C.S.V., Chicago, June 5, 1963. See also Matthew Hoehn, O.S.B., ed., *Catholic Authors* (Newark, N.J.: St. Mary's Abbey, 1948), pp. 581–83.

30. Senate Committee on Educational Policy, "Report of July 7, 1920," AUI, Kinley, General Correspondence, box 20, University Senate.

31. To O'Brien, April 15, 1920, as published in O'Brien, "The Catholic Foundation at the University of Illinois," pamphlet, 1922, p. 20, Personel Files, John A. O'Brien, University of Notre Dame.

32. See architect's drawing and caption describing "a Catholic college, almost upon the campus of a state university" in *NCWC Bulletin* 4 (November 1922), 21. Keogh claimed that the donor of $100,000 to the project insisted upon the term to Joseph Connerton (Chicago), September 7, 1954, AACHSP, Keogh Papers, box I.

33. "A Ghost in Its Flight," pamphlet, 1925, pp. 4–6, 16, Personal Files, O'Brien, University of Notre Dame; emphasis O'Brien's.

34. "The Need of Jesuit Universities," *Woodstock Letters* 54 (1925), 238–48.

35. For exposures of secular campuses and arguments favoring Catholic ones see "Catholics at Non-Catholic Universities," *America* 33 (August 22, 1925), 455–56; "Morals at Non-Catholic Universities," 33 (August 29, 1925), 479–80; "Courses at Catholic Universities," 33 (September 18, 1925), 552–53; "Are Catholic Universities Inferior?" 33 (September 26, 1925), 576–78; "Catholic Colleges for Women," 33 (October 3, 1925), 599–600; and "A Reply to Mr. Quinlan," 34 (November 7, 1925), 83. For personal attacks on O'Brien see "A Catholic Foundation Unmasked," 34 (December 19, 1925), 226–28, and "Catholic Foundations and Canon Law," 34 (February 2, 1926), 277–78.

36. Mario Barbera, S.J., "Fondazioni Cattoliche nelle Universita Dello Stato in America," *Civiltà Cattolicà* 2 (May 1926), 337–45, and "Stato Presente Della Scuole e La Questione Delle 'Fondazioni Cattoliche' Negli S. U.," ibid., 4 (October 1926), 113–26.

37. "In Place of the Foundation," *America* 34 (February 13, 1926), 425–26; emphasis LaFarge's.

38. "Chaplaincy, Newman Club, or Catholic College?" *America* 34 (September 4, 11, 18, 1926), 488–89, 515–17, 536–37.

39. Quoted in *The Catholic Review* (Baltimore), May 21, 1926.

40. "Resolutions," *NCEA Reports* 23 (1926), 86–87.

41. To Henry C. Hengell (Madison, Wis.), November 19, 1925, SPC, Hengell Papers.

42. A copy of this ms., "The Catholic Foundation at the University of Illinois" is in AAB, Curley Papers, 1922–27, O–O'Connell.

43. *Catholic School Interests* 5 (April 1926), 3–5.

44. "No Substitute for Catholic College," ibid. (June 1926), 99.

45. To Curley, February 11, 1926, AAB, Curley Papers; see also February 1 and 3.

46. To O'Brien, March 2, 1926, AAB, Curley Papers.

47. "Father O'Brien Replies to Archbishop Curley," typescript, ribbon copy, "Catholic Foundation News Services" release, April 18, 1927, ANNA, Former Chaplains.

48. Curley to John K. Cartwright (Washington, D.C.), April 26, 1917, AAB, Curley Papers.

49. Issues of January 8, 11, and 12, 1927.

50. Gabriel Zema, S.J., "Catholic Foundations in Secular Universities," *Woodstock Letters* 57 (1928), 14–32.

51. According to John W. Keogh, "Report to Cardinal Dougherty, 1926," typescript, ribbon copy, n.p., AAP, Keogh Papers, Newman Club.

52. O'Brien was researching a book on evolution for which he wanted Pierre Teilhard de Chardin to write the foreword (see correspondence with Edward C. Messenger [Ware, England], October 14, 1928, ANHUI, Evolution). He submitted four articles on the subject to *Newman News*. The first appeared because the student editor did not submit it to Keogh. Upon its publication, Keogh would not allow the others to be printed because they seemed "to over-favor the scientists against the theologians." See their exchange of letters of February 1931, AACHSP, Keogh Papers, Files, E; and O'Brien, "Evolution and Religion," *Newman News* 15 (November 1930), 5. Keogh discussed what he regarded as O'Brien's aloofness with Alvin R. Kutchera (Madison, Wis.), December 22, 1938, SPC, Kutchera Papers, and with Agnes Collins (Washington, D.C.), May 18, 1931, ANNA, Misc. Box. O'Brien confirmed his preoccupation with local affairs in an interview, Notre Dame University, July 5, 1964.

53. Keogh, "Report to Cardinal Dougherty, 1926," covering letter dated September 2, 1926, AAP, Keogh Papers, Newman Club.

54. "Report to Cardinal Dougherty, 1930," typescript, ribbon copy, p. 6, in ibid.

55. Minutes of the Quarterly Meeting, March 13, 1926, Executive Committee, Federation of College Catholic Clubs, n.p., ANNA, Minutes of Executive Meetings, 1926. Father James Ryan Hughes, M.M., confirmed this account in his letter to this writer from Kyoto, Japan, September 4, 1965.

56. See Hughes, "Encyclical 'Acerbo Nimis' of Pius X," pamphlet, Philadelphia, 1929, 4 pp. unnumbered, AACHSP, Keogh Papers, box II; also

issued with a cover reading "School of Religion in *Acerbo Nimis* of Pius X," copy in SPC, Kutchera Papers.

57. Monsignor Joseph M. Corrigan, the archdiocesan censor, quoted in Keogh to Harry J. Towey (St. Paul), October 14, 1947, AACHSP, Keogh Papers, box labeled "Keogh."

58. Letter to the writer, September 4, 1965.

59. As related by Parsons to Edward J. Duff, S.J., and by Duff (Worcester, Mass.), to this writer, April 7, 1976.

60. See Pius XI, "On the Christian Education of Youth" in Gerald Treacy, S.J., ed., *Five Great Encyclicals* (New York: Paulist Press, 1939), p. 43. Father John A. O'Brien confirmed Parsons' influence in his letter to this writer of April 19,1976.

61. H. G. Takkenberg, "The Iowa School of Religion," *America* 44 (February 28, March 7, 1931), 504–06, 527–29.

62. See *America* 46 (January 23, 1932), 377–79.

63. In his letter of February 7, 1965 to this writer, Father Edward F. Hagemann, S.J., "quite distinctly" remembered being told this by Father James F. Donovan, S.J., associate editor at *America* from October 15, 1932 to September 9, 1933. Some Newman chaplains knew of the rebuke. See George B. Ford (Columbia University) to Msgr. Francis McIntyre (New York), January 22, 1940, Personal Files, John Ricketts, Philadelphia.

64. See William J. McGucken, S.J., *The Catholic Way in Education* (Milwaukee: Bruce Publishing Co., 1934), pp. 84–87.

65. Garvin (New York) to David Kinley (Urbana, Ill.), December 16, 1925. AUI, Kinley, General Correspondence, 1925, box 126, Columbus Foundation (an earlier name for O'Brien's project.)

66. Father Robert Drinan, S.J., quoted by Richard Butler, O.P., *Witness to Change* (River Forest, Ill.: The Priory Press, 1976), p. 121.

67. Ryan, "Catholic College Week—April 30 to May 6," p. 2.

68. See above, n. 36.

69. See John J. McDevitt, "Catholic Action in the Newman Club," *Newman News* 23 (October 1938), 2.

7. EDUCATIONAL APOSTOLATE OR YOUTH MOVEMENT?

1. See John Higham, *Strangers in the Land: Patterns of American Nativism 1860-1925* (New York: Athaneum, 1963), pp. 264ff.

2. Interview, Earl Harrington, Milwaukee, June 24, 1964.

3. "Catholic Institutions for Higher Education," *NCWC Bulletin* 8 (June 1926), 12.

4. "Secular Universities and Catholic Students," *The Acolyte* 3 (April 9, 1927), 10ff; see also "Marquette Student" to Hengell (Madison, Wis.), June 7, 1926, SPC, Hengell Papers.

5. To O'Brien (Champaign, Ill.), February 14, 1922, AUND, Burns' Papers.

6. James E. Moran quoted Keogh in "The Newman Idea," *Newman Quarterly* 7 (Spring, 1923), 6; see also "Newmanism," ibid., 5 (Summer 1921), 142.

7. "The Convention," ibid., 11 (November 1926), 10, 14.

8. "Pittsburgh Convention, 1927," *Newman News* 12 (November 1927), 11; Cuthbert Goeb, O.S.B., "What is the Mass?" ibid., 12 (March, April, May 1928), 1, 8, 16; 1, 5, 10; 10–11; Keogh, "Newman Clubs' Interest in Liturgical Music," typescript, ribbon copy, 1928, n.p., AACHSP. Keogh Papers, File 1.

9. Account of this conversation is in Keogh, "Notebook," holograph, entry for September 8, 1916, AACHSP, Keogh Papers, box labeled "Keogh."

10. Hengell's comment appears in *Our Sunday Visitor* (Fort Wayne, Ind.), July 21, 1918. Keogh wrote Hengell for verification (July 31, 1928, Hengell Papers). Giobbio, a priest of the Archdiocese of Milan, became a monsignor on December 29, 1901. For unknown reasons he resigned from curial work in 1909 to become a Jesuit. See Mark A. Calegari, S.J. (Rome) to the writer, June 23, 1966.

11. "Minutes of the Thirteenth Annual Conference, July 2–4, 1928," pamphlet, 1928, p. 5, AACHSP, Keogh Papers, box II.

12. "Report . . . , 1930," pp. 7–8, 12–13, AAP, Keogh Papers, Newman Club.

13. See above, ch. 2, p. 26.

14. Keogh (Philadelphia) to George Garrelts (Minneapolis), July 30 and 31, 1959, AACHSP, Keogh Papers, box II; and to Angela Perone (Washington, D.C.), February 9, 1951, ANNA, History.

15. Quoted in Arthur Alonso, O.P., *Catholic Action and the Laity* (St. Louis, Mo.: Herder, 1961), p. 117.

16. Callahan, *Mind of the Catholic Layman,* pp. 86–87. In January 1932 the *NCWC Review* began to appear under the new title, *Catholic Action.*

17. Minutes of the Quarterly Meeting, February 1, 1941, National Executive Committee of the Federation of College Catholic Clubs, n.p., ANNA, Executive Committee Minutes, 1941.

18. John J. McDevitt, "Catholic Action in the Newman Club," *Newman News* 23 (October, 1928), 2.

19. "The Cincinnati Convention," ibid., 14 (November, 1929), 3.

20. See Pius XI, *"Non Abbiamo Bisogno"* (Washington, D.C.: NCWC Press, 1931), p. 15, and *"Mortalium Animos"* (Washington, D.C.: NCWC Press, 1928), passim.

21. Minutes of the Eighteenth Annual Convention, July 6–8, 1933, National Federation of College Catholic Clubs, n.p., ANNA, Convention Minutes.

22. To "Miss White" (address unknown), December 12, 1931, ANNA, Pax Romana, 1937–40; and to John Ricketts (Philadelphia), December 12, 1943, AACHSP, Keogh Papers, box labeled "Keogh."

23. "Open Letter," *Newman News* 20 (March 1936), 13.

24. Margaret Bighain (Poughkeepsie, N.Y.) to Margaret Ann Hogan (Natick, Mass.), May 8, 1936, ANNA, External Affairs Dept. 1956–57.

25. Quoted in *The Philadelphia Record,* July 12, 1936.

26. Quoted in *The Evening Union* (Atlantic City), July 11, 1936.

27. "The American Student Union, the Y.M.C.A. and the Y.W.C.A.," typescript, ribbon copy of address, 1936, p. 4, AACHSP, Keogh Papers, box labeled "Keogh."

28. Keogh recounted these reactions to Boyd S. Newborne (New York), January 18, 1938, ANNA, Convention Minutes, 1936.

29. Same to same, February 22, 1938.

30. Charles Schwartz, "Catholics Don't Co-operate," *Newman News* 22 (February 1938), 2; also Schwartz (New York) to Edward Hawkes (Philadelphia), March 27, 1937, ANNA, *Newman News* Correspondence.

31. To Peter B. Duffee (New York), March 10, 1938, AACHSP, Keogh Papers, box labeled "Letters."

32. Johanna Doniat, "A Brief History of Childerly," pamphlet, 1946, p. 3, Personal Files, Johanna Doniat, Milwaukee, Wis.

33. See Doniat, "The Chapter of St. Thomas," *The Dominican Bulletin* (Winter 1950), pp. 14–16; also interviews, Johanna Doniat, Milwaukee, June 10, 1964, and George Dunn, Washington, D.C., September 3, 1964.

34. Minutes of the Quarterly Meeting, October 25, 1936, Executive Committee of the Federation of College Catholic Clubs, ANNA, Executive Committee Minutes, 1936.

35. Quoted in Keogh (Philadelphia) to John F. Cullinan (Altoona, Pa.), July 27, 1937, ANNA, Misc. Correspondence, 1937–40.

36. See above, ch. 6, pp. 78ff.

37. *Catholic Telegraph* (Cincinnati), December 5, 19, 1929; Keogh, "Report of the Chaplain," *Newman News* 15 (November 1930), 13.

38. Interview, Joseph B. Hearn, Philadelphia, August 4, 1964.

39. "Responsibility of the Church for Catholic Students Attending Secular Colleges," *CCD Proceedings,* 1938, 35–38.

40. NCWC News Service, July 12, 13, 1937; see also "Proceedings of the National Catechetical Congress of the Confraternity of Christian Doctrine" for these years, on file in the Confraternity Center, United States Catholic Conference, Washington, D.C.

41. Minutes of the Annual Conference, September 8–10, 1939, National Newman Club Federation, p. 64, ANNA, Convention Minutes.

42. Ibid., pp. 36–37.

43. Minutes of the Quarterly Meeting, December 28–29, 1950, Executive Committee of the National Newman Club Federation, p. 15, ANNA, Executive Committee Minutes, 1950.

44. Quoted in "Symposium," *America* 66 (November 15, 1941), 148.

45. Keogh, "Report . . . , 1930," pp. 6–10.

46. "Treasurer's Report, 1939," ANNA, Financial Reports, 1939.

47. Minutes of the Twenty-third Annual Conference, September 2–4, 1938, National Newman Club Federation, n.p., ANNA, Convention Minutes, 1938.

48. To Vincent Mooney, C.S.C. (Washington, D.C.), December 21, 1938, ANNA, National Chaplains, 1929–40.

49. Mooney to Donald Cleary (Ithaca, N.Y.), December 29, 1941, in ibid., Chaplains' Letters, 1929–46. For officers see list in Sister M. Alexander Gray, O.S.F., "The Development, Organization, and Operation of the Newman Club Movement in American Education" (Diss., Catholic Univ. of America, 1962), app. III, pp. 290–301.

50. *Catholic Action* 16 (March 1934), 14. Mooney to Joseph Van Horn (Philadelphia), August 15, 1939, ANNA, Historical Information, 1934–38.

51. Pius XI, "De Actione Catholica Aptius Provehenda," *Acta Apostolicae Sedis* 27 (October 27, 1935, 159–64.

52. Mooney to Paul Tanner (Milwaukee), December 11, 1939, ANNA, National Chaplains, 1929–40.

53. Ibid.

54. Mooney to William Ferree (Washington, D.C.), July 6, 1939, and Ferree to Mooney, July 7, 1939, ANNA, Pax Romana, 1937–46.

55. Figures from Damien Lyons, O.F.M., "Statistical Survey of the Catholic Youth Movement in the United States," *Franciscan Educational Conference* 20 (June 1938), 52.

56. "DALsj" [Daniel A. Lord, S.J.], "Confidential Report on the Catholic Youth Meeting," quoted in full in Mooney to Tanner, December 11, 1938, ANNA, National Chaplains, 1929–40. See also Mooney to Keogh, December 30, 1938, in ibid.

57. Tanner to Mooney, January 20, 1939, in ibid.

58. National Office, NFCCS, "National Federation of Catholic College Students" (Washington, D.C.: NCWC Youth Department, 1941), pp. 2–9.

59. Keogh to Mooney, December 21, 1938, ANNA, National Chaplains, 1929–40.

60. See the papal letter in *Catholic Action* 22 (June 1940), 20; and interview, Msgr. Paul Tanner, Executive Secretary, NCWC, Washington, D.C., August 5, 1964.

61. *Catholic Action* 22 (August 1940), 5, 13.

62. Ibid., 23 (January 1941), 8.

63. Quoted in *Newman News* 25 (Fall 1940), 2.

64. Mooney to Cleary, December 1, 1941, ANNA, National Chaplains, 1929–46.

65. Cleary to Ann Metzger (Cincinnati), June 23, 1942, in ibid.; list of officers is in Gray, "The Development . . . of the Newman Club Movement . . . ," pp. 296ff.

66. Mooney to Cleary, December 29, 1941, ANNA, National Chaplains, 1929–46.

67. Compare "The Constitution and By-Laws of the Newman Club Federation," leaflet, 1938, 2 pp., AACHSP, Keogh Papers, box labeled "Keogh," with Donald M. Cleary, ed., *Newman Club Federation: A Manual for Newman Leaders* (Washington, D.C.: NCWC Youth Department, 1942), pp. 36–41.

68. A. G. Cigognani, "To the Reverend Diocesan Youth Directors," pamphlet, August 25, 1941, NCWC Youth Department, pp. 4–5.

69. See Cleary, *Newman Club Federation*, passim.

70. See *America* 35, 536.

71. See Minutes of the Quarterly Meeting, November 16, 1941, National Executive Committee of the National Newman Club Federation, ANNA, National Executive Committee Minutes.

72. John LaFarge, *The Jesuits in Modern Times* (New York: The America Press, 1928), p. 84; see also Charles A. Hart, "Catholic Action and the Catholic College," *Catholic Action* 28 (August 1946), 6–7, and (September 1946), 6–8, which, in listing collegiate organizations for Catholic Action, omit any reference to Newman clubs or the federation.

8. FEDERATION RUNNING STRONG

1. Statistics on file in ANNA, Executive Secretary. However, Martin W. Davis estimated Catholic enrollments in secular institutions to be closer to

200,000 in 1940. See *The Sister as Campus Minister* (Washington, D.C.: Center for Applied Research in the Apostolate, 1970), pp. 7–9.

2. Interview, The Most Rev. Leo Pursley, Fort Wayne, Ind., July 10, 1964.

3. Robert E. Welch and Paul J. Hallinan, *The Newman Club in American Education* (Cleveland: National Association of Newman Club Chaplains, 1953), p. 4.

4. Minutes of the Quarterly Meeting, April 15–16, 1950, National Executive Committee of the National Newman Club Federation, ANNA, National Executive Committee Minutes.

5. "Dear Father—A Lay Youth Speaks about Youth Groups," *Orate Fratres* 24 (January 1950), 82–85.

6. Butler, *Witness to Change*, p. 94.

7. James W. Trent, *Catholics in College* (Chicago: University of Chicago Press, 1967), pp. 234–42.

8. Lawrence Menard, "Effect of the Newman Club on the Religious Commitment of Its Members," paper read at annual meeting of the American Catholic Sociological Society, Miami, 1966, in Robert Hassenger, ed., *The Shape of Catholic Higher Education* (Chicago: University of Chicago Press, 1967), p. 160, n. 252.

9. Kenneth Underwood, *The Church, The University, and Social Policy,* Vol. I: *Report of the Director* (Middletown, Conn.: Wesleyan University Press, 1969), pp. 129–38, 194–96. Although concerned principally with Protestant students, these conclusions appear to be representative of their Catholic counterparts.

10. See "Keep Your Members—Active," pamphlet, National Newman Club Federation, 1955, pp. 9–11; Butler, *Witness to Change*, p. 91, conversations with dozens of chaplains while attending annual meetings.

11. Clarence Manion to William V. Pinkel (Washington, D.C.), August 2, 1950, ANNA, National Officers' Reports, 1949–50.

12. Interviews, Alvin R. Kutchera, Madison, Wis., June 10, 1964, and Johanna Doniat, Milwaukee, June 25, 1964. See also George Barry Ford, *A Degree of Difference* (New York: Farrar, Straus, and Giroux, 1969), pp. 73ff.

13. Quoted from Newman's *Loss and Gain* in Paul J. Hallinan, ed., *Newman Club Manual* (Washington, D.C.: National Newman Club Federation, 1954), p. 22.

14. Robert Tracy (Baton Rouge, La.) to Robert J. Reynolds (New York), June 24, 1957, ANNA, Executive Secretary, 1956–57.

15. Religious Vocation Survey Reports, in ibid.

16. Minutes of the Quarterly Meeting, March 11, 1945, National Executive Committee of the National Newman Club Federation, n.p., ANNA, National Executive Committee: "Annual Report, December, 1948, Executive Secretary, Newman Club Federation," in ibid., Executive Secretary.

17. Philip Des Marais (Washington, D.C.) to Leonard Cowley (Minneapolis), October 1, 1948, ANNA, National Chaplains, 1956–58; emphasis is Des Marais'.

18. Virginia M. Morrissey (Boston) to "Dear Newmanite," July 2, 1943, in Minutes of Quarterly Meeting, September 9, 1945, National Executive Committee of the National Newman Club Federation, ANNA, Executive Committee.

19. Minutes of the Quarterly Meeting, April 15–16, 1950, National Executive Committee, in ibid.

20. Minutes of the Quarterly Meeting, December 4, 1950, National Executive Committee, in ibid.

21. Minutes of the Quarterly Meeting, December 29–31, 1955, National Executive Committee, ANNA, Convention Minutes.

22. Edward Duncan, "Newmanism Comes of Age," typescript, ribbon copy, May 15, 1951, n.p., AACHSP, Keogh Papers, box I.

23. Vincent A. Brown, ed., *The Responsible Catholic,* rev. ed. (Washington, D.C.: National Newman Club Federation), 1950, p. 19.

24. Quarterly Report, May 15, 1955, National Chaplain, Newman Club Federation, p. 1, ANNA, National Chaplains, 1954–56.

25. Sister Mary Aloysia Zuczuski, S.S.M., "The Nature and Function of the Newman Club in the Modern University" (Thesis, Canisius College, 1955), p. 17.

26. See above, ch. 5, p. 64.

27. Minutes of the Annual Convention, July 11–13, 1947, National Newman Club Federation, n.p., ANNA, Convention Minutes.

28. *Newman World* (Minneapolis), February 22, 1949; Minutes of the Quarterly Meeting, Winter 1953, National Executive Committee of the National Newman Club Federation, n.p., ANNA, Executive Committee; and Minutes of the Annual Convention, September 2–6, 1958, Newman Club Federation, in ibid., Convention Minutes.

29. Minutes of the Quarterly Meeting, Winter, 1953, National Executive Committee of the National Newman Club Federation, n.p., in ibid., Executive Committee.

30. Copies of these publications are in the writer's files; in some cases back issues are available from the clubs at the universities indicated.

31. "Report on 'Newman Magazine,'" 1959, ANNA, National Officer's Reports, 1956–59.

32. "Address to Participants in the World Congress of the Universal Movement for World Federation, April 6, 1951," in Vincent A. Yzermans, ed., *The Major Addresses of Pope Pius XII* (St. Paul, Minn.: North Central Publishing Company, 1961), I, 143.

33. See "External Affairs Department—NNCF," ANNA, National Officers' Reports, 1955.

34. "Newmanmission," typescript, ribbon copy, n.d., 4 pp. in ibid. for 1962 to 1963.

35. See "Report Filed by Four Newman Federation Representatives of the Chicago Congress, December 28–30, 1946," ANNA, Misc. Box. See also Henry W. Briefs, "After the International Union of Students: The Great Challenge," *Catholic Action* 39 (April 1948), 10–11; John L. Meyers, "History of the National Student Association," Report of the Chairman of the Newman Club Federation Delegation to the NSA Convention, April 1, 1948, and "Confidential Memorandum to All Chaplains" (1953), ANNA, External Affairs Department.

36. Meyers, "History of the National Student Association," p. 5.

37. Thomas A. Carlin (Washington, D.C.) to James J. Hannon (Jackson, Miss.), December 14, 1954, in ANNA, Executive Secretary, 1954–55.

38. Carlin to John W. Keogh (Philadelphia), July 24, 1959, AACHSP, Keogh Papers, box II. See also Bill Eckert, "Vienna Autopsy," *World Campus* 3 (October 1959), 1.

39. "External Affairs, The Apostolate to the Non-Catholic," ANNA, Na-

tional Officers' Reports, 1950–51; also letters in ibid., External Affairs Department, 1946–59.

40. See for example, "Report of Foreign Students' Committee, 1926," Federation of College Catholic Clubs, in ibid., Convention Minutes, 1926.

41. Donald Cleary (Ithaca, N.Y.) to Tess Marie Gorka (Washington, D.C.), April 10, 1942, in ibid., Exchange Program.

42. See "Report of the Aid to Foreign Students Committee, Newman Club, University of Texas, 1959," in ibid., External Affairs Department, 1956–57; "Special Project" in ibid., National Officers' Reports, 1949–50; and Gray, "The Development, Organization, and Operation of the Newman Club Movement in American Education," p. 123.

43. Herman Neusch (Washington, D.C.) to Leonard de Hoog (Fribourg), November 14, 1949, ANNA, Pax Romana, 1949–53, and to Edward Kirchner (Munich), December 6, 1949, and to Gannon F. Ryan (Syracuse, N.Y.), February 16, 1950, in ibid., D. P. Correspondence; Andrew J. O'Reilly, "The Foreign Student Opportunity," pamphlet, 1956, Newman Club Federation, pp. 2–4; Annual Report, November, 1957, Episcopal Moderator, Newman Club Federation, in ANNA, Episcopal Moderator.

44. Minutes of the Quarterly Meeting, December 2–3, 1949, National Executive Committee of the National Newman Club Federation, p. 7; same for March 25, 1956, and April 15, 1962 all in ANNA, Executive Committee.

45. Same for February 5, 1938, in loc. cit.; also William A. Bachman, "Catholics and Other People: Cooperation with Non-Catholics in Colleges and Universities," pamphlet, 1950, National Newman Chaplains' Association, n.p.

46. Annual Report, 1954, Executive Secretary, National Newman Club Federation, n.p., ANNA, Executive Secretary.

47. Quoted in NCWC News Service, September 13, 1948.

48. Minutes of the Thirty-sixth Annual Convention, June 15–18, 1950, National Newman Club Federation, ANNA, Convention Minutes; also NCWC News Service, June 19, 1950.

49. Editorial, "Newman Clubs at Mid-century," *America* 83 (June 3, 1950), 263.

50. "Newman Clubs—New Tasks and Opportunities," ibid., (September 9, 1950), pp. 583–88.

51. See above, ch. 6, p. 74.

9. WORKING ON THE SYSTEM

1. To Denis J. O'Connell (Washington, D.C.), January 8, 1907, ANCEA, Howard Papers.

2. See above, ch. 3, pp. 34ff.

3. See "Report to Cardinal Dougherty, 1926" and covering letter dated September 2, 1926, AAP, Keogh Papers, Newman Club.

4. Interviews, Alvin T. Kutchera and Helen C. White, Madison, Wis., June 9 and 12, 1964; Edward Lange, Austin, July 21, 1965; Bartholomew Fair, John H. Donnelly, and Rose Shovlen, Philadelphia, April 3, August 5, 1964, and December 15, 1965 respectively; also John A. O'Brien, Notre Dame, July 4–5, 1964.

5. Title of a promotional leaflet bound in *Newman Chaplains' Manual* (Washington, D.C.: National Newman Chaplains' Association, 1962), p. 22. The leaflet is dated 1959.

6. See James W. Trent, *Catholics in College: Religious Commitment and the Intellectual Life* (Chicago: University of Chicago Press, 1967), pp. 231ff.

7. See comments of professors in ch. 11, pp. 139ff; and see Christopher Dawson, *The Crisis of Western Education* (New York: Sheed and Ward, 1961), pp. 89, 99, 113–15, 169ff.

8. "A Few Facts about the National Newman Chaplains [sic] Association," typescript, ribbon copy, 1965, 2 pp., ANNA, National Chaplain, 1965–66.

9. Leonard Cowley (Minneapolis) to "Dear Father," August 10, 1949, ANNA, Chaplains' Reports.

10. Quarterly Report, December, 1953, National Chaplain, Newman Club Federation, p. 3, in ibid.

11. Hallinan (Cleveland) to Thomas Carlin (Washington, D.C.), May 17, 1954, in ibid.; and Minutes of the Annual Convention, September 1–5, 1954, Newman Club Federation, n.p., in ibid., Convention Minutes.

12. Quarterly Report, December 29, 1952, National Chaplain, Newman Club Federation, n.p., in ibid., Chaplains' Reports.

13. Minutes of the Annual Convention, August 30–September 4, 1955, Newman Club Federation, n.p., in ibid., Convention Minutes.

14. Same for September 2–6, 1958, in loc. cit.

15. Annual Report, 1958, National Chaplain, National Newman Club Federation, in ANNA, National Chaplain, 1958.

16. Quarterly Report, 1954, National Chaplain, Newman Club Federation, n.p., in ibid., Chaplains' Reports.

17. Annual Report, November, 1958, Episcopal Moderator, Newman Club Federation, in ibid., Episcopal Moderator.

18. Same for 1960, in loc. cit.

19. Robert E. Welch and Paul J. Hallinan, *The Newman Club in American Education* (Washington, D.C.: National Association of Newman Club Chaplains, 1953).

20. Hallinan and Welch, Washington, D.C., 1956.

21. By the Chaplains' Association, Washington, D.C., 1955.

22. No longer available; cited in Annual Report, November, 1956, Episcopal Moderator, Newman Club Federation, ANNA, Episcopal Moderator.

23. Published at Woodstock, Md., Woodstock College, 1951.

24. Fort Wayne, Ind., Our Sunday Visitor Press, 1955–56.

25. Claire Murphy, Washington, D.C., Newman Club Federation, 1957.

26. Cited in Annual Report, November, 1956, Episcopal Moderator, Newman Club Federation, ANNA, Episcopal Moderator.

27. Minutes of the Quarterly Meeting, December 17, 1958, National Executive Committee of the National Newman Club Federation, n.p., in ibid., National Executive Committee.

28. Charles W. Albright (Washington, D.C.) to Alex Sigur (Lafayette, La.), June 28, 1957, in ibid., Chaplains' Correspondence, 1956–58.

29. Minutes of the Annual Convention, July 20–22, 1941, Newman Club Federation, n.p., in ibid, National Chaplain, 1948–53.

30. Same for September 4–7, 1952, in loc. cit.

31. Hallinan (Atlanta) to "Dear Father," form letter, 1963, in ANNA, National Chaplain, 1962–63.

32. Joan Ellen Hickey (Washington, D.C.) to J. Desmond O'Connor (Durham, N.H.), February 5, 1952, and Marian Andert (Washington, D.C.) to Edward J. Duncan (Champaign, Ill.), January 5, 1951, in ibid., National Chaplains, 1948–53. See also R. E. Tracy, "On the Present Condition of National Newman Club Affairs," memorandum, July 5, 1954, p. 4, in ibid., National Chaplain, 1952–54.

33. To Alcuin Greenberg, O.S.B. (Conception, Mo.), February 27, 1953, in ibid., Executive Secretary, Survey, 1953.

34. "The Status of the Priest in the Local Newman Club and in the National Newman Club Federation," December, 1952, pp. 5–6, in ibid., National Chaplain, 1952–54.

35. Quarterly Report, September, 1953, National Chaplain, Newman Club Federation, p. 1, in ibid., Convention Minutes.

36. See Hallinan to "Dear Father."

37. To Frank McPhillips (Ann Arbor, Mich.), May 5, 1955, ANNA, Executive Secretary, 1954–55. Tracy saw a necessity for "getting Tom [Carlin] back into closer touch with the priests on the Board and getting him and them to look upon his office as part of the Chaplains' Association as well as part of the NEC [National Executive Committee]" in "On the Present Condition of National Newman Club Affairs," p. 12.

38. Tracy (Baton Rouge, La.) to Howard J. Carroll (Washington, D.C.), June 19, 1955, AACHSP, Keogh Papers, box I.

39. Carroll to Tracy, June 19, 1955, and Joseph Schieder (Washington, D.C.) to Tracy, June 6, 1955, ANNA, Executive Secretary, 1955–56.

40. Tracy to Schieder, June 22, 1955, in ibid. Tracy believed that "in dealing with the Youth Department, 'eternal vigilance is the price,' etc., etc. ..." in "On the Present Condition ... ," p. 4.

41. Gerard E. Maguire, C.S.P., (Washington, D.C.) to Tracy, June 28, 1955, ANNA, Executive Secretary, 1955–56.

42. Tracy to Schieder, July 1, 1955, and his Report to the Advisory Board, National Association of Newman Club Chaplains, July 11, 1955, in ibid.

43. See criticisms of Catholic scholarship in R. H. Knapp and H. B. Goodrich, *Origins of American Scientists* (Chicago: University of Chicago Press, 1952); Knapp and J. J. Greenbaum, *The Younger American Scholar* (Chicago: University of Chicago Press, 1953); Joseph Cunneen, "Catholics and Education," *Commonweal* 58 (August 7, 1953), 437–41; "Where are the Catholic Scientists?" *America* 91 (April 10, 1954), 36; John Tracy Ellis, "American Catholics and the Intellectual Life," *Thought* 30 (Autumn 1955), 356–88.

44. Philip Des Marais, "Newman Club and Catholic College," *Catholic World* 182 (May 1956), 444–48; John P. Sullivan, "Catholic Higher Education," *America* 101 (September 19, 1959), 714–20; Alfred F. Horrigan, "Can the Small College Survive?" *Commonweal* 61 (January 28, 1955), 452–54.

45. Letter to the Editor, *Contact* (May 1955), n.p., ANNA, Permanent Files.

46. "Subversion of Faith by Intellectuals," *America* 92 (October 1954), 39–41.

47. "Another Look at Subversion of the Faith," ibid. (December 4, 1954), pp. 269–71.

48. See letters to the editor, ibid. (January 22, February 25, 1955), pp. 423–24 and 553–56. See also Albright to Lawrence Murtagh (Rochester, Minn.), July 30, 1957, ANNA, Chaplains' Correspondence, 1956–58.

49. Herm Sittard, "The Newman Idea in Action," *Catholic Digest* 18 (September 1954), 64–74.

50. "Formal Statement," October, 1954, ANNA, National Chaplain, 1954–56.

51. Tracy to Robert L. Reynolds (New York), June 24, 1957, in ibid., Chaplains' Correspondence, 1956–58.

52. National Association of Newman Club Chaplains, "A Statement of the Principles and Policies of the Newman Club Movement," May 7, 1955, 1 page, in ibid., National Chaplain, 1954–56.

53. Tracy to Reynolds; and "Statement of the Chaplains of the North Central Province," in Minutes of the Meeting, March 1, 1963, Newman Chaplains and Catholic College Representatives, n.p., Files, Newman Hall, University of Minnesota.

54. Minutes of the Annual Convention, August 28–September 2, 1961, Newman Club Federation, n.p., ANNA, Convention Minutes.

55. Minutes of the Quarterly Meeting, October 1955, National Executive Committee, National Newman Club Federation, n.p., in ibid., Executive Committee.

56. See above, ch. 3, p. 37.

57. See above, ch. 8, pp. 108ff.

58. "Report of the Education Committee" in Minutes of the Annual Meeting, August 31–September 5, 1959, Newman Club Federation, n.p., ANNA, Convention Minutes; "Editorial," *Newman* (Boston) 1 (Lent 1957), 3, and 2 (Christmas 1957), 2.

59. Minutes of the Quarterly Meeting, August 29–31, 1956, National Executive Committee of the National Newman Club Federation, ANNA, Executive Committee, 1956.

60. "Report on the National Consultative Conference, Ann Arbor, November 16–19, 1959" in ibid., National Chaplain, 1958–60.

61. "The Outlook for Religious Education," *Religious Education* 54 (March–April 1959), 144.

62. Hallinan to Carlin, November, 1954, and Carlin to Hallinan, November 19, 1954, ANNA, Executive Secretary, 1954–56; Minutes of the Quarterly Meeting, May 18, 1956, Chaplains' Advisory Board, Newman Club Federation, n.p., in ibid., National Chaplains, 1954–56.

63. Annual Report, November 1959, Episcopal Moderator, Newman Club Federation, in ibid., Episcopal Moderator.

64. Interview, Charles Albright, Chicago, June 5, 1964.

65. Carlin to Mary Heffernan (Slippery Rock, Pa.), December 17, 1954, in ANNA, Executive Secretary, 1954–55.

66. Annual Report, November 1959, in ibid., Episcopal Moderator.

67. Annual Report, December 1959, in ibid., National Chaplain, 1958–59.

10. OUT FROM THE SHADOWS

1. See theological opinions cited in Francis J. Connell, C.S.S.R., "The Catholic Student in a Non-Catholic College," *American Ecclesiastical Review* 149

(April 1959), 229–36. A "justifying reason" for attending secular colleges did not remove "the obligation to continue the study of Catholic doctrine" (p. 234). How this was to be accomplished, given the restrictions placed upon the Newman Movement, Connell does not discuss.

2. See Donald M. Cleary, ed., *Newman Club Federation: A Manual for Newman Leaders* (Washington, D.C.: NCWC Youth Department, 1942), preface.

3. Annual Report, December 29, 1959, National Chaplain, Newman Club Federation, n.p., ANNA, National Chaplain, 1958–60.

4. Minutes of the Annual Convention, August 29–September 5, 1959, pp. 29–30, in ibid., Convention Minutes, 1959.

5. Hallinan, quoted in ibid., p. 22; emphasis Hallinan's.

6. "Summer Summit Session," July 17–20, 1961, National Association of Newman Club Chaplains, pp. 5–12, and "Province Chaplains' Reports, July 17–20, 1961," pp. 1–35 in ibid., National Chaplain, 1960–62.

7. Annual Report, December 29, 1959, National Chaplain.

8. "Summer Summit Session," pp. 7–8.

9. See ch. 13, p. 170.

10. Based on conversations with members of several religious orders during the summers of 1964 and 1965. See also "Jesuits and Catholic Students in American Higher Education," *Woodstock Letters* 93 (July 1964), 253–68.

11. For the origin, constitution, and bylaws of this group see ANNA, Faculty and Staff Association, 1959–61.

12. NC News Release, May 26, 1960.

13. Hallinan (Charleston, S.C.) to Sigur (Baton Rouge, La.), October 9, 1961, in ANNA, National Chaplain, 1960–62.

14. *Newman News* 45 (February 1962), 2.

15. Orlett to Sigur, February 2, 1962, ANNA, National Chaplain, 1960–62.

16. Same to same, March 16, and Orlett to Albright, March 18, 1962, in ibid.; also "Memorandum: A Proposed Newman 'Summit' Meeting, March 17, 1962," in ibid.

17. Albright to Orlett, February 8 and 23, 1962, in ibid.

18. See "Exchange," Newsletter of the National Newman Chaplains' Association, December, 1961, n.p., in ibid.

19. Orlett to Albright, May 19, 1962, in ibid., President's Papers, box 11.

20. Albright to Sigur, March 21, 1962, in ibid., National Chaplain, 1960–62.

21. Albright to Orlett and Sigur to Orlett, March 22, 1962, in ibid.

22. Hallinan to Orlett, March 23, 1962. Some students also asked Orlett not to endanger the favorable developments by acting unilaterally, as evidenced by Allene Guss (Washington, D.C.) to Orlett, March 26, 1962, in ibid.

23. To Frederick Stevenson (Washington, D.C.), April 27, 1962, in ibid.

24. NC News Release, April 18, 1962.

25. Orlett to Sigur, March 24, 1962, claimed that "the first and most enthusiastic" responses to his summons of March 17 had come "from chaplains — hardly evidence of its engendering a negative reaction on their part," ANNA, National Chaplain, 1960–62.

26. Minutes of the Newman Apostolate Meeting, June 22–24, National Newman Apostolate, p. 1, in ibid.

27. Compare the penciled outline of objectives in Hallinan to Sigur, October 9, 1961, with the contents of the detailed letter of same to same, March 19, 1962, both in ibid.

28. The writer, arriving at the Gabriel Richard Center to attend the first Newman Chaplains' Training School (June 23–July 10), heard this remark from one of the departing, and unidentified, delegates. A spirit of optimism and general satisfaction percolated abroad.

29. Minutes of the Newman Apostolate Meeting, p. 6.

30. Ibid. Sigur expanded on this theme during his lectures at the chaplains' school which followed the meeting.

31. See "Building a Newman Club," *Catholic Property Administration* 27 (January 1963), 18–21; "Meeting Expenses at a Newman Club," ibid., pp. 22–24; "A Policy Regarding Newman Centers: Chapels of Ease to Mother Parishes," ibid., (October 1963), 60; and "Modern Building Materials in the LaCrosse State Newman Center," *Catholic Market* 2 (July 1963), 40.

32. "Survey of Opinion (Confidential), July–August, 1962," ANNA, Executive Secretary, 1961–62.

33. "An Outline of the Proposed Public Relations and Fund-Raising Program Developed as a Result of a Survey Conducted During July and August, 1962," n.p., in ibid.

34. For examples see Richard Butler, "The End of the Newman Club," *Commonweal* 82 (September 3, 1965), 627–30; Joseph Quinn, "Crash Program for the Newman Apostolate," *Catholic World* 202 (December 1965), 116–17; Eldon K. Somers, "Newman Club: A False Hope?" *Catholic High School Journal* 45 (January 1965), 53–56.

35. "Statistics, 1962," ANNA, Executive Secretary, 1961–62.

36. *Newman Apostolate Newsletter* 4 (Fall 1967), n.p., in ibid., National Director, 1965–69.

37. "Report to the Bishops of America [sic] from the National Newman Chaplains' Association" (Washington, D.C.: By the Association, 1965), pp. 1–4, copy in ANNA, Episcopal Moderator, 1960.

38. Annual Report, November, 1960, Episcopal Moderator, Newman Club Federation, n.p., in ibid.

39. They were John J. Burns (May 1962 to December 1962); Joseph S. McGrath, Jr. (December 1962 to June 1963). Jerry Burns occupied the position from June 1963 until December 1968. William F. Tonne, Jr., took on the job in January 1970.

40. Interviews, John T. McDonough and William Tonne, Washington, D.C., April 14, 1969; also Minutes of the Semi-Annual Meeting, September, 1966, Coordinating Board, National Newman Apostolate, p. 59, ANNA, National Coordinator, 1965–69.

41. *Newman Apostolate Newsletter* 2 (Summer 1966), n.p., and 4 (Fall 1967), n.p., ANNA, National Director, 1965–69.

42. Interview, John T. McDonough, Washington, D.C., April 14, 1969; McDonough also supplied printed material from his files regarding the dates and locations of these schools.

43. Ibid.

44. Minutes of the Semi-annual Meeting, September 2, 1966, Coordinating Board, National Newman Apostolate, pp. 21–27.

45. Quoted in Edward Duff, "Newman Club: Problems and Prospects," *America* 80 (November 13, 1948), 153.

46. Quoted in Clark Kerr, *Uses of the University* (Cambridge, Mass.: Harvard University Press, 1964), p. 96.

11. RELIGION SUCCEEDED IN COLLEGE

1. In Hunter Guthrie, S.J., and Gerald G. Walsh, S.J., eds., *A Philosophical Symposium on American Catholic Education* (New York: Fordham University Press, 1941), p. 112.

2. Erik H. Erickson, "Memorandum on Youth," *Daedalus* 96 (Summer 1967), 862.

3. Malcom M. Willey (Minneapolis) to Guy Stanton Ford (Minneapolis), January 2, 1940; also W. C. Coffey (Minneapolis) to W. T. Middlebrook (Minneapolis), July 30, 1941, AUMinn, Papers of the President's Office, Religion, 1940–41.

4. In AUW-M, E. B. Fred Papers, Addresses, 1945–46.

5. Charles B. Ketchum (Alliance, Ohio) to W. C. Coffey, March 12, 1945, AUMinn.

6. Jeanne S. Brown, "Administrative Attitude Toward Religion in State Universities and Colleges," Term Paper (c. 1948), p. 53, ADSYU, Shedd Collection, File Drawer I, State University and Religion.

7. Report of Robert Rankin cited in "Recommendations," JCUM, Brady Papers, Series 233, Religion.

8. "Practices of Land-Grant Colleges and State Universities Affecting Religious Matters," *School and Society* 76 (December 6, 1952), 359–63.

9. G. W. Harrod, "Religious Activities in Campuses of Colleges and Universities," *Personnel and Guidance Journal* 38 (March 1960), 355–57.

10. Lloyd A. Bates, "The Administrator's Concept of the Organizational Relationships of the Campus Ministry to the Publicly Sponsored University" (Diss., Indiana Univ., 1964), pp. 92–98.

11. "Religion in the Life of a College Professor," *AAUP Bulletin* 43 (May 1957), 351.

12. Quoted in Knox C. Hill, et al., "Report of the Lilly Committee on Studies in Religion, January 25, 1962," p. 7, Personal Files, Knox C. Hill, University of Chicago.

13. Interview, Byron Atkinson, Los Angeles, July 28, 1965.

14. Philip C. Nash, "University Chapel—New Style," *School and Society* 51 (January 27, 1940), 123–24.

15. Report of Faculty Committee on Religious Education, October 14, 1943, Louisiana State University, n.p., AUMinn, Papers of the President's Office, Coffey Papers, 1943, Religion. See also DeWitt Redick (Austin, Tex.) to Emil R. Kraettli (Oklahoma City), December 14, 1943, AUT, box UF, 5–C, Committees, 1929–44, Folder, Religious Life, 1943; and Minutes of the Meeting, May 2, 1944, Committee on Religious and Spiritual Activities, n.p., AUOre, Department of Religion, Religious Activities, 1944.

16. J. Edward Dirks, *The Faculty Christian Fellowship* (New York: National Council of Churches, 1954), pp. 11–15.

17. Conference on Science, Philosophy and Religion in Their Relation to the Democratic Way of Life, *Science, Philosophy and Religion: A Symposium* (New York: By the Conference, 1941), pp. 1–2.

18. A. S. Nash, *The University and the Modern World* (New York: Macmillan, 1943), pp. 102, 144–45, 225.

19. "Education versus Western Civilization," *American Scholar* 10 (Spring 1941), 184.

20. In Gail Kennedy, ed., *Pragmatism and American Culture* (Boston: D. C. Heath and Co., 1950), pp. 67–76, passim.

21. Lymon Bryson and Louis Finkelstein, eds., *Science, Philosophy and Religion: A Third Symposium* (New York: Conference on Science, Philosophy and Religion in Their Relationship to the Democratic Way of Life, 1943), pp. xi–xvi.

22. "The New Failure of Nerve," in Gail Kennedy, ed., *Evolution and Religion* (Boston: D. C. Heath and Co., 1957), pp. 108–10; also "The New Medievalism" in Kennedy, *Pragmatism and American Culture*, pp. 76–80.

23. William Cecil Dampier, *A History of Science and Its Relations with Philosophy and Religion* (Cambridge: Cambridge University Press, 1958), pp. 493–94.

24. Quoted in Christian Gauss, ed., *The Teaching of Religion in American Higher Education* (Chicago: The Ronald Press, 1951), p. 84.

25. See A. J. Brumbaugh, "College Life in the United States" in Frank C. Abbott, ed., *Student Life in the United States*, Series I, No. 57 (Washington, D.C.: American Council on Education, 1953), p. 13; David Riesman, "The Uncommitted Generation," *Encounter* 15 (November 1960), 25–30.

26. Gaylon C. Caldwell, "Reinhold Neibuhr and the Crisis of Our Times," *Ethics* 70 (July 1960), 306–15; George H. Edwards, "How Is't with Thy Religion?" *Journal of Higher Education* 24 (December 1953), 500; and Oron J. Hale, "Faculty and Students," *Christian Scholar* 41 (March 1959), 9–10.

27. Report of the President, 1953–55, University of Wisconsin, p. 11, AUWisc, President's Papers, Reports, 1955; also Cyrus R. Pangborn, "Trim the Ivy But Don't Raze the Chapel," *AAUP Bulletin* 44 (December 1958), 755–60.

28. Dirks, *The Faculty Christian Fellowship*, pp. 3–8; see also Werner A. Bohnstedt, "The Faculty Christian Fellowship: Its Meaning and Task," *Christian Scholar* 36 (June 1953), 1950–55.

29. Robert E. Fitch, "Why Is Protestantism in Disrepute with American Colleges and Universities?" *Religious Education* 45 (July–August 1950), 237.

30. A. J. Coleman, "Faith and Learning in the University," *Christian Scholar* 47 (Winter 1964), 369.

31. Interview, J. Edward Dirks, New Haven, Conn., December 22, 1965.

32. Kenneth E. Boulding, "Religion and the Social Sciences" in Erich A. Walter, ed., *Religion and the State University* (Ann Arbor: University of Michigan Press, 1958), p. 153.

33. Elijah Jordan, "The Philosophical Problem of Religion," *Ethics* 65 (April 1955), 192, 200; also Hugh van Rensselaer Wilson, "How Valid Is Jordan's Disillusionment with Life and Thought?" ibid., 66 (July 1956), 279–83.

34. "Aims of Courses in Religion," *Journal of Social Psychology* 31 (February 1950), 305–09.

35. Philip E. Jacob, *Changing Values in College* (New York: Harper and Brothers, 1957), pp. 1–11.

36. Edward D. Eddy, Jr., *The College Influence on Student Character* (Washington, D.C.: American Council on Education, 1959), pp. 175–78, 181. Religion also seemed to have little impact on the views and practices of teachers in church-related colleges. R. H. Edwin Espy, "The Theism of Teachers in Church-Related Colleges," *Religious Education* 45 (September 1950), 301–06.

37. Tuttle, "Aims of Courses in Religion," p. 309.

38. T. R. McConnell, *Urbanization and the College Student* (Minneapolis: University of Minnesota Press, 1966), p. 36.

39. C. Robert Pace, "The College Environment as an Exemplar of Values," in *Higher Education in California: Its Responsibilities for Values in American Life* (Commission on Higher Education of the California Teachers Association, 1962), pp. 10-20.

40. Lawrence G. Thomas, "Collegiate Opportunities for Developing Moral and Spiritual Values," in ibid., pp. 27-32; see also Lois E. Olive, "Relationships of Values and Occupational Role Perceptions for Freshmen and Senior Students in a College of Engineering," *Journal of Counseling Psychology* 16 (March 1969), 114-20, which reviews the findings of three studies during the 1940s and 1950s; and John E. Smith, *Value Convictions and Higher Education* (New Haven, Conn.: The Hazen Foundation, 1958), pp. 5, 34.

41. *Church, State and Freedom* (Boston: Beacon Press, 1953), p. 102.

42. Paul Kauper, "Law and Public Opinion," in Walter, *Religion and the State University*, p. 79; Robert Michaelson, "The Legal Syndrome and the Study of Religion," *Journal of Higher Education* 35 (October 1964), 373-78.

43. *Religion, A Humanistic Field* (Englewood Cliffs, N.J.: Prentice-Hall, 1963), p. 176.

44. Quoted from School District of Abington Township v. Schempp, 374 U.S. 203, 215 (1963) in Wilbur G. Katz, *Religion and the American Constitution* (Evanston, Ill.: Northwestern Univesrity Press, 1964), p. 95.

45. Quoted in Ann Oriel and Jeanne Fortier, "Report from Minneapolis," *The Nation* 182 (January 14, 1956), 29.

46. Robert E. Cushman, "Address to the Pacific Lutheran Synod, May 9, 1943," AUOre, Department of Religion, Committee on Religious and Spiritual Activities, 1944-45.

47. Quoted in E. W. Blakeman, "Curricular Religion in State Universities," *Religious Education* 48 (July-August 1953), 266-67; see also Charles Linton, "Religion in the Tax Supported Colleges and Universities of the United States" in Abbott, *Student Life in the United States*, p. 42.

48. S. I. Clark, "Religion in Public Education," *AAUP Bulletin* 40 (Winter 1954-55), 652-54. See also Anthony Nemetz, "Religion as an Academic Discipline," *Journal of Higher Education* 30 (April 1959), 200; George Edwards, "Teaching Religion in a Tax Supported College," *Religious Education* 48 (July-August 1953), 257-61; Deane W. Ferm, "Teaching Religion in a State University," ibid., 51 (July-August 1956), 287; and Paul Reinert, "What More Emphasis on Religion Might Contribute to General and Professional Objectives," *Educational Record* 35 (July 1954), 232.

49. Jacques Maritain, quoted in Edmund Fuller, ed., *The Christian Idea of Education* (New Haven, Conn.: Yale University Press, 1957), p. 181.

50. Bernard Iddings Bell, "Studying Religion in the University," *Christian Century* 65 (September 22, 1948), 975.

51. Stephen F. Bayne in Fuller, *The Christian Idea of Education*, p. 265.

52. Gerard Sloyan, "Religion in the State University," *The Commonweal* 71 (October 2, 1959), 7-8.

53. Nemetz, "Religion as an Academic Discipline," p. 199.

54. *Biennial Survey of Education, 1918-20* (Washington, D.C.: Government Printing Office, 1923), p. 281; *Biennial Survey of Education, 1956-58* (Washing-

ton, D.C.: U.S. Department of Health, Education, and Welfare, 1961), 2:2.

55. Charles F. Kent, "The Undergraduate Course in Religion at the Tax Supported Colleges and Universities of America," *Bulletin IV of the National Council on Religion in Higher Education* (1924), pp. 26–27; Seymour A. Smith, "Religious Instruction in State Universities: A Report on Recent Trends," *Religious Education* 53 (May–June 1958), 293.

56. Ferme, "Teaching Religion at a State University," p. 286; and Kent, "The Undergraduate Course in Religion," p. 28.

57. "Studying God on Campus," *Time* 87 (February 4, 1966), 72.

58. Weldon Lee Estes, "The Curricular Status of Religion in Land Grant Colleges and Universities" (Diss., Univ. of Tennessee, 1963), pp. 112ff.

59. See lists of courses in Milton D. McLean and Harry H. Kimber, *The Teaching of Religion in State Universities* (Ann Arbor: University of Michigan Press, 1960), and Robert Michaelson, *The Study of Religion in American Universities* (New Haven, Conn.: The Society for Religion in Higher Education, 1965).

60. Claude Welch, *Graduate Education in Religion: A Critical Appraisal* (Missoula, Mont.: University of Montana Press, 1971), pp. 231–32.

61. Robert Michaelson, "The Study of Religion: A Quiet Revolution in American Universities," *Journal of Higher Education* 37 (April 1966), 181–86.

62. Robert Michaelson, "Religion and Academia," in Claude Welch, *The Study of Religion in College and University* (New York: Department of Higher Education, National Council of Churches, 1967), pp. 5–6.

12. CRISIS OF FAITH IN COLLEGE

1. "Catholic Action and the Catholic College," *Catholic Action* 28 (August 1946), 6.

2. See above, ch. 6, p. 78.

3. See above, ch. 3, pp. 32f.

4. E. E. Y. Hales, "Letter to the Editor," *The London Tablet* 217 (March 23, 1963), 318.

5. James W. Trent, "Progress and Anxiety," *The Commonweal* 81 (October 2, 1964), 41.

6. See Andrew M. Greeley, *The American Catholic: A Sociological Portrait* (New York: Basic Books, 1977), pp. 67ff.

7. John LaFarge, S.J., *The Jesuits in Modern Times* (New York: The America Press, 1928), p. 90.

8. John M. Cooper, "Catholic Education and Theology," in Roy Deferrari, ed., *Vital Problems of Catholic Education* (Washington, D.C.: Catholic University of America Press, 1939), p. 137. See also "Report of the Commission on Educational Policy and Progress," *NCEA Reports* 33 (1937), 88–91; and John E. Walsh, C.S.C., "Aspects of the Reverend James A. Burns' Philosophy of Education," *Bulletin of the Educational Conference of the Priests of the Holy Cross* 24 (December 1956), 40–52.

9. Charles M. O'Hara, "An Integrated Curriculum for the Catholic College Today," *Jesuit Educational Quarterly* 1 (June 1938), 26.

10. Bakewell Morrison, S.J., "An Interpretation of the Work of the Convention of Religion Teachers," ibid. (October 1938), pp. 18–27.

11. "Report on College Teachers of Religion," *NCEA Reports* 33 (1937), 124.

12. See William H. Russell, "Religion for College Students," ibid., 43 (August 1946), 216–17; Walter Farrell, O.P., "Argument for Teaching Theology in Catholic Colleges," ibid., pp. 239–44; C. W. Phillips, "Needed: Lay Theologians," *Catholic Educational Review* 45 (November 1947), 541–43; "Report of the Committee on Educational Problems and Research," *NCEA Reports* 37 (August 1940), 116, 137, 140; ibid., 38 (August 1941), 220–21; ibid., 39 (August 1942), 128; Robert Henle, S.J., "The Future Challenge to Catholic Education," ibid., 45 (August 1948), 277, 282–83; Paul L. O'Connor, S.J., "Religion in the Undergraduate Jesuit College," *Jesuit Educational Quarterly* 11 (June 1948), 41–48; Mary Gratia Maher, *The Organization of Religious Instruction in Catholic Colleges* (Washington, D.C.: Catholic University of America Press, 1951), pp. 134–35, 142–43, 150–51; and Roy Deferrari, *Essays on Catholic Education in the United States* (Washington, D.C.: Catholic University of America Press, 1942), p. 213.

13. See above, ch. 5, pp. 66f.

14. "Editorial," *America* 33 (September 2, 1925), 520.

15. "Present Tendencies in Our Educational System," *Jesuit Educational Quarterly* 1 (June 1938), 7.

16. Walter Farrell, O.P., "Wisdom in the Colleges," *Catholic Educational Review* 48 (May 1950), 289–98; Roland G. Simonitsh, C.S.C., *Religious Instruction in Catholic Colleges for Men* (Washington, D.C.: Catholic University of America Press, 1952), pp. 301–03; Kevin O'Sullivan, O.F.M., "The Integration of Theology in College Life and Curriculum" in *Theology and Daily Life* (Washington, D.C.: Franciscan Educational Conference, 1953), pp. 79–86.

17. Study Committee of the International Federation of Catholic Universities, "Statement on the Nature of the Contemporary Catholic University," *America* 117 (August 12, 1967), 154–56; "Says College Theology Not under Local Bishop," *National Catholic Reporter* (Kansas City, Mo.), March 15, 1967.

18. Charles F. Donovan, "Implications for the Future of Catholic Higher Education," *NCEA Reports* 60 (August 1963), 138.

19. "The Responsibility of American Catholic Higher Education in Meeting National Needs," ibid., 61 (August 1964), 134–36, 142.

20. "Minutes of the Executive Committee, April 2, 1964," ibid., pp. 215–218.

21. George Shuster, "Catholic Education Once More," *The Catholic World* 201 (April 1965), 53.

22. Archbishop John Krol of Philadelphia quoted in Gene Currivan, "Catholics Debating Unplanned Growth of Small Colleges," *New York Times*, June 8, 1964.

23. See Charles E. Ford and Edgar J. Roy, *The Renewal of Catholic Higher Education* (Washington, D.C.: The National Catholic Educational Association, 1968), pp. vii–ix, passim.

24. Logan Wilson, ed., *Emerging Patterns in American Education* (Washington, D.C.: American Council on Education, 1965), pp. 174–79, 199–203.

25. Mary Delores Salerno, D.M., "Patterns of Inter-institutional Cooperation in American Catholic Higher Education," *NCEA Bulletin* 62 (May 1966), 5.

26. Urban H. Fleege, "Our Resources: Actual and Potential in Catholic Higher Education," *NCEA Reports* 56 (August 1959), 115.

27. " 'Ecumenical' Claremont," *Newsweek* 65 (March 1, 1965), 53. See also

Eldon L. Johnson, "College Federation," *Journal of Higher Education* 37 (January 1966), 1–9.

28. St. Louis *Post-Dispatch,* January 15, 1967.

29. John J. McGrath, *Catholic Institutions in the United States: Canonical and Civil Law Status* (Washington, D.C.: Catholic University of America Press, 1968), pp. 22–24, 33–36; Fred M. Hechinger, "The Future of Church-Related Schools," *New York Times,* January 26, 1967.

30. Editorial, "A Sense of the Past in Adapting Catholic Colleges to the New Vogue of 'Secularization'," *The Christian Century* 84 (February 8, 1967), 165–66.

31. Philip Gleason, "Academic Freedom: Survey, Retrospect, and Prospect," *NCEA Reports* 64 (August 1967), 77; John P. Leary, "The Wisdom of Being Apart," *America* 115 (September 3, 1966), 224–27.

32. William J. Mehok, "An Analysis of National Statistics," *Jesuit Educational Quarterly* 17 (January 1955), 166.

33. "Comment," ibid., 25 (March 1963), 223.

34. Robert Fitzgerald, ed., "Jesuits and Catholic Students in American Higher Education," *Woodstock Letters* 93 (July 1964), 253–86.

35. See John J. Jansen, *Personnel Services in Catholic Four-Year Colleges for Men* (Washington, D.C.: Catholic University of America Press, 1955), pp. 79–81; "Faith and the College Student: A Continuing Discussion," *Newman: A Review* Winter 1966, pp. 27–49; "Students' Views on Education," *America* 110 (May 23, 1964), 722–23; "The Cool Generation and the Church," *The Commonweal* 87 (October 6, 1967), 11–23.

36. Ralph Martin, "Letter from a Catholic College Graduate to the President," *Ave Maria* 103 (April 16, 1966), 7ff.

37. "Dayton Students Show Reservations on Church," *The Witness* (Dubuque, Iowa), December 21, 1967.

38. R. W. Gleason, S.J., quoted in ibid., August 1, 1968.

39. John Leo, "Young Catholics Altering Values," *New York Times,* February 13, 1968.

40. Leo A. Piguet, "The Change in Catholic Piety," *U.S. Catholic* 34 (May 1968), 22–25; Kevin Ranaghan and Dorothy Ranaghan, *Catholic Pentecostals* (New York: Paulist Press, Deus Books, 1969), pp. 38ff.

41. Bruce M. Ritter, O.F.M., quoted in Leo, "Young Catholics Altering Values."

42. Jansen, *Personnel Services in Catholic Four-Year Colleges for Men,* pp. 79–81.

43. Miriam Imelda Murphy, C.S.J., "The Chaplain in Catholic Colleges for Women in the United States, 1965," (Thesis, Catholic University of America, 1965), p. 72; see also John N. Ryan, O.S.F.S., "The Chaplain in United States Catholic Colleges for Men," (Thesis, Catholic University of America, 1965), pp. 7–17; and William J. Nessel, O.S.F.S., "The Canonical Status of the Catholic College Chaplain," *The Jurist* 25 (July 1965), 324–25.

44. William J. Farrell, "Where are the Catholic Catholics?" *Anselmian News* 9 (December 1966), 10–14. The first draft of the full report is in this writer's files.

45. Andrew M. Greeley and Peter H. Rossi, *The Education of Catholic Americans* (Chicago: Aldine Publishing Company, 1966), pp. 219–32.

46. William J. Whelan, "The Role of Newman Club Education in American Catholicism," *NCEA Reports* 59 (August 1962), 513.

47. "The Responsibility of Catholic Higher Education," ibid., 60 (August 1963), 149–51; see also Richard Butler, O.P., "The Cultural Contribution of the Newman Apostolate to Secular Higher Education" and Egbert Donovan, O.S.B., "The Newman Apostolate and High School Graduates," ibid., 61 (August 1964), 148–55, 273–80.

48. George R. Fitzgerald, "Catholics in Secular Colleges," *America* 103 (May 21, 1960), 278–81.

49. "Catholic Values on the Secular Campus," ibid., p. 276.

50. See above, ch. 3.

51. Editor's note accompanying O'Brien article, *America* 105 (April 18, 1961).

52. John A. O'Brien, "Catholics on the Secular Campus," ibid., pp. 52–56.

53. Richard J. Clifford and William R. Callahan, "Catholics in Higher Education," ibid., 111 (September 19, 1964), 291.

54. Ibid., pp. 288–89.

55. Ibid., pp. 289–90. The writer worked out the ratios for women religious from data in the *Official Catholic Directory* for 1965.

56. Clifford and Callahan, "Catholics in Higher Education," p. 291.

57. See, in addition to citations in ch. 3, pp. 28, 35, the comments of Timothy Harrington in "Discussion," *NCEA Reports* 4 (1907), 173.

58. *The Training of a Priest: An Essay on Clerical Education, with a Reply to the Critics* (New York: Longmans, Green and Co., 1908), p. 398.

59. The Paulist Fathers appeared on the scene in the winter of 1889–90 when they organized a Catholic club at Cornell University while conducting a mission in Ithaca (see Frederick Zwierlein, *Life and Letters of Bishop McQuaid* [Rochester, N.Y.: Art Print Shop, 1926], p. 396). Catholic students had organized a year before (see *Newman Quarterly* 1 [March 1917], 7), something McQuaid probably had not heard about until the "liberal" Paulists appeared to be meddling in his diocese. Dominicans first joined the Newman Movement in Austin, Texas, around 1918 (see above, ch. 3, pp. 30f); the fact that Archbishop McNicholas of Cincinnati, who opened a Newman foundation there in 1929, was a Dominican, combined with the fact that about the same time Dominican priests took up work at the University of Washington in Seattle, suggests a topic for additional research. For a brief summary of Dominican effort see Butler, *Witness to Change,* pp. 90ff.

60. "Annual Report 1965–66," *Newman Apostolate Newsletter* 2 (Summer 1966), n.p.

13. TO LIVE IS TO CHANGE

1. See Godfrey Hodgson, *America in Our Time* (New York: Doubleday and Company, 1976), pp. 100, 491ff.

2. See David J. O'Brien, *The Renewal of American Catholicism* (New York: Oxford University Press, 1972), pp. 194ff; also Halsey, *The Survival of American Innocence,* pp. 169ff.

3. Minutes of the Quarterly Meeting, August 27–29, 1966, National Executive Committee of the National Newman Club Federation, p. 1, ANNA, box 13, President's Office.

4. "Final Report from the Office of the President," n.p., in ibid., box 8, NNCF, 1964.

5. Butler, *Witness to Change,* p. 120.

6. Minutes of the Quarterly Meeting, March 23, 1964, National Executive Committee of the National Newman Club Federation, n.p., ANNA, box 8, NNCF, 1964.

7. Rory Ellinger, "Newman Jamboree," *The Commonweal* 72 (September 24, 1965), 682–83.

8. Quoted in Hans Kung, et al., eds., *Council Speeches of Vatican II* (Glen Rock, N.J.: Paulist Press, Deus Books, 1964), p. 231.

9. "The Newman Apostolate: Bringing the Church to Catholic Students on Secular Campuses," pamphlet, Washington, D.C., 1962, title page.

10. See Walter M. Abbott, S.J., and Joseph Gallagher, *The Documents of Vatican II* (New York: Guild Press, America Press, Association Press, 1966), par. 30, p. 56.

11. Ibid., par. 3, p. 492.

12. Ibid., par. 2, p. 679.

13. Ibid., pars. 19 and 21, p. 361.

14. Ibid., par. 2, p. 661.

15. Ibid., par. 34, p. 232.

16. Anthony F. C. Wallace quoted by William A. Osborne, "The Church as a Social Organization" in Philip Gleason, ed., *Contemporary Catholicism in the United States* (Notre Dame, Ind.: University of Notre Dame Press, 1969), p. 44.

17. *The Order of Mass,* English language ed. (Washington, D.C.: United States Catholic Conference, 1969), par. 66, p. 15.

18. Abbott and Gallagher, *The Documents of Vatican II,* "Dogmatic Constitution on the Church," pars. 23 and 28, pp. 44, 54.

19. "Memorandum, November 25, 1963," ANNA, box 12, NNCF, 1963.

20. "Memorandum, May, 1964," in ibid., box 11, NNCF, 1964.

21. Minutes of the Special Meeting of the Advisory Board, June 27–28, 1964, National Newman Chaplains' Association, pp. 1–2, in ibid., National Chaplain, 1964.

22. Michele Fearing (Washington, D.C.) to Peter Foote (Chicago), October 27, 1965, in ibid., box 8, Administrative Director.

23. "College Student Groups Form United Movement," *National Catholic Reporter* (Kansas City, Mo.), September 14, 1966.

24. Michele Fearing (Washington, D.C.) to Ron Del Bene (Toledo, Ohio), September 23, 1966, ANNA, box 8, Administrative Assistant.

25. Fearing to Marty Kleist (Notre Dame, Ind.), November 9, 1966, in ibid.

26. Interview, Charles Albright, C.S.P., Chicago, June 27, 1964.

27. John Cogley, "Parley of 17 Campus Chaplains Calls for Sharing of Communion," *New York Times,* September 4, 1966.

28. See "Campus Ministries Index," CARA CMD Project No. 69–02, Files, Campus Ministries Department, Center for Applied Research in the Apostolate, Washington, D.C.

29. Minutes of the Annual Meeting, August, 1966, National Apostolate Coordinating Board, pp. 57–66, ANNA, Director, 1964–69.

30. "Catholic Student News Service" (Washington, D.C.) 3 (October 5, 1966), 1–2, mimeographed bulletins, in ibid.

31. Catholic Commission on the Church and the American University, "Working Papers for Reevaluation Meeting, March 19–21, 1967," pp. 20–28, 30–62, and Minutes of the "Evaluation Meeting," January 3–5, 1967, National Newman Chaplains' Association, pp. 1–6, ANNA, Director, 1964–69.

32. *Newman Apostolate Newsletter* (Washington, D.C.) 3 (Spring 1967), "Supplement," 4 pp.

33. "A Critique of the Recommendations of the Catholic Commission on the Church and the American University: A Proposal for Restructuring the National Newman Apostolate" (Hyattsville, Md., June 30–July 3, 1967), p. 9, mimeograph, ANNA, box 8, Notebook, 1967–68.

34. *Newman Apostolate Newsletter* 4 (Fall 1967), 1–3.

35. Interview, Mr. William Tonne, Washington, D.C., October 3, 1969.

36. See "Correspondence," *The Commonweal* 83 (March 25, 1966), 38; also Robert E. Tracy, *American Bishop at the Vatican Council* (New York: McGraw-Hill, 1966), pp. 217–20.

37. Quoted in Mark J. Hurley, *The Declaration on Christian Education of Vatican Council II* (Glen Rock, N.J.: The Paulist Press, 1966), pp. 154–57.

38. See above, ch. 6, pp. 81ff.

39. Laurence T. Murphy (Washington, D.C.) to Patrick LaBelle (Eugene, Ore.), May 6, 1971, Files, Director, Division of Campus Ministry, United States Catholic Conference, Washington, D.C.

40. *Newman Apostolate Newsletter* 5 (Fall 1968; Spring 1969), n.p.

41. "CARA Campus Ministries Department Data Bank Preliminary Overview of Catholic Campus Ministry, June, 1971," 7 pp., Center for Applied Research in the Apostolate.

42. Martin W. Davis, S.D.S., *The Sister as Campus Minister* (Washington, D.C.: Center for Applied Research in the Apostolate, 1970), pp. 49, 63, 85–92, 112. See also Ann Elizabeth Kelley, *Women in Campus Ministry* (Cambridge, Mass.: National Center for Campus Ministry, 1973), p. 19.

43. See files of *Newman Apostolate Newsletter* for Winter 1969, and other entries.

44. George A. MacLean (Iowa City) to John R. Mott (East Northfield, Mass.), September 11, 1909, SCUI, MacLean Papers, General Correspondence, 1909–10.

45. See F. Thomas Trotter, "The Campus Ministry as Normative," *The Christian Century* 86 (June 4, 1969), 766–67; Paul Goodman, "Student Chaplains," *The New Republic* 156 (January 7, 1967), 29–31; and Kenneth Underwood, *The Church, The University and Social Policy*, Vol. I: *Report of the Director* (Middletown, Conn.: Wesleyan University Press, 1969), 68–69, 135–38.

46. See John J. Ryan, O.S.F.S., "The Chaplain in United States Catholic Colleges for Men" (Thesis, Catholic University of America, 1965), pp. 35–41, 49–51, 66; also Miriam Imelda Murphy, C.S.J., "The Chaplain in Catholic Colleges for Women in the United States" (Thesis, Catholic University of America, 1965), pp. 31–38, 42–44, 54–55, and 67–68.

47. Minutes of the Annual Meeting, April 8, 1969, National Newman Chaplain's Association, n.p., Files, Director, Division of Campus Ministry.

48. See John Whitney Evans, *An Evaluative Study of Institutional Guidelines for Campus Ministry* (Cambridge, Mass.: National Center for Campus Ministry, 1973), pp. 8ff.

49. Minutes of the Annual Meeting, November 11–12, 1971, East Coast Diocesan Directors, p. 1, Files, Director, Division of Campus Ministry. See also "CARA Campus Ministries Data Bank Preliminary Report on the Office of Diocesan Director of Catholic Campus Ministry, June 14, 1971," 10 pp., Center for Applied Research in the Apostolate.

50. Quoted in Laurence T. Murphy and John Whitney Evans, eds., *Perspec-*

tives for Campus Ministers (Washington, D.C.: Division of Campus Ministry, United States Catholic Conference, 1973), p. xv.

51. See above, ch. 3, p. 25.

52. The NCEA no longer publishes full texts of addresses and minutes of its meetings. See Ray Sullivan, "Campus Ministry on the Secular Campus: Perspectives and Problems," *Counselling and Values* 16 (Winter 1972), 102–06; also James Blumeyer, "Campus Ministry in Jesuit Colleges and Universities," ibid., pp. 107–09. The writer was present at the 8:00 P.M. meeting of April 14, 1971, at which Murphy made this announcement.

53. Murphy summarized the state of affairs in "A Letter to All in Campus Ministry," May 8, 1970, Files, Director, Division of Campus Ministry. See *Campus Ministry Report* (Washington, D.C.) 2 (October 1970) and 3 (October 1971), for subsequent developments.

54. Between 1968 and 1971 the hierarchy issued a statement on selective conscientious objection, established the Human Life Foundation for research into sexuality, set in motion a multimillion dollar Human Development Campaign, set up a Center for Urban Ethnic Affairs and an Office for Black Catholics. Some bishops also criticized the Vatican-issued *Lex Fundamentalis* as an attempt to use canon law to squelch the reformist spirit of Vatican II; for example, see Felician A. Fox, O.F.M., ed., *1972 Catholic Almanac* (Huntington, Ind.: Our Sunday Visitor Press, 1971), pp. 106–22. In questions of ecumenism and social action, "bishops tend to be even more 'liberal' than the clergy under [age] thirty-six;" see *American Priests* (Chicago: National Opinion Research Center, 1971), p. 146.

55. Percentages of entering freshmen from Catholic homes checking this response increased from 6.9 percent in 1966 to 14.4 percent in 1971. See *The American Freshman: National Norms for Fall, 1971* (Washington, D.C.: American Council on Education, 1971), p. 40; and *National Norms for Entering College Freshmen — Fall, 1966* (Washington, D.C.: American Council on Education, 1966), p. 22.

56. "The Second Spring" in *Sermons Preached on Various Occasions* (London: Longmans, Green and Co., 1921), pp. 180–81.

APPENDIX I

1. *The Secular City* (New York: Macmillan, 1965), pp. 20–21, 61.

2. "Toward Eliminating the Concept of Secularization" in Julius Gould, ed., *Penguin Survey of the Social Sciences, 1965* (Baltimore: Penguin Books, 1965), pp. 169, 177–78, 182.

3. Cox, *Secular City*, p. 61.

4. *Beyond Belief* (New York: Harper and Row, 1970), p. 246.

5. Langdon Gilkey, *Naming the Whirlwind: The Renewal of God Language* (Indianapolis: Bobbs-Merrill, 1969), pp. 32–33, 39.

Discussion of Principal Sources

Materials contributing to this study comprised two major categories: those that presented the changing condition of religious life and study in American nondenominational higher education during the twentieth century, and those that described the Roman Catholic response to these changes.

I

A comprehensive history of religion on the secular campus is hard to find. Laurence Russ Veysey produced an admirable history of higher education from primary sources, *The Emergence of The American University* (Chicago: University of Chicago Press, 1965), but ended his study at 1910 and suggested that religion was a nineteenth century thing. Harry E. Smith offered helpful insights in *Secularization and The University* (Richmond, Va.: John Knox Press, 1968), but he was answering questions that were more abstract than mine. Martin Lang's doctoral dissertation at The Catholic University of America, "Religion in the Undergraduate Curriculum of the American State University" (1964) was thorough but based almost exclusively on published sources. More relevant for this study was David Cottrell's *College Reading and Religion* (New Haven, Conn.: Yale University Press, 1948), especially for the years between the wars. Most suggestive was Merrimon Cunniggim's *The College Seeks Religion* (New Haven, Conn.: Yale University Press, 1947), but he includes only two state institutions among the eight he investigated and I found him to be somewhat overly optimistic about the return of religion to academia prior to World War II.

Such works examined the question more or less primarily from the point of view of ideology or administration; others attempted to approach the subject from the point of view of students and non-institutional figures. Among the more useful of the latter were Harry Melvin Philpott's doctoral dissertation at Yale, "A History of The Student Young Men's Christian Association" (1947); Howard Hopkin's *History of the YMCA in North America* (New York: Association Press, 1951); Edna and James French, *The Pioneer Years of the University Pastorate* (Ann Arbor, 1959); William Fred Urbach, *Religious Coopera- tion in State Universities* (Ann Arbor: University of Michigan Press, 1957); Clarence Prouty Shedd, *The Church Follows Its Students* (New Haven, Conn.: Yale University Press, 1938); John Sayre's *A History of Disciples' Student Work* (Indianapolis, Ind.: Joint Commission on Campus Christian Life, 1955); and Ronald B. Flowers, "The Begin- nings of The Bible Chair Movement among the Disciples of Christ," a seminar paper submitted in June 1955 to a graduate seminar in the School of Religion, Iowa State University, which the author kindly allowed me to use. The Disciples of Christ Historical Society in Nashville, Tenn., contains many informative pamphlets which its interim director, Harold C. Kime, generously shared with me in thermofax copy.

To develop the setting for the Newman Movement a search of archival and periodical collections became mandatory. With two travel grants from The National Newman Foundation I was able to examine institutional records in a dozen Midwestern and Western schools, ten of which were public, during the summers of 1964 and 1965. Another grant from the Committee on Co-Institutional Cooper- ation at the University of Minnesota provided travel for additional visits to five Eastern public and private campuses and also to a year's residency at the University of Michigan, where rich archival as well as periodical sources were at hand. This research program was somewhat biased because I selected schools characterized, wherever possible, by two traits: the presence of a school or department of religious studies, and that of an older, well-developed Newman Center, e.g., the University of Missouri.

Of each collection (there were nineteen in all) I asked four general questions: What did administrators say and do about religious life and study since 1900? What did professors and faculty committees say and do? What did student personnel staffs say and do? and, finally, What did these holdings contain that was relevant to Catholics and the Newman Movement? Although each "secular" institution I ap- proached yielded abundant information for the study, the Ora D. Foster Papers at Iowa, the Charles Foster Kent Papers at Michigan, and the Clarence Prouty Shedd Papers at Yale proved to be the richest lodes. Holdings at Iowa, Minnesota, Texas, and Wisconsin were especially rewarding because they contained surveys that their administrators conducted among their counterparts in different regions regarding various issues connected with religion in higher education.

Along with this manuscript material, the following periodicals contributed to telling the stories in chapters 1 and 5: *American Association of University Professors' Bulletin, American Journal of Psychology, American Journal of Religious Psychology and Education, American Journal of Sociology, Christian Education, Current Opinion, Forum, International Journal of Ethics, Literary Digest, The Outlook, Proceedings of the National Education Association, Religious Education,* and *School and Society.* In addition to providing opinions and programs of administrators and faculty and the findings of survey research into campus piety and practice, these files also yielded views of students, parents, clergymen, and businessmen.

The section in chapter 5 on the "school of religion" movement depends also upon an interview with M. Willard Lampe, the first director of the school at Iowa, who also offered insights about the work of Ora D. Foster. Carl Murchison's volume, *A History of Psychology in Autobiography* (Worcester, Mass.: Clark University Press, 1930) provided direct accounts of some professors' "crisis of faith" after the turn of the century. Correspondence and reports by Fathers John W. Keogh and Henry C. Hengell (collections described below) offered opinions of students and priests about faculty treatment of traditional religion. (Father Hengell, who served at Wisconsin in a full-time capacity from 1906 to 1936, at times employed a "truth squad" of students that reported unorthodox utterances of professors to be refuted in the following Sunday's sermon; many of these refutations were summarized in *Our Sunday Visitor* [Fort Wayne, Ind.]. Naturally, one must be cautious in using such biased material). Two histories of student personnel professionals were valuable: Ruth Barry and Beverly Wolf, *Modern Issues in Guidance and Personnel Work* (New York: Teachers' College, 1957), and E. G. Williamson, *Trends in Student Personnel Work* (Minneapolis: University of Minnesota Press, 1949).

Chapter 11 presents the changed attitudes of university presidents, faculty, and personnel workers toward religious life and study. Especially helpful for the general picture was Lloyd A. Bates' doctoral dissertation at Indiana University, "The Administrator's Concept of the Organizational Relationship of the Campus Ministry to the Publicly Sponsored University" (1964); Henry Allen's volume, *Religion in the State University: An Initial Exploration* (Minneapolis: Burgess Publishing Co., 1950) was likewise informative about developing trends. Representative in tracing the "quiet revolution" that saw religious studies return to the campus were William Adams Brown, *The Case for Theology in the University* (Chicago: University of Chicago Press, 1938); Lyman Bryson, *Science, Philosophy, and Religion* (New York: Conference on Science, Philosophy, and Religion in Their Relation to the Democratic Way of Life, 1941) with the companion volumes of 1942 and 1943; Erich Walter, ed., *Religion and the State University* (Ann Arbor: University of Michigan Press, 1959), Robert Michaelson, *The Study of Religion in American Universities* (New Haven, Conn.: Society for Religion in Higher Education, 1965); and Claude Welch, *Religion in the Undergraduate Curriculum* (Washington, D.C.: Association of American Colleges, 1972). Files of the *Journal of Higher Education* during these years contain a number of pivotal articles; those of the *Christian Scholar* help also to tell the story of the Christian Faculty Forum. An Interview with J. Edward Dirks, who was closely associated with this movement, threw considerable light upon its ambitions and difficulties. Work of Robert Pace and Lawrence Thomas on the inculcation of values summarized in *Higher Education in California: Its Responsibilities for Values in American Life* (California Teachers' Association, 1962) represented one of the better models for understanding this elusive subject. I am indebted to Professor Pace for an interview.

II

To develop an overview of Catholic life in the United States since the turn of the century I have relied principally upon Daniel Callahan's *The Mind of the Catholic Layman* (New York: Charles Scribner's Sons, 1963) which offers a refreshing view of the first years "from the bottom"; John Tracy Ellis' *Documents of American Catholic History* (Milwaukee: Bruce Publishing Co., 1965) whose explanatory introductions supply the necessary context for the same span of years; Thomas T. McAvoy's *A History of the Catholic Church in the United States* (Notre Dame, Ind.: University of Notre Dame Press, 1969) which provides institutional and cultural interpretations up to mid-century; and David J. O'Brien's *The Renewal of American Catholicism* (New York: Oxford University Press, 1972) which, in addition to discussing recent Catholic history, also presents political and theological interpretations. William Michael Halsey's *The Survival of American Innocence: Catholicism in an Era of Disillusionment, 1920-1940* (Notre Dame, Ind.: University of Notre Dame Press, 1980) provides a graceful intellectual and cultural interpretation; despite the period indicated in its title, this work also treats of recent Catholicism in the United States.

Sister M. Alexander Gray's doctoral dissertation at The Catholic University of America, "The Development, Organization, and Operation of the Newman Club Movement in American Education" (1962) represents the most thorough investigation of the Catholic response to the growth of secular higher education after 1900; it appeared in shortened form as "Development of the Newman Club Movement" in *Records of the American Catholic Historical Society of Philadelphia* (June 1963). Her careful work proved to be very helpful as I tried to approach the subject from a more chronological and broader perspective as well as include developments since 1962. Among the more instructive unpublished local histories and dissertations were Peter Alegi's seminar paper in American Studies, "A History of Catholicism at Yale to 1943" (1956, Main Library, Yale University); Michael Burke's "History of St. Mary's Chapel" (c. 1926; in files of The Gabriel Richard Center, Ann Arbor, Mich.); Barry McDermott's Master's thesis at the University of Illinois, "History of the Newman Foundation at the University of Illinois" (1958); Robert Melvin's "History of St. Thomas Aquinas Parish at Purdue University" (1963, Parish Files); Mary Ruth Torpey's historical paper, "The Newman Club of the University of Iowa" (1945; Special Collections of the University); Harry James Towey's Master's thesis at the St. Paul Seminary, "A History of the Principal Catholic Student Groups on the Main Campus of the University of Minnesota" (1945); and Sister Mary Aloysia Zuczuski's Master's thesis at Canisius College, "The Nature and Function of the Newman Club in the Modern University" (1955).

Six principal manuscript depositories yielded information about national as well as local developments in the Newman movement. The files of St. Paul's Chapel and Catholic Student Center at the University of Wisconsin (SPC) comprise approximately two file drawers of uncatalogued letters; pamphlets; six scrapbooks of newspaper clippings that include sermons preached by the chaplain, Father Henry C. Hengell, between 1906 and 1936; information indispensable for understanding origins at Wisconsin as well as at Berkeley, Ithaca, and Austin, and also events surrounding the Catholic Student Association of America (1908–c.1915) and the early years of the Federation of College Catholic Clubs. The archives of the National Catholic Educational Association (ANCEA), especially the Francis W. Howard Papers and the James A. Burns Papers, must be consulted to understand the pre-1920s conflict between the Newman Movement and the Catholic colleges. The archives of The Catholic University of America (ACUA), Denis J. O'Connell Papers also contain material germane to this period, while the Edward A. Pace Papers constitute one important source for writing about the relationship between the movement and the Department of Education in the National Catholic Welfare Council during the early 1920s.

The papers of Father John W. Keogh, chaplain at the University of Pennsylvania, 1913–1938, and chaplain general of the Federation of College Catholic Clubs, 1917–1935, reside in two collections. His section in the files of the Archdiocese of Philadelphia (AAP) contains his reports of 1926, 1930, and 1931 describing local and national conditions of the movement and, as well, provides letters to his superior, Cardinal Denis Dougherty, that throw light on its internal tensions. The major source for Keogh's work is the American Catholic Historical Society in Overbrook, Pa. (AACHSP). It holds fifteen boxes of uncatalogued letters; pamphlets; minutes of various meetings; and addresses bearing dates from 1906 to 1960, including the reports of the chaplain general of 1918 and 1921. I am grateful to the late Father Bartholomew Fair for permission to examine these records as well as for helpful comments during my approximately fifteen days with him; he also made available a microfilm copy of the *Newman Quarterly/Newman News* (1917–1934), an almost complete series collected from issues at the society, and others were loaned for the occasion by two former presidents of the federation, Joseph B. Hearn and Joseph VanHorn, whom, along with another former president, John L. Ricketts, I also thank for interviews. Keogh's correspondence indicates that a third collection, one of minutes and papers of the Federation of College Catholic Clubs, which he intended to forward to the National Catholic Welfare Conference in Washington, D.C., was destroyed after he resigned from his post. His personal letters between 1948 and 1960 attempted to convey much of this history, but they are filled with many inaccuracies and exaggerations.

The archives of the National Newman Apostolate (ANNA), now housed at The Catholic University of America as part of its National Catholic Welfare Conference Collection, were stored in an abandoned garage when I examined them in the summer of 1964. The collection comprised something over a hundred boxes of only roughly catalogued materials, a condition that reflected not only the differing systems of organization employed by federation officers who changed frequently, but also the press of business that at times made systematic filing impossible and disrupted established groupings. Though not always complete or uniformly identified, the most significant of these are: minutes and reports of the annual conventions of the Federation from 1916 to 1969 (with many gaps filled by consulting the same as published in the *Newman Quarterly*); letters, minutes, and quarterly and annual reports by its Executive Committee, 1916–1969, and its External Affairs Department, 1947–1962; letters and interoffice memoranda by the Director of the Youth Department, and the same along with reports by the Executive Secretary and Episcopal Moderator of the Federation, 1940–1962; similar material exists for its President and National Chaplain, 1916–1962, although with huge gaps. Groupings for 1962 to 1969 include letters and reports by the Director of the National Newman Apostolate, its Episcopal Moderator and National Chaplain, and of the President and Secretary of the Federation. Also included are a variety of pamphlets, promotional materials, Newman Club aids and manuals, and educational materials; four boxes of Sister M. Alexander Gray's research are also on hand. I am very grateful to Paul F. Tanner, Bishop of St. Augustine, who served as Director of the Youth Department from 1942 to 1945, and at the time of my four-week visit was Executive Secretary of the conference; he granted permission to examine the materials and offered instructive comments about them.

Additional material for chapter 2, which describes the condition of Catholic students entering public universities around the turn of the century, came from interviews with Raymond V. Achatz and Clarence Luhn, both of whom helped to organize the Newman Society at Purdue and the Catholic Student Association of America, and with Edward M. Kerwin, who recalled the situation at the University of Chicago. Contemporary statements can be found in the letters and reports of Catholic students, professors, and clergymen. The Austin O'Malley Papers at the University of Notre Dame contain accounts and descriptions collected in 1897 from priests in college towns. Newman centers at Austin, Berkeley, and Illinois have letters and reports by chaplains writing before World War I. In 1904 John LaFarge prepared a "Report on the Condition of Catholic Students at Harvard University" (ribbon copy, 13 unnumbered pp.) that discusses the relative merits of having Jesuits rather than Paulists set up a chaplaincy there; this valuable document was found in the papers of LaFarge's classmate at Innsbruck, Thomas H. McLaughlin, later Bishop of Paterson, N.J., by Monsignor Francis Rodimer, who forwarded it to Monsignor John Tracy Ellis, who in turn sent it to the writer, a splendid example of historical preservation for which I am deeply grateful. Some published statements are also available. Accounts of the Melvin Club (Wisconsin) and the first Newman Club (Pennsylvania) were provided by Timothy Harrington, member of the former and founder of the latter, in the *Newman Quarterly* (Summer 1921); an interview with Harrington's son, Earl, helped to fill out biographical data. The first four volumes of *Reports and Proceedings of the Catholic Educational Association* (1904–07) supply a number of comprehensive summaries by professors and priests. The files of *The*

Catholic Student (1909–1915) offer comments from undergraduates on a dozen midwestern and eastern campuses; unfortunately, only four issues of this publication are extant, and I thank Quinlan Halbeisen, president of the federation, 1953–54, for making them available.

Diocesan weeklies published in San Francisco, Milwaukee, and Cleveland to be found in collections at Notre Dame and The American Catholic Historical Society of Philadelphia, provided considerable coverage of the efforts of bishops to establish Catholic chapels and halls at state universities around 1906–08, which is the story of chapter 3. *The American Ecclesiastical Review* (January 1912) carried an account of the origins at Wisconsin; Michael J. Murphy presents an excellent summary, "The Cornell Plan of Bishop Bernard J. McQuaid," in *Essays in U.S. Church History* (May 1959), and the diocesan archives of Rochester, along with the Daniel Hudson Papers at Notre Dame, include many of McQuaid's letters on the project; the Catholic Archives of Texas hold materials telling the story of St. Austin's student parish at the University of Texas which is also recounted in Volume VII of Carlos E. Castaneda's *Our Catholic Heritage in Texas, 1919–1936* (Austin: Von Boechmann-Jones, 1958); although both Newman Hall and the archives of the University of California at Berkeley hold materials on the former, I am also grateful to my friend, Father James P. Gaffey, who shared his notes with me as he prepared *Citizen of No Mean City: Archbishop Patrick Riordan of San Francisco (1841–1914)* (Wilmington, N.C.: Consortium Books, 1976).

Statistics indicating the number of Catholics matriculating to secular campuses over the decades of the twentieth century are difficult to find. *Proceedings and Reports of the Catholic Educational Association* (1907) and *Catholic Colleges and Schools in the United States* (Washington, D.C.: NCWC Department of Education, 1942) provide figures; but comparison with other sources, such as John A. O'Brien's "Catholic Students in Secular Colleges and State Normal Schools" (mimeograph, 4 pp.) in the Pace Papers, suggests how difficult it is to determine an accurate picture. Newman Club officials collected census data but these are usually not reliable. Unless otherwise indicated, I have relied upon the work of my late friend, Father Martin W. Davis, S.D.S., whose training in statistics allowed him to develop some significant tables and comments in *The Sister as Campus Minister* (Washington, D.C.: Center for Applied Research in the Apostolate, 1970).

How a handful of Catholic college leaders exploited the emerging "Catholic hall" movement to rally their colleagues around the faltering College and University Division of the Catholic Educational Association comes clear from an examination of the Burns, Howard, Hudson, and O'Connell Papers. Although Coleman Barry offers substantially the same interpretation in *The Catholic University of America, 1903–09* (Washington, D.C.: The Catholic University of America Press, 1959), he was writing from a different point of view and did not have at hand all the materials the present account uses, a packet of letters and broadsides identified as "Varia: Education, 1907–20", as yet not included in the otherwise completely catalogued Farley and Hayes papers in the archives of the Archdiocese of New York, Dunwoodie, when I visited there in the summer of 1965. These materials reveal efforts by Catholic college leaders to repulse the Newman Movement as well as attempts by the bishops to place Catholic colleges under episcopal jurisdiction; they also show how Cardinal Gibbons moderated extremists in both camps. I am grateful to Monsignor Ellis for making available copies of the meetings of the archbishops for 1906, 1907, and 1908, which he found in the archives of the Archdiocese of St. Louis, John J. Glennon Papers. Published accounts to be found in the above-mentioned *CEA Reports* and *The Catholic University of America Bulletin* (July 1907) are also essential.

Citations of *The Catholic Student* in chapter 4 may cause some confusion. The periodical began with "Volume I" in 1909, ran into trouble around 1911, may have missed some issues thereafter, and then apparently started up again with a second "Volume I" in 1915. Two collections are crucial for understanding the development of the Federation of College Catholic Clubs in the early 1920s. The Frank Demuth Papers in the files of the Catholic Chaplain's Office, Columbia University, New York, and the records of the NCWC Department of Education, 1919–23, in the Pace Papers. Demuth was one of the organizers of the FCCC and was deeply involved in the "Tenth Legion Affair." His correspondence supplies much information missing from the NCWC files as well as that about quarrels between Newman leaders; an important diary was unavailable to me when I examined these records in 1965, but Sister M. Alexander Gray quotes from it and its more important entries can be found in letters from Demuth to Keogh in the Overbrook depository.

In addition to the Demuth and Pace Papers, chapter 6 is based upon accounts published in the *Newman Quarterly,* the *NCWC News Service* (Washington, D.C.), and the *NCWC Bulletin* for 1921 to 1926; also indispensable for the story of how the Newman Movement was regarded as "part of the Catholic educational system" are some news

releases and leaflets issued by the NCWC Department of Education in
its behalf that have been lost to Washington, where the department's
records are very incomplete for these years, but survive in the packet
at Dunwoodie identified as "Varia: Education, 1907–20." Without
joining the complementary elements of these fragmented collections
the story cannot be told, and even then it remains tentative in some
minor details. The often unfair and bitter attacks on Father John A.
O'Brien's efforts to provide a center for the accredited study of
religion at the University of Illinois are chronicled in the David A.
Kinley Papers at the University of Illinois, a few files in the chaplain's
office of the Newman Foundation at Champaign–Urbana, and in
O'Brien's personal files at Notre Dame University; I thank him for
permission to examine these files, for two interviews, and for several
letters during the preparation of this study. O'Brien's exchanges with
Archbishop Curley along with the draft of an article explaining his
project are in the latter's papers in the archives of the Archdiocese of
Baltimore. I am also grateful to the following Jesuit fathers: George
Dunne, who opened up some leads in an interview; Edward F.
Hagemann and Edward J. Duff, both of whom knew of the inside
workings at *America* during these years from conversations with its
editors; and Mark A. Calegari of the American Assistancy, Jesuit
Headquarters, Rome. The candor of these and other Jesuits in discussing this very embarrassing episode gives evidence of a commendable
spirit of historical accuracy and honesty. Published sources for the
conflict include contemporary files of the *Woodstock Letters* and *America* for the Jesuit "side" and of *Catholic School Interests* for O'Brien's;
those of *The Osservatore Romano* and the *Civiltà Cattolicà* fill out the
international implications of the "foundation plan." Circumstances
surrounding the authoring of "School of Religion in *Acerbo Nimis* of
Pius X," Keogh's attempt to blunt the Jesuit assault, were narrated in a
letter from its author, Father James Ryan Hughes, M.M., Tokyo,
whom I thank for permission to cite.

Additional sources for chapter 7, which describes the fate of the
Newman Movement during the "Catholic Action" decade, are the files
of the *NCWC Bulletin,* which became *NCWC Review* in 1930, and
Catholic Action in 1932. I am grateful to Johanna Doniat for materials
and an interview telling of her work with Professor Jerome Kerwin at
Chicago in the 1930s. *Proceedings and Reports of the National Catechetical
Congress of the Confraternity of Christian Doctrine* (1938–1940) should also
be consulted.

Information on the spirituality of Newman Club members discussed in chapter 8 can be found also in Richard Butler, O.P., *Witness*

to Change: A Cultural Memoir (River Forest, Ill.: The Priory Press, 1976). Helpful interpretive material is in James W. Trent and Jenette Golds, *Catholics in College* (Chicago: University of Chicago Press, 1967), Robert Hassenger, ed., *The Shape of Catholic Higher Education* (Chicago: University of Chicago Press, 1967), and Kenneth Underwood, *The Church, The University, and Social Policy,* Vol. I: *Report of the Director* (Middletown, Conn.: Wesleyan University Press, 1969). Conversations with former Newman Club members one meets everywhere are also instructive, as was my own experience in Newman centers from 1962 to 1969. *America* (June 3 and September 9, 1950), contains significant material on the state of the movement at mid-century.

Chapters 9 and 10, which narrate how the youth movement became a mandated pastoral-educational apostolate depend upon interviews with the following persons, whom I thank: the late Archbishop Paul J. Hallinan, National Chaplain, 1952–54, and Episcopal Moderator, 1960–64; these other national chaplains: Edward J. Duncan (1950–51), George Garrelts (1958–60), Alexander Sigur (1960–62), Richard Butler, O.P. (1962–64), and the late John Bradley (1965–66). (Technically, Bradley had the title, "President of the Chaplains' Association" because in 1964 the students began to elect their own national chaplain. For several months in 1964–65, when I was living with Bradley at the Gabriel Richard Center, the Apostolate Office in Washington lacked a priest-director; he filled the post from Ann Arbor with the very able assistance of Joan Orlosky, who also supplied an interview.) Also helpful were Father Charles Albright, C.S.P., Coordinating Secretary of the Apostolate (1962–64) and Father John T. McDonough, its Director (1965–69); and Mr. William Tonne, Director of the National Newman Foundation (1969–72). Also informative are monthly issues of the *Newman Apostolate Newsletter* which began to appear in October 1963.

Articles appearing in *Catholic Action, The Catholic Educational Review, The Jesuit Educational Quarterly,* and the *NCEA Bulletin* from the 1930s on are useful for documenting the transformation of "religion" in Catholic colleges from catechetical indoctrination to academic study, one of the themes of chapter 11. John LaFarge, S.J., *The Jesuits in Modern Times* (New York: America Press, 1928) offers a fine statement of the religious ideal of Catholic higher education. Roy Deferrari, ed., *Vital Problems of Catholic Education* (Washington, D.C.: Catholic University of America Press, 1939) and Roland G. Simontitsch, C.S.C., *Religious Instruction in Catholic Colleges for Men* (Washington, D.C.: Catholic University of America Press, 1952) document the reality of the enterprise. Proposals for over-all improvement in Charles E. Ford and Edgar J. Roy, *The Renewal of Catholic Higher Education* (Washington, D.C.: The National Catholic Educational Association, 1968) do not include the complete statement of problems besetting these institutions as listed in the 1966 *Working Paper* by the advisory committee of the association. Andrew M. Greeley, *The American Catholic: A Sociological Portrait* (New York: Basic Books, 1977) offers data for assessing the progress of Catholic colleges and universities. The religious situation on Catholic campuses studied by Trent and Golds in their *Catholics in College* takes much more dramatic form in articles on the subject in *Newman: A Review* (Winter 1966), *The Commonweal* (October 6, 1967), *America* (May 23, 1964), and *Ave Maria* (April 16, 1966) which includes a number of responses from the presidents of prominent Catholic colleges and universities. Works like John J. Jansen, *Personnel Services in Catholic Four Year Colleges for Men* (Washington, D.C.: Catholic University of America Press, 1955) indicate how fragmented was the extra-curriculum, including religious counseling. This can also be inferred from two Master's theses completed at Catholic University in 1965, Sister Miriam Imelda Murphy, "The Chaplain in Catholic Colleges for Women in the United States" and John N. Ryan, O.S.F.S., "The Chaplain in United States Catholic Colleges for Men." William J. Farrell's "Liturgical Involvement: A Survey of Student Attitudes," prepared for the National Conference of Catholic Bishops in 1966, sets forth some gloomy conclusions from its survey of seven Catholic colleges; I am grateful to Professor Farrell for making this report available. Files of *America* and *Woodstock Letters* for the 1960s indicate the massive review Jesuits were making of their educational and religious apostolates.

The dismantling of the Newman apostolate after 1966 so it could return to its pre-1910 diocesan-centered form, the central theme of chapter 13, can be understood by comparing Richard Butler, O.P., *God on the Secular Campus* (Garden City, N.Y.: Doubleday and Company, 1963) with the vision of the Church found in Walter M. Abbott, S.J., and Joseph Gallagher, *The Documents of Vatican II* (New York: Guild Press, America Press, Association Press, 1966); Robert E. Tracy, *American Bishop at the Vatican Council* (New York: McGraw-Hill, 1966) gives a former national chaplain's view of the Vatican II statement on education and the campus ministry. Other publications relevant to the shape of the Newman Movement forming in these years are papers by chaplains published in *Counseling and Values* (Winter 1972) and the files of *Campus Ministry Report* (Washington, D.C.). Much information for the final section of the book came from my close contact with the

Director of the Division of Campus Ministry in the United States Catholic Conference (formerly the NCWC), Father Laurence T. Murphy, M.M., and with the dozens of diocesan directors I met at meetings all over the country from 1969 to 1971 as Coordinator of Research in the Campus Ministries Department, Center for Applied Research in the Apostolate, Washington, D.C.

Index

O

P